IMAGES
of America

OLD YORK

I0806352

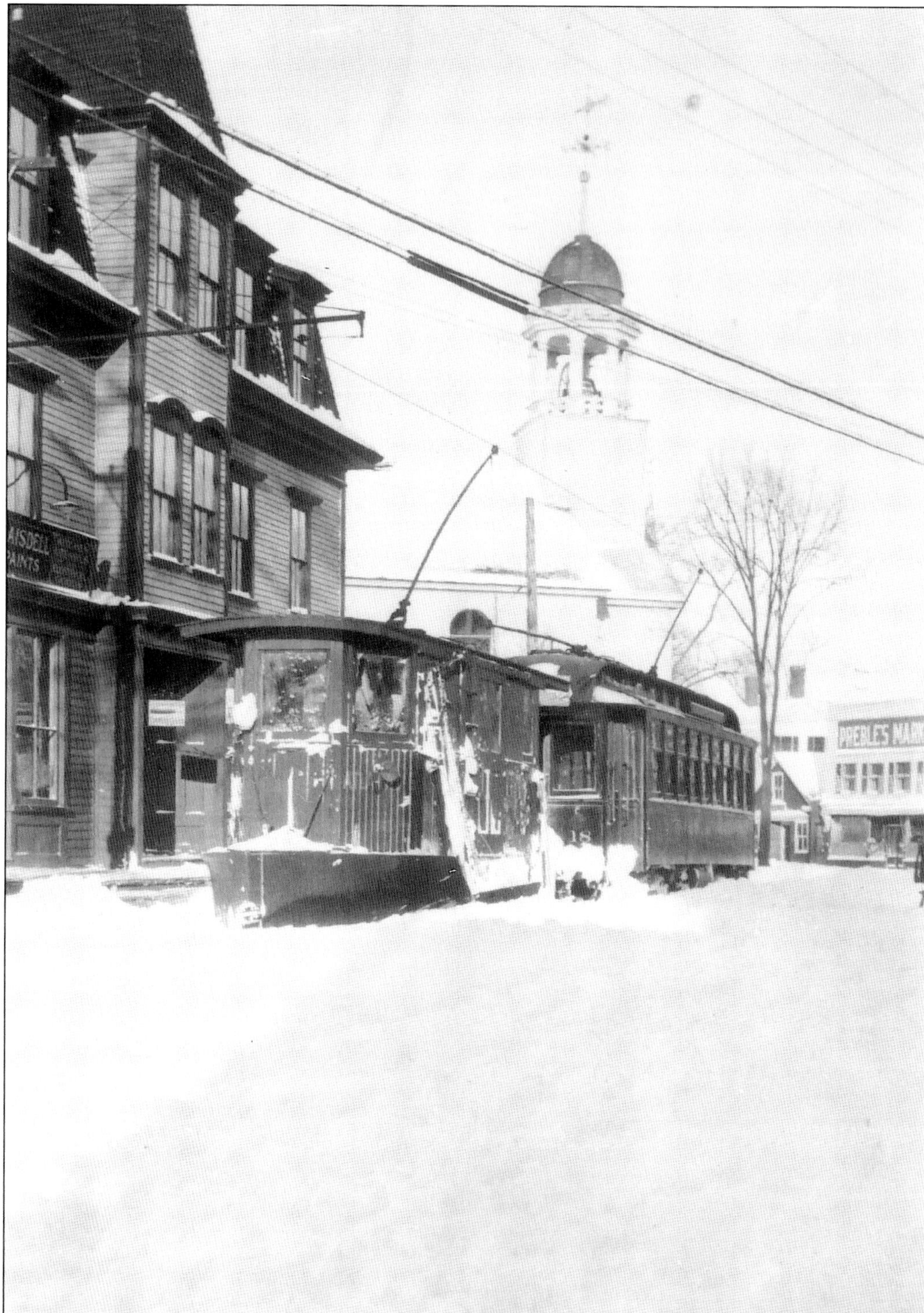

A TROLLEY CAR PLOWING THE TRACKS in front of the Methodist Church and the Golden Cross building in the village square.

IMAGES
of America

OLD YORK

Compiled by
John D. Bardwell

ARCADIA
PUBLISHING

ISBN 978-0-7385-8838-4

Published by Arcadia Publishing
Charleston, South Carolina

Printed in the United States of America

For all general information contact Arcadia Publishing at:
Telephone 843-853-2070
Fax 843-853-0044
E-mail sales@arcadiapublishing.com
For customer service and orders:
Toll-Free 1-888-313-2665

Visit us on the Internet at www.arcadiapublishing.com

To Esther E. Wood, a long-time history professor from the Gorham campus of the University of Southern Maine and a 1994 inductee in the Maine Women's Hall of Fame. She introduced me to the writings of Kenneth Roberts and made history a special part of my life. For that, I will be ever grateful. Great teachers are rare. Esther Wood was among the very best.

OTHER PUBLICATIONS BY JOHN D. BARDWELL

A Diary of the Portsmouth, Kittery and York Electric Railroad (1986)
A History of the Country Club at York, Maine (1988)
The Isles of Shoals: A Visual History (1989)
A History of York Harbor and the York Harbor Reading Room (1993)
Old York Beach (1994)

PUBLICATIONS BY JOHN D. BARDWELL AND RONALD P. BERGERON

Images of a University: A Photographic History of the University of New Hampshire (1984)
The White Mountains of New Hampshire: A Visual History (1989)
The Lakes Region of New Hampshire: A Visual History (1989)

PUBLICATIONS BY JOHN D. BARDWELL AND PETER A. MOORE

A History of the York Beach Fire Department: 1890-1990 (1990)

Contents

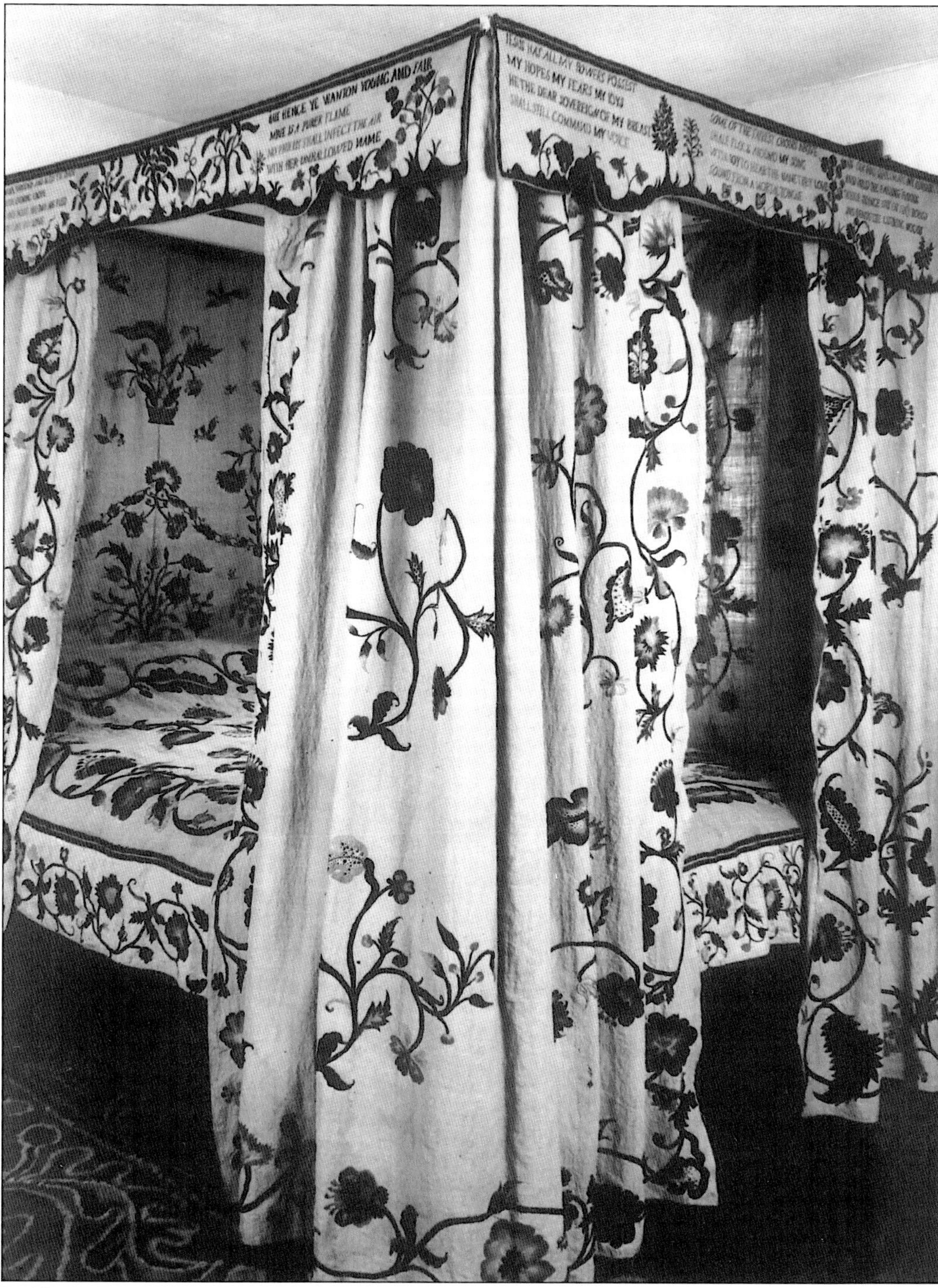

MARY BULMAN, WHO LIVED IN THE HOUSE ACROSS FROM THE OLD GAOL, worked on these famous bed hangings while her husband, Dr. Alexander Bulman, served as personal physician to General William Pepperrell during the attack on Louisbourg in 1745. The expedition was successful but an epidemic of "distemper" broke out and Dr. Bulman died from the disease.

Introduction

Early in 1982, the editor of the Old York Weekly asked if I would write a weekly feature on local history. I had access to a box of old photographs by Myron Cox and suggested a column featuring an old photograph with appropriate caption and historical background. My offer was for about a year because at that point I expected to run out of photographs. As it turned out, The Unknown History of York carried my byline from February 10, 1982 until December 9, 1992. Stories and photographs from interested readers arrived from all parts of the country and I received enough material to write over five hundred weeks of Unknown History. Peter Moore continued the column when I began spending winters in Florida and was unable to meet the weekly deadlines. During the ten years that I wrote the columns, readers urged me to put them together in book form and I promised to give the proposal careful consideration.

Old York Beach was published by Alan Sutton and it included several hundred of the images with appropriate captions. Photographs, postcard views, and ephemera were used to illustrate the history of Cape Neddick, York Beach, Long Sands Beach, the Nubble and Mount Agamenticus. It was my approach to sharing the region's visual history while emphasizing the need for identifying and preserving the images in the old photo albums and personal collections of the seniors in our community.

Old York is the second book in this series and it features pictures of York Village, York Corner, Cider Hill, Scotland, Beech Ridge and the other areas that were not covered in the first book. The images are arranged to illustrate how people lived in this community between 1850 and 1950. York's rich colonial heritage has been well documented and this story does not begin until after the invention of photography in 1840. It is a story of gradual change brought about by improvements in transportation and the arrival of summer residents who had the resources to improve the quality of life for those who lived here. Trains, trolleys and automobiles also made it possible for York residents to travel within and beyond the community.

Pictured are homes, places of business, methods of transportation, types of recreation, educational facilities, unusual characters, prominent citizens, people at work, historic sites and significant landmarks. Whenever possible, the images are matched to emphasize changes and show trends. The captions provide appropriate historical background and identification of people and places. The emphasis is on what the pictures communicate as opposed to a straightforward chronological treatment.

Old York and Old York Beach, includes many of the more interesting photographs from my collection. Together they contain hundreds of images that have been shared by the people who contributed to the collection while I was writing for the newspaper. Others have been contributed specifically for use in the two books.

These books are my response to those people who asked me to share the collection by publishing it in some form.

John D. Bardwell

One

The Village

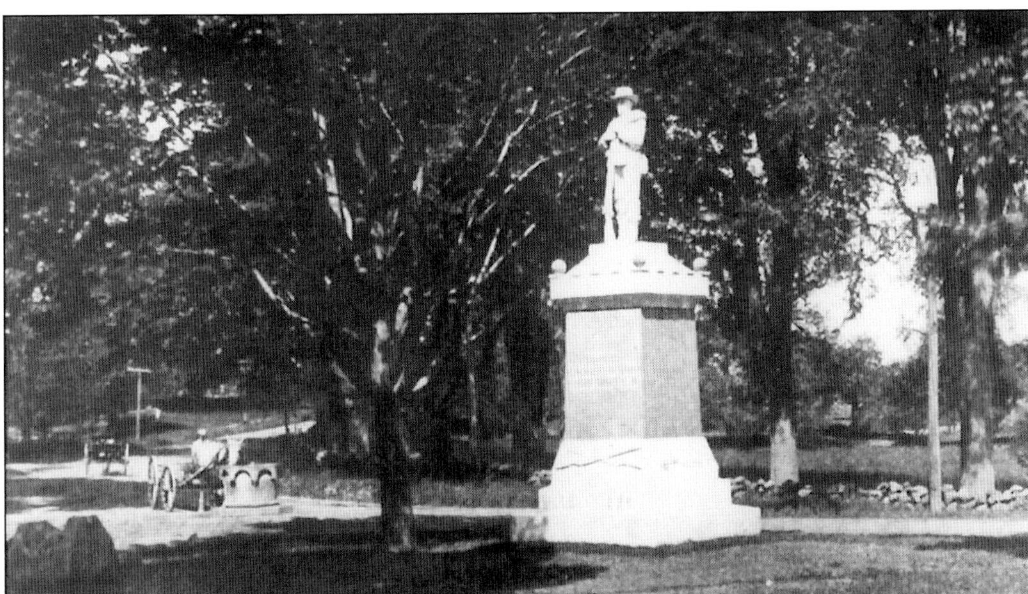

CIVIL WAR MONUMENT in the village square.

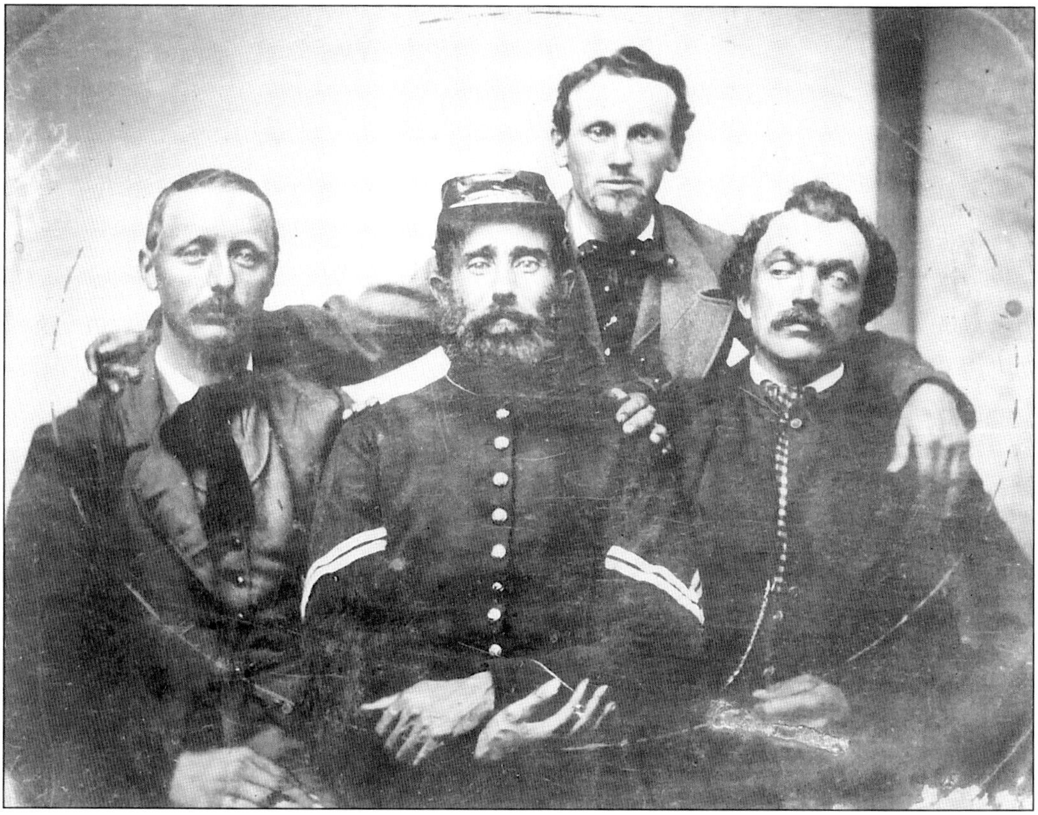

"RETURNED FROM THE WAR" was written on the back of this picture. The Civil War soldiers are, left to right: Joseph Howard Preble, Jeremiah Linscott McIntire, Andrew Jackson McIntire and Hiram Hobbs Thompson.

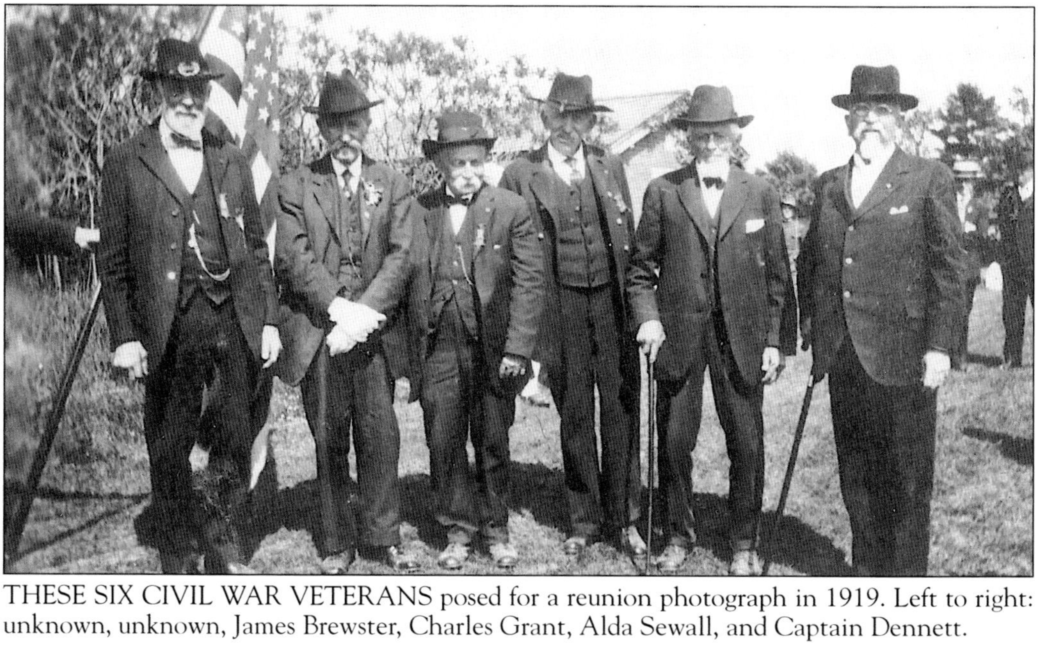

THESE SIX CIVIL WAR VETERANS posed for a reunion photograph in 1919. Left to right: unknown, unknown, James Brewster, Charles Grant, Alda Sewall, and Captain Dennett.

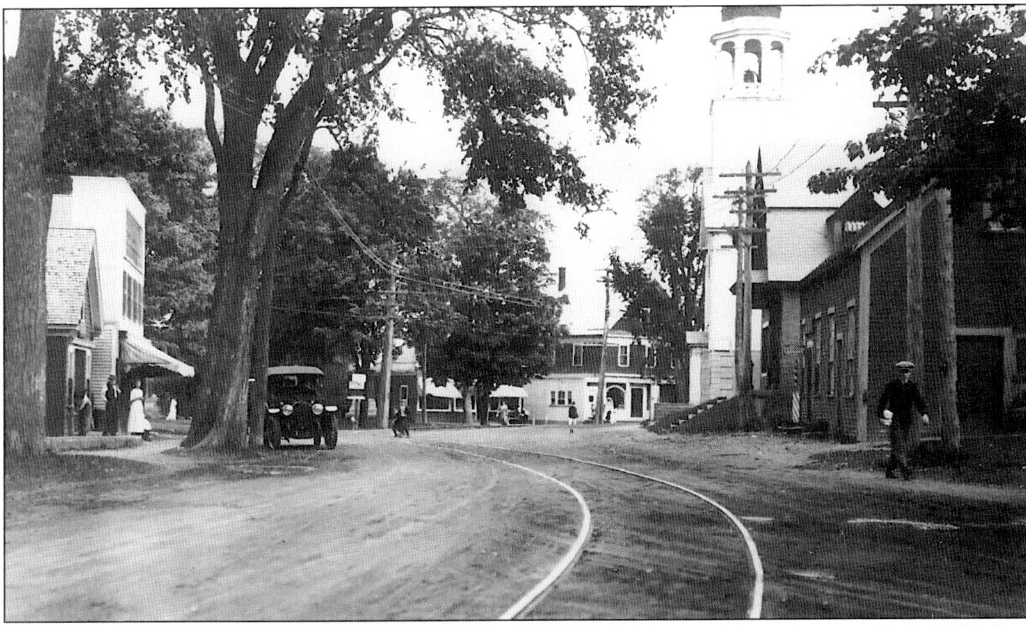

YORK STREET, YORK VILLAGE IN 1912. This view is looking north toward York Harbor. The trolley car tracks run down the middle of the unpaved road.

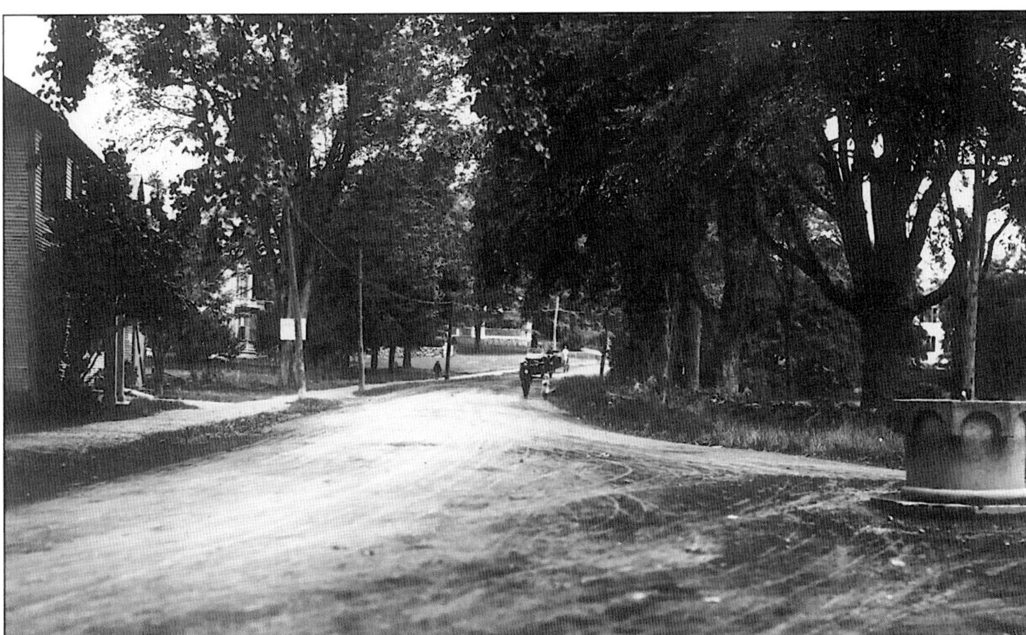

LOOKING DOWN LONG SANDS ROAD from the village square. On the right of the picture is the granite water fountain that was used by the horses that passed through the village.

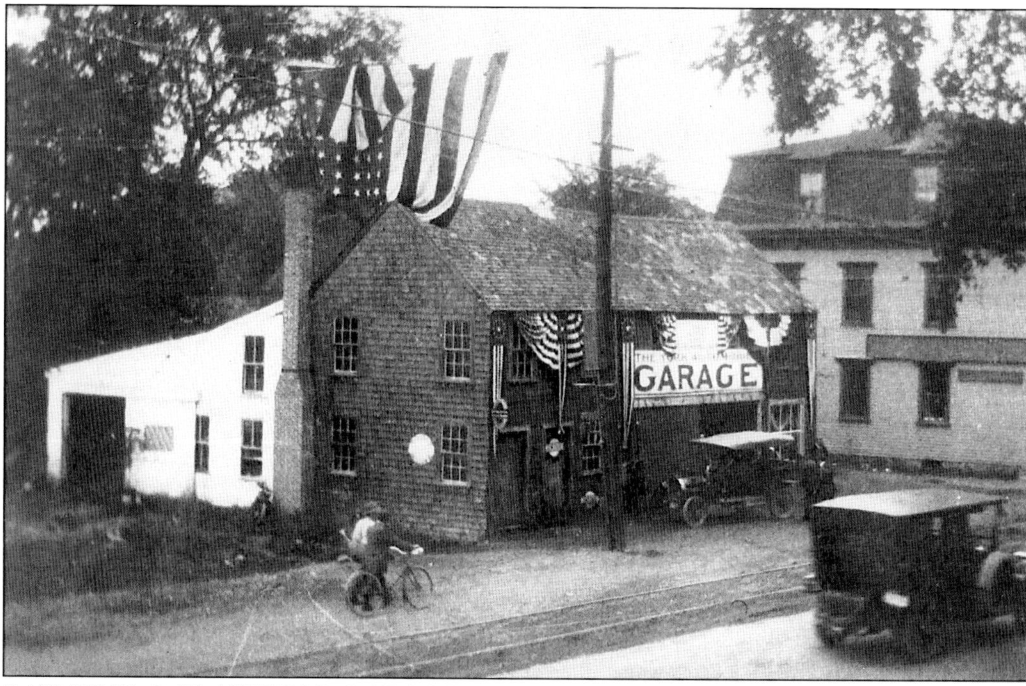

RAYMOND C. BLAISDELL'S GARAGE AND FORD AGENCY was adjacent to the Golden Cross building. Blaisdell also sold Chevrolet, Overland, Nash, and Willis-Knight automobiles. The building, a former blacksmith shop, also housed a ticket agency for the Atlantic Shore Railway. This was the electric trolley system that evolved from the Portsmouth, Kittery, and York Electric Railway.

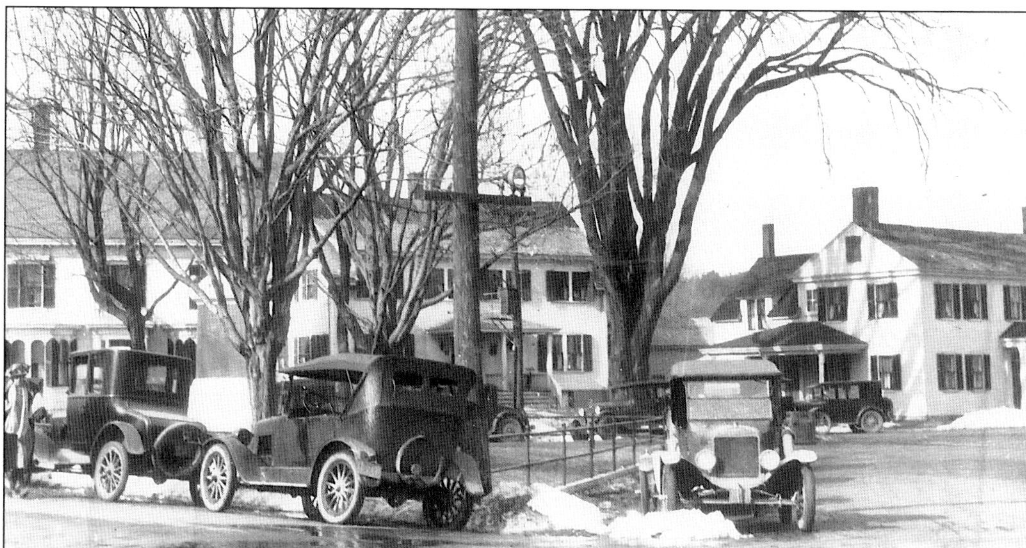

VILLAGE SQUARE ON TOWN MEETING DAY IN THE 1920s. Voters studied the town report carefully and tested their views on neighbors before driving to the village on town meeting day. For many residents, it was their first trip to town in many months and the local merchants had a busy day. The barbershop was especially busy and potential customers could talk politics while waiting for a brief turn in the chair.

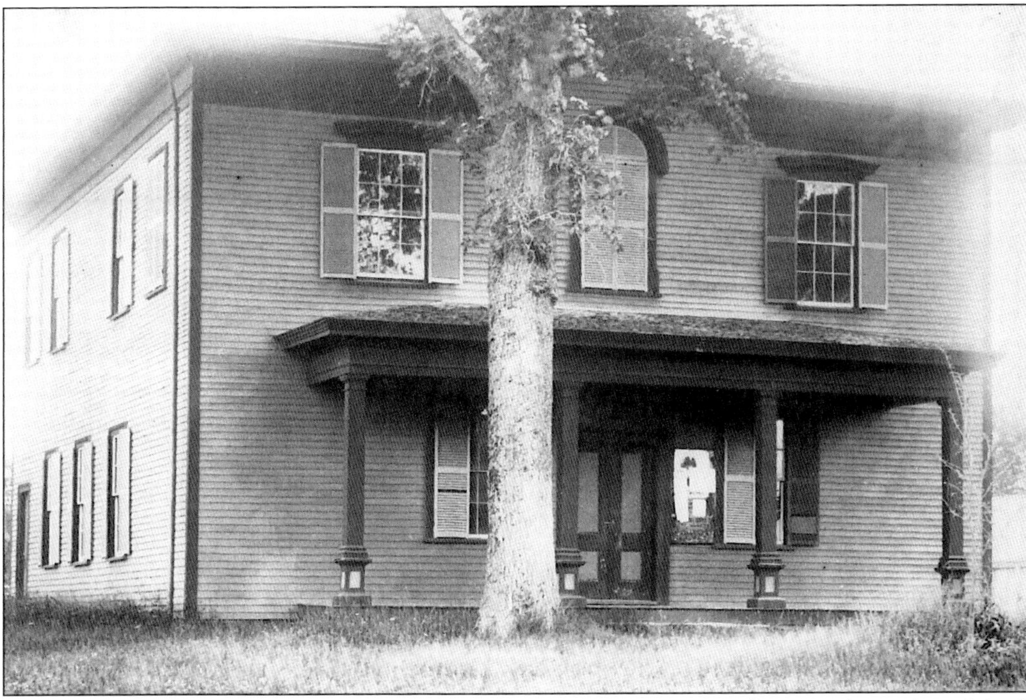

THE OLD COURTHOUSE, now known as the York Town Hall, was planned and built in 1733-74. It was to be used as a courthouse and meeting house. The building became the York Town Hall in 1811 and was remodeled in 1873. A 16-foot addition was added in the back in 1893.

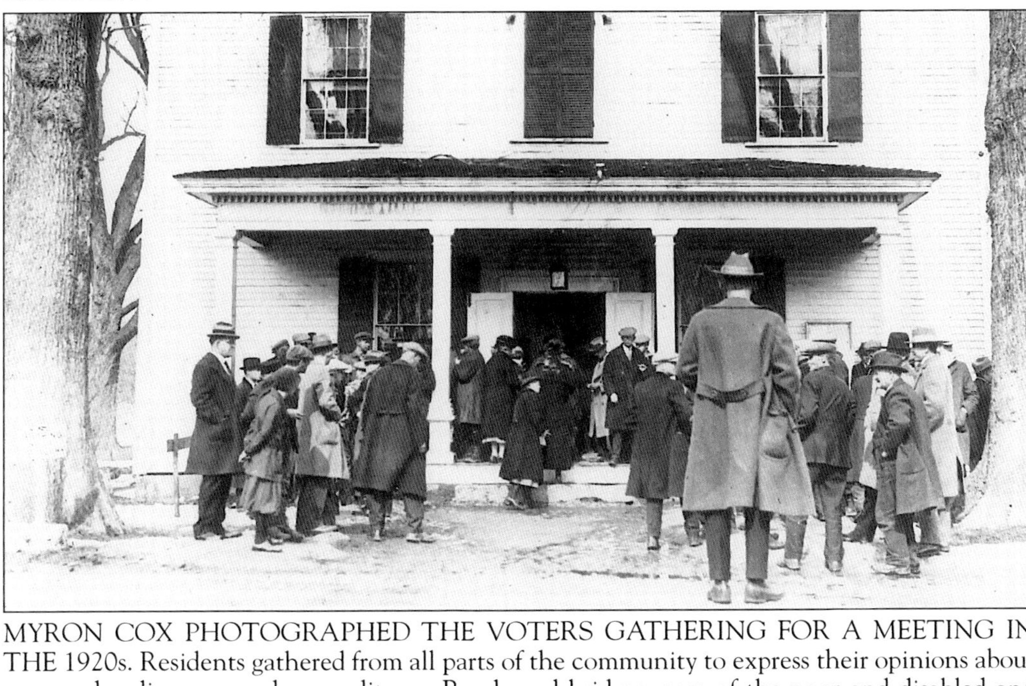

MYRON COX PHOTOGRAPHED THE VOTERS GATHERING FOR A MEETING IN THE 1920s. Residents gathered from all parts of the community to express their opinions about proposed ordinances and expenditures. Roads and bridges, care of the poor and disabled and schools received the largest appropriations.

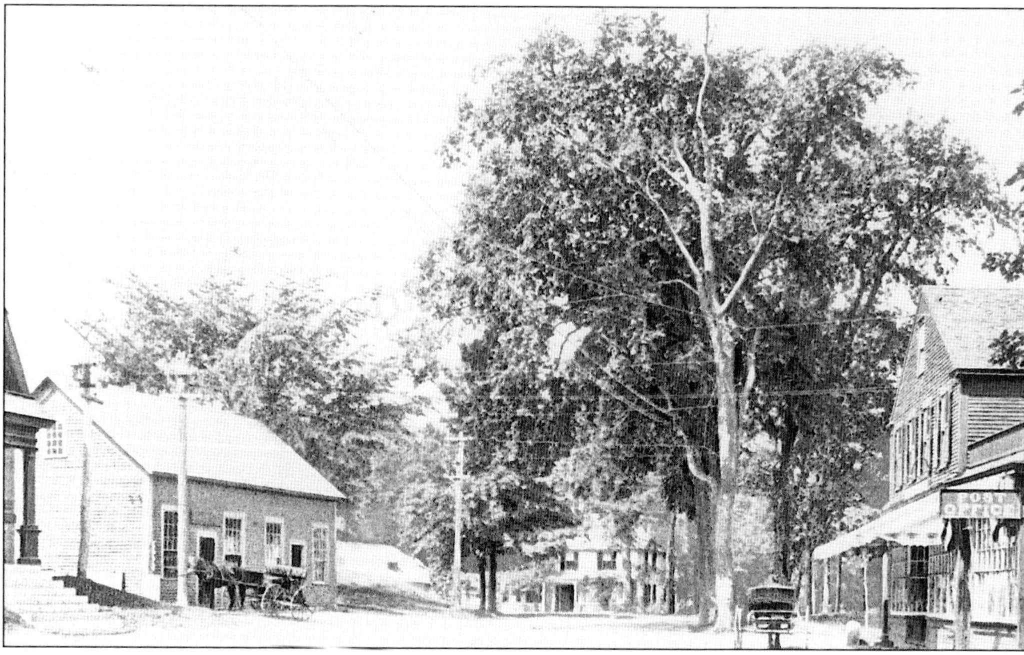

THE EMERSON-WILCOX HOUSE is in the center of this postcard view taken from Monument Square. On the left is the building housing Aaron Fellow's barbershop. On the right is the grocery store and post office.

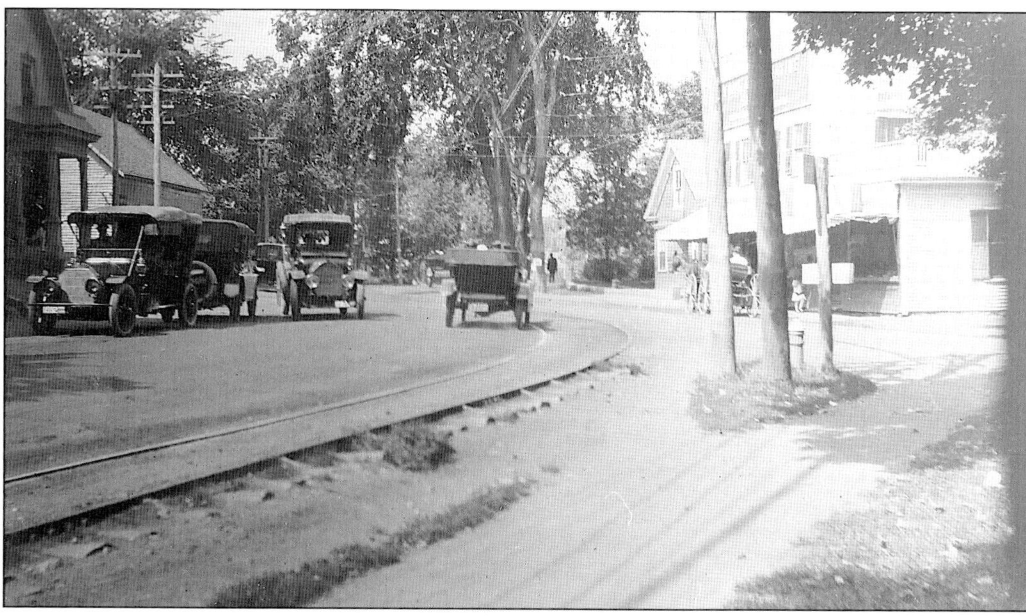

A LATER PICTURE FROM THE SAME LOCATION has automobiles and trolley tracks as well as the grocery store and post office.

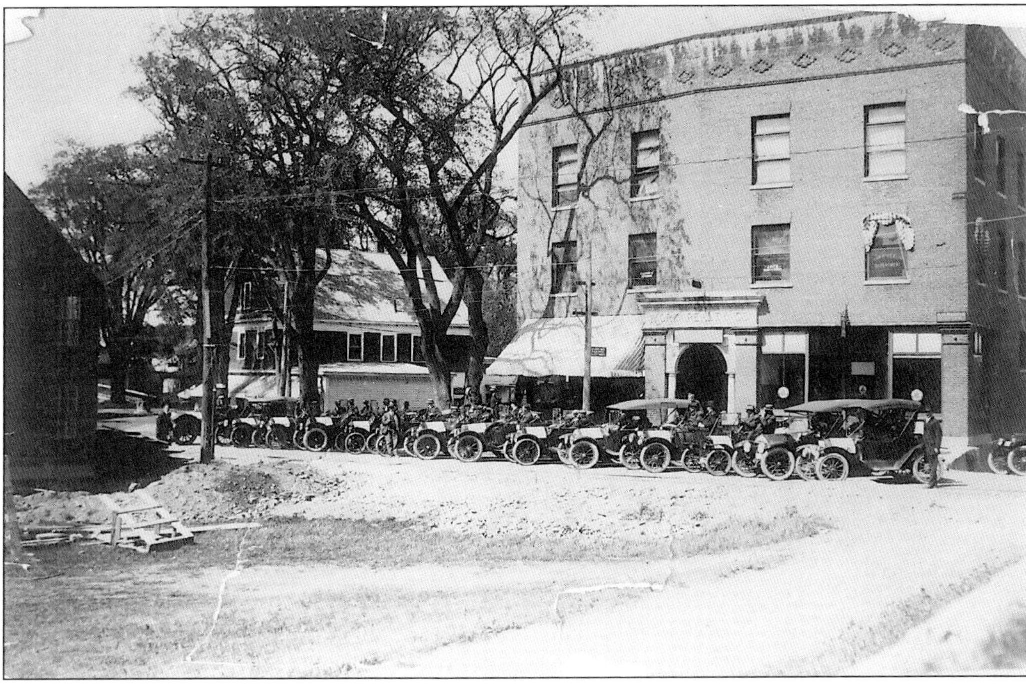

WAITING FOR A PARADE? Automobiles are lined up in front of the Realty building in the center of the village. It appears that they are waiting for a parade to pass by on the traditional parade route.

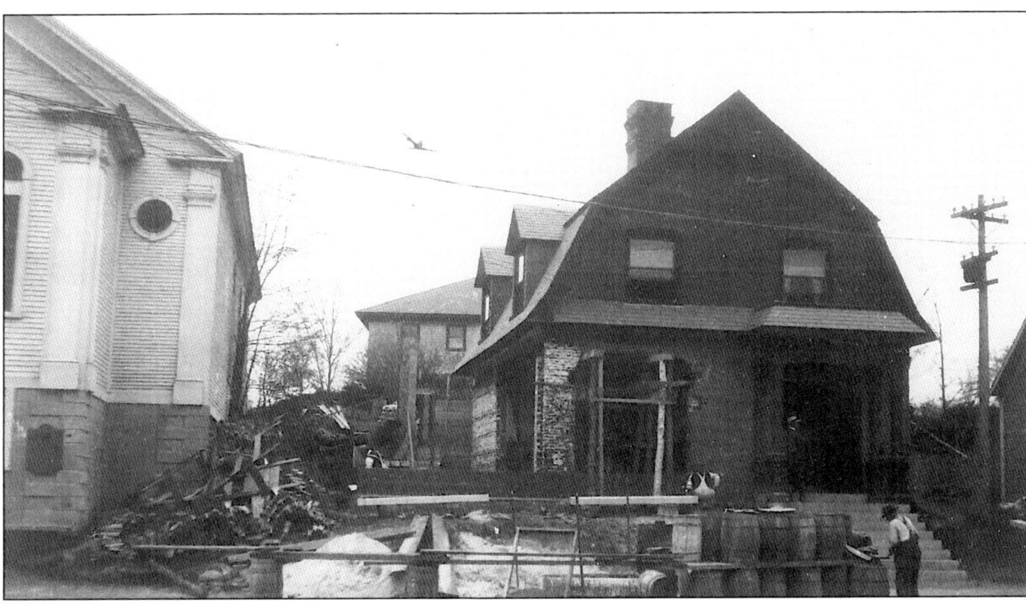

THE BANK BUILDING which housed the Community Trust Company was expanded with an addition on the side next to the Methodist Church.

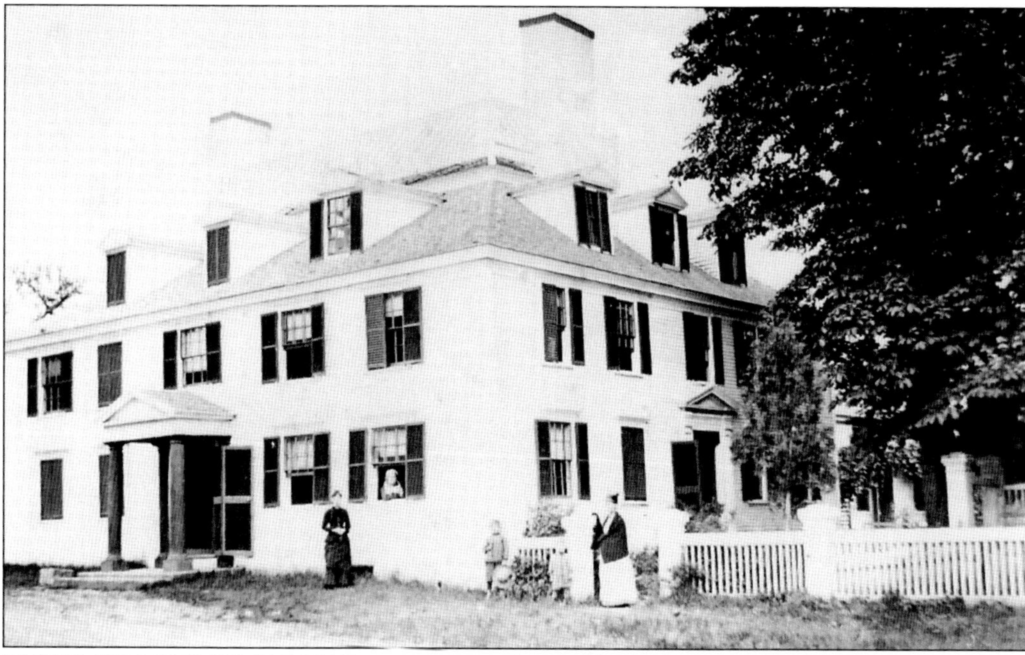

THE EMERSON HOMESTEAD was once Paul Woodbridge's Tavern. John Adams, the second President of the United States, told in his diary of four occasions when he rested at this tavern, during the years from 1770 to 1774. The building was originally located at the edge of the road. It was moved back to its present location at a later date.

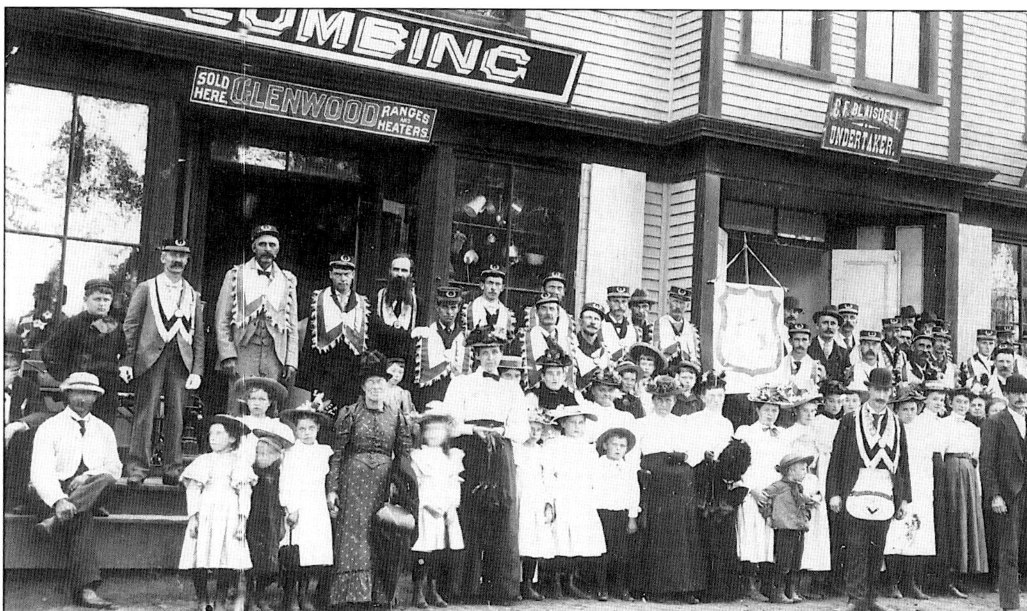

THE GOLDEN CROSS BUILDING WAS LOCATED TO THE LEFT OF THE METHODIST CHURCH NEAR THE HOSPITAL ENTRANCE. A group of Masons and their relatives gathered on the steps to be photographed by Angevine Gowen. The building was the commercial center of York for many years. It housed a hardware store, a furniture store, an undertaker's parlor, a restaurant, a bakery shop, the first A&P store and an attorney's office.

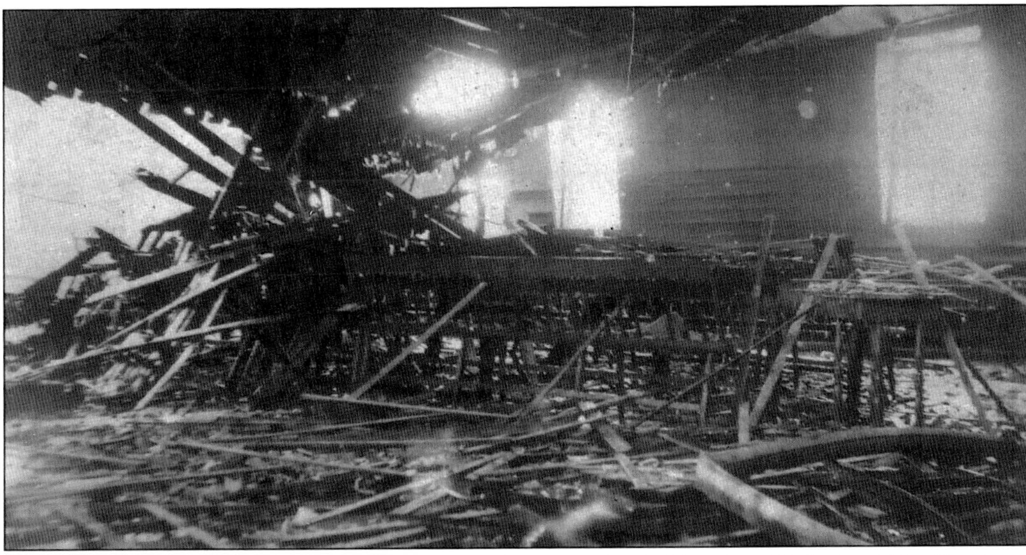

THE MAIN HALL ON THE THIRD FLOOR OF THE GOLDEN CROSS BUILDING was used for many public events including movies and basketball games. In 1917 or 1918, a fire destroyed the third floor which was later removed. A fire eventually damaged the building beyond repair and it had to be torn down.

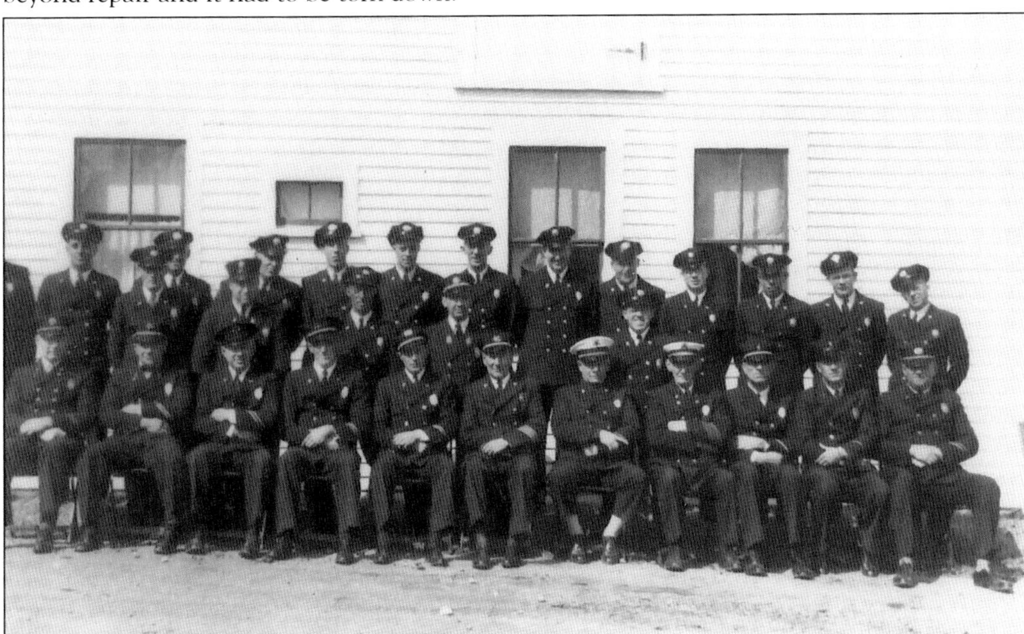

MEMBERS OF THE YORK VILLAGE FIRE DEPARTMENT. Rear, left to right: Walter Maddox, Russell Marston, Charles Ramsdell, Oliver Starkey, Kenneth Dorr, Pearl Freeman, Jack LaPlante, Herbert Bennett, Carl Dennett, Edward Cooper, Gordon Drew, Roland Hall and LeRoy Salls. Center: John Raynes, Ernest Moulton, Charles Ballentine, Henry Fogg and Eddie Gilchrist. Front: Donald McIntire, Chester Tobey, John Thyng, Brad Woodward, Harold Goodwin, William Sullivan, Roy Sturtevant, Tom Thumith, Leon Ramsdell, Floyd Avery and James McIntire.

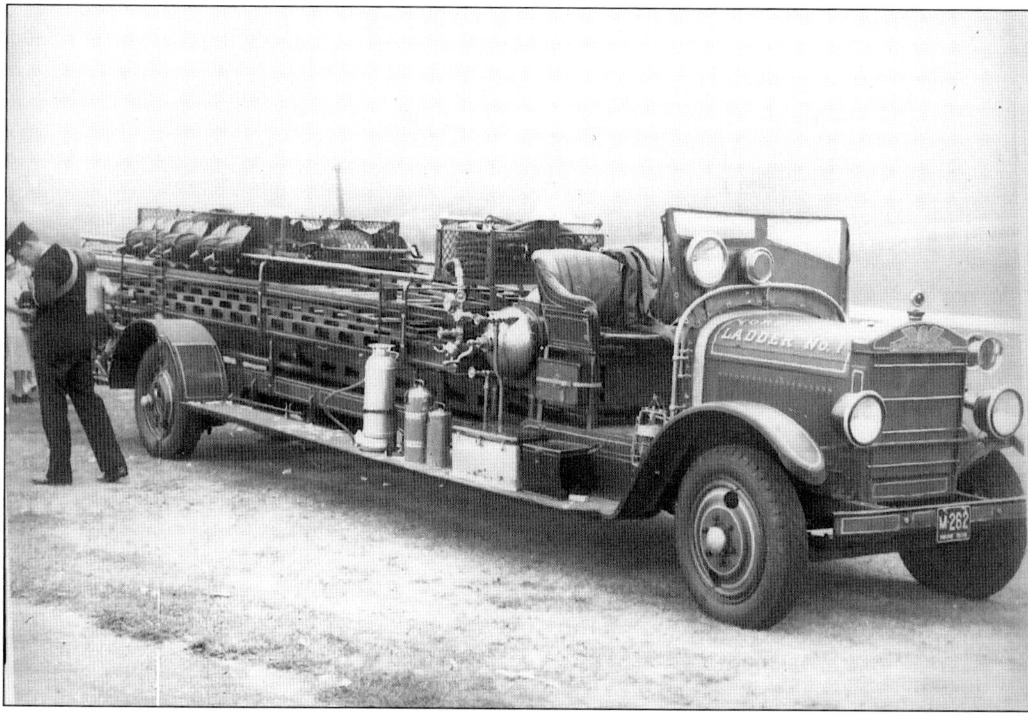

YORK FIRE DEPARTMENT LADDER NUMBER 1.

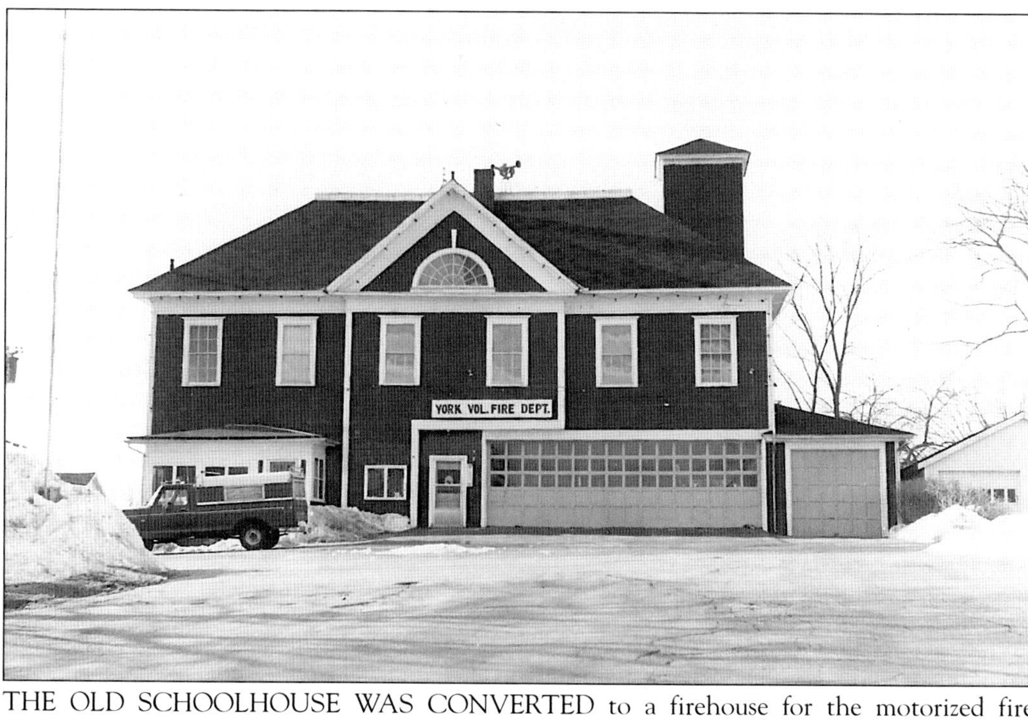

THE OLD SCHOOLHOUSE WAS CONVERTED to a firehouse for the motorized fire equipment that was purchased for fire protection in the community.

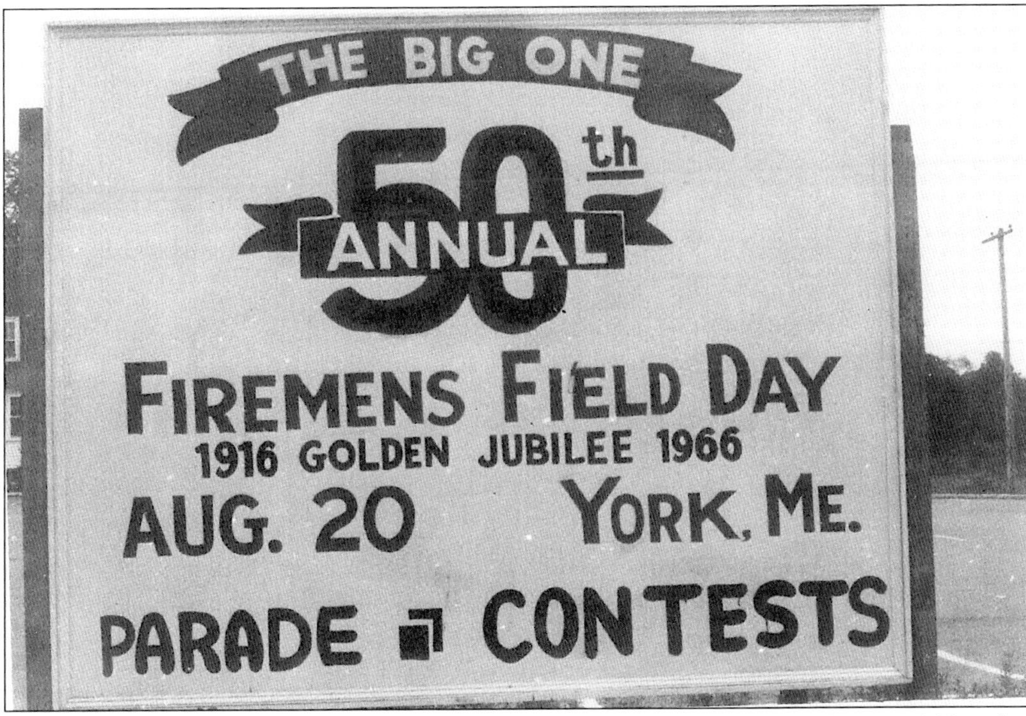

THE VILLAGE FIREMEN CELEBRATED THEIR 50TH ANNIVERSARY in 1966 with a huge parade and display of fire equipment.

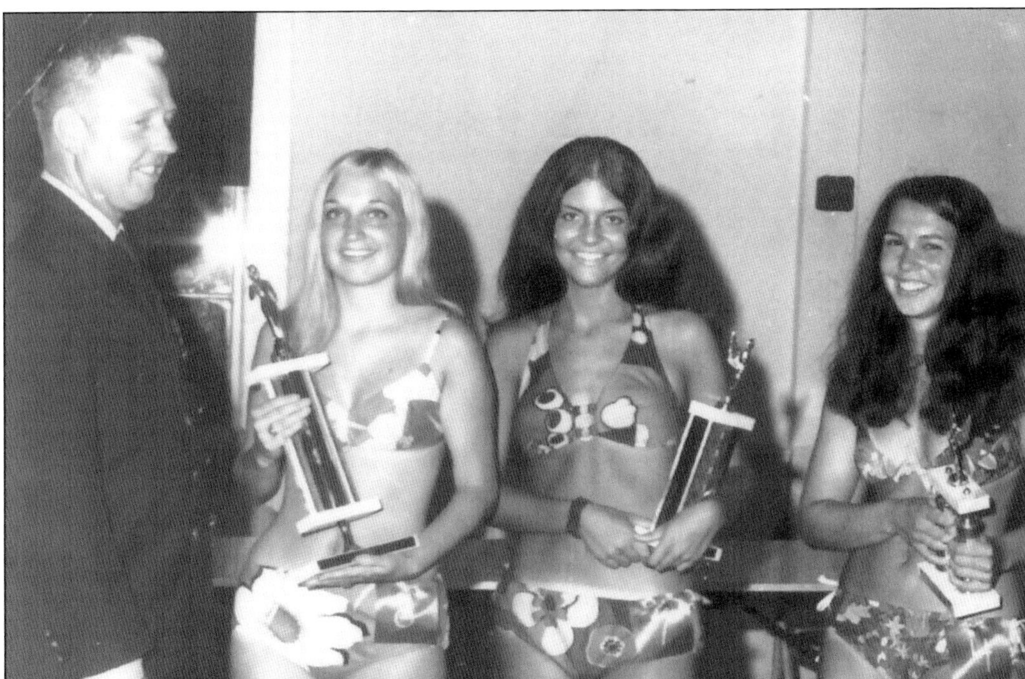

FIREMAN CHARLES BALLENTINE had the pleasant duty of awarding the trophies to the winners of the "Miss Flame" contest at the annual Firemen's Field Day.

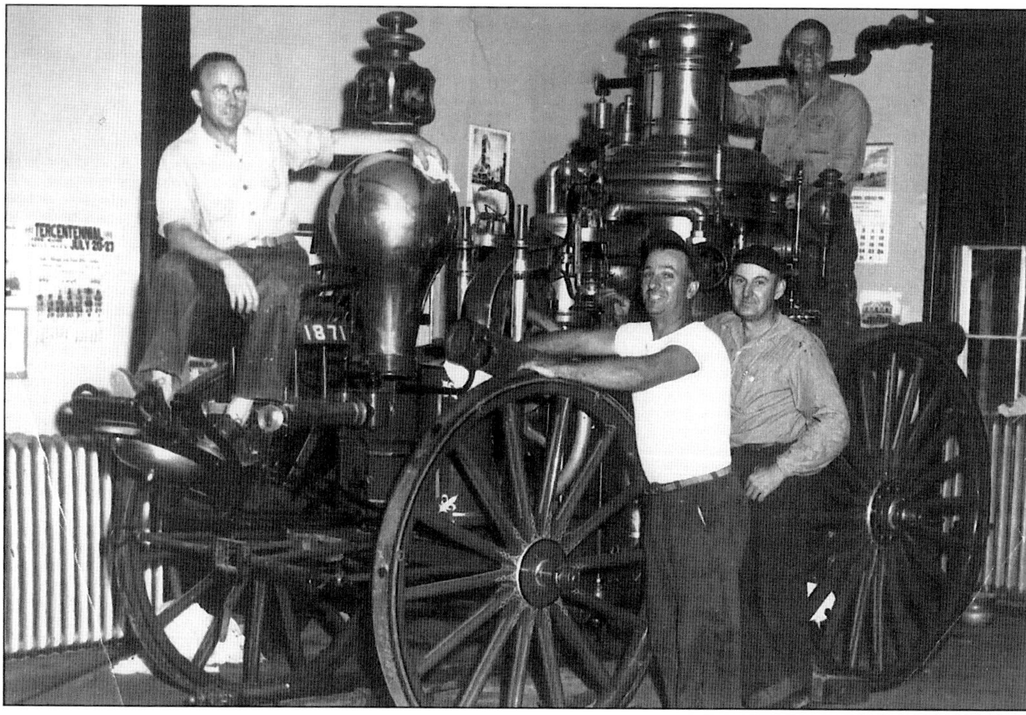

THIS EARLY STEAM PUMPER was on loan for the July 26, 1952 Field Day. It is being examined by York firemen LeRoy Salls, Russell Marston, Charles Ramsdell and Andrew Ramsdell. When they fired it up to compete against a modern pumper, it pumped 750 gallons per minute.

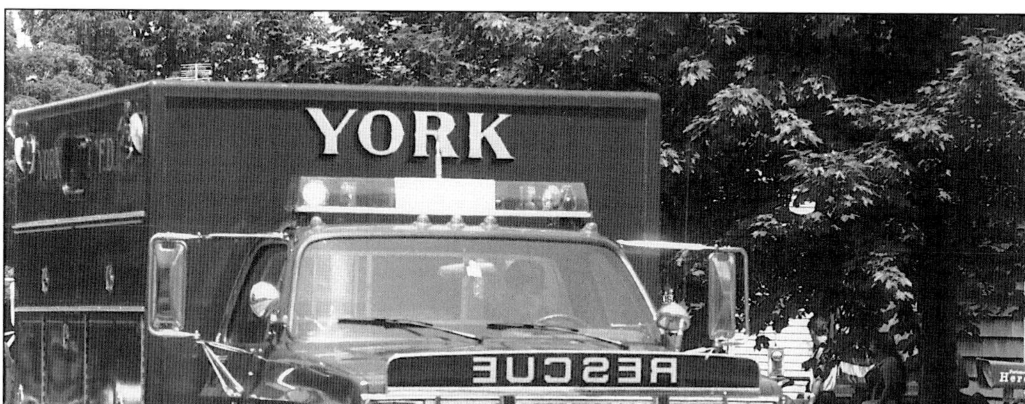

THE NEW SQUAD TRUCK of the York Village Fire Department was exhibited in the York Beach Fire Department's 100th Anniversary Parade.

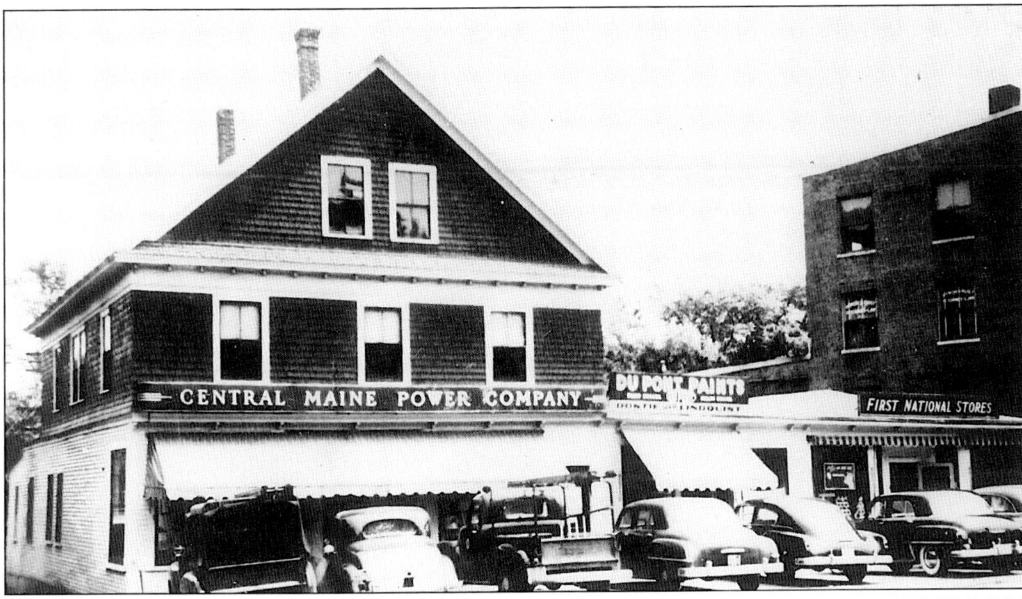

THIS BUSINESS BLOCK BETWEEN THE COX STORE AND THE REALTY BUILDING housed the offices of the Central Maine Power Company, a paint store, a First National Store and the office of Dr. Alvin Hoffman.

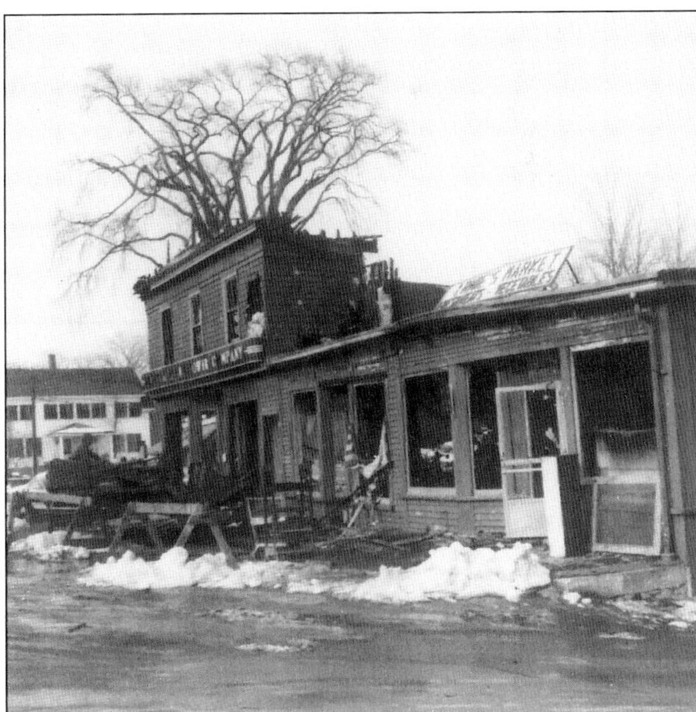

A FIRE DESTROYED THE BUSINESS BLOCK on February 13, 1959. Firemen from York Village, York Beach and Ogunquit battled the flames and were able to save the Cox Store which was just across the alley.

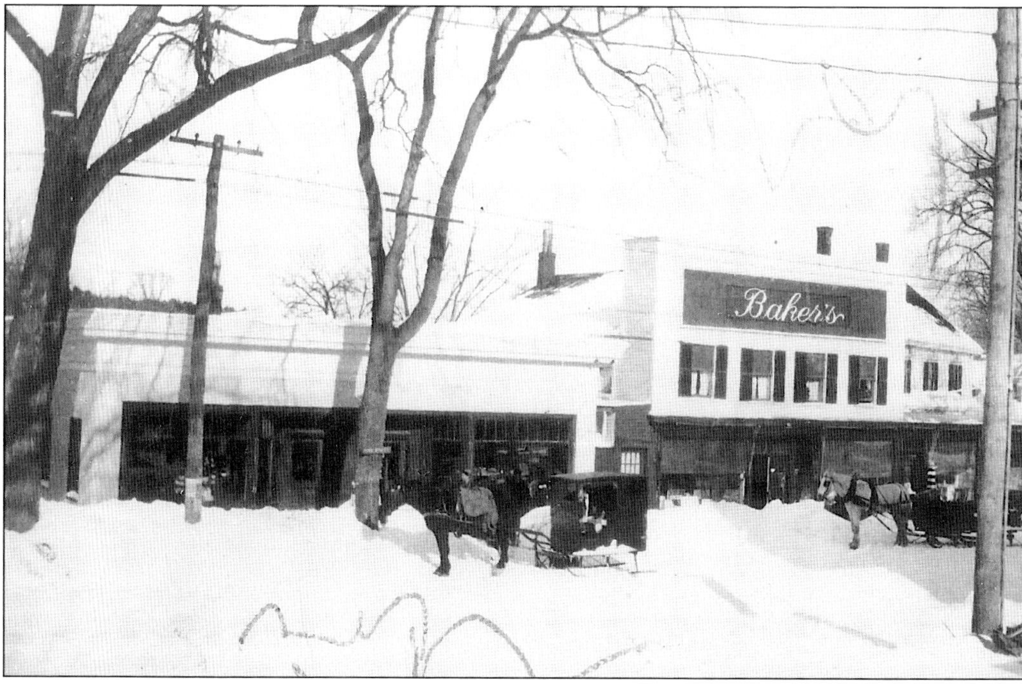

BAKER'S MARKET was once the "shopping center" of York Village. This busy store operated in the early 1900s. Horse-drawn wagons or sleighs, and later, trucks, were used to deliver grocery orders to the kitchens of York's homes. The building was razed to provide space for the construction of the Maine National Bank.

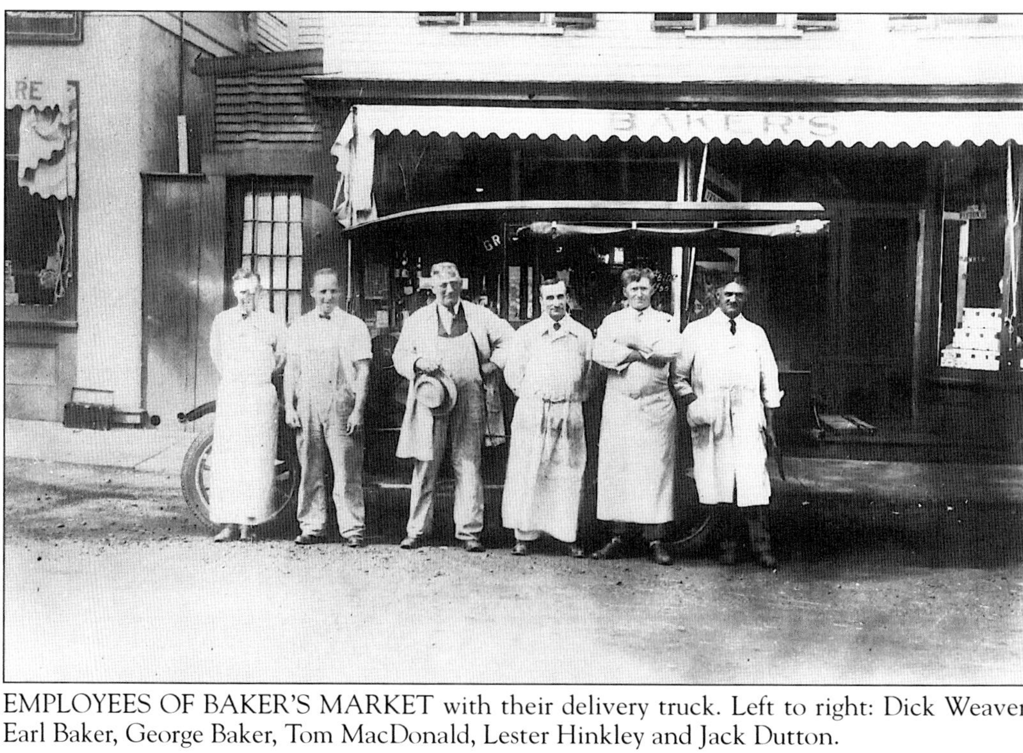

EMPLOYEES OF BAKER'S MARKET with their delivery truck. Left to right: Dick Weaver, Earl Baker, George Baker, Tom MacDonald, Lester Hinkley and Jack Dutton.

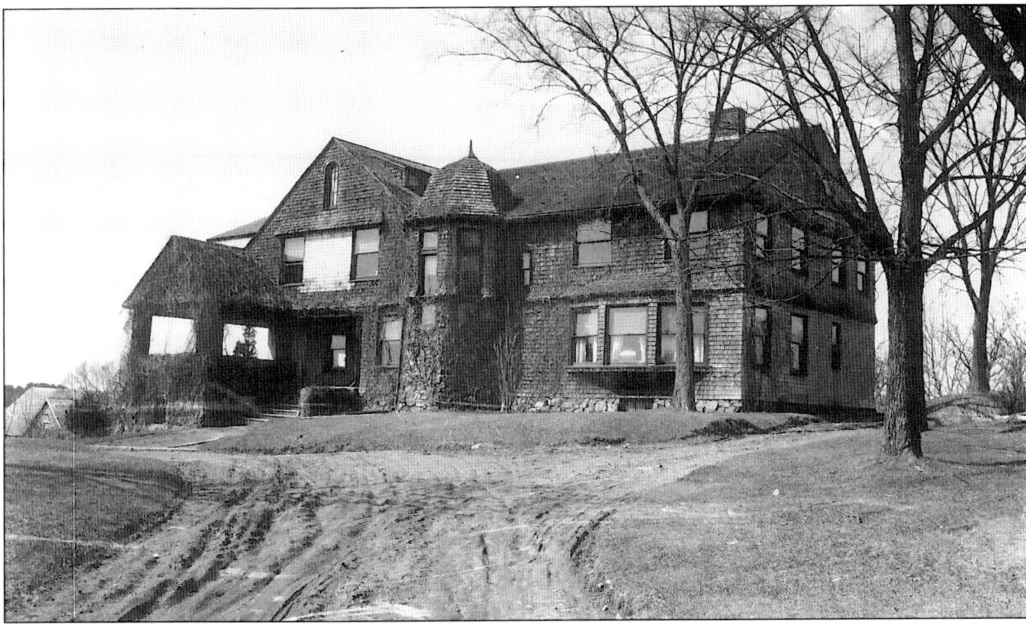

YORK HOSPITAL was founded and incorporated on 5 November 1904. The Davidson estate was purchased for $15,000 and another $3,000 was spent on remodeling and repairs.

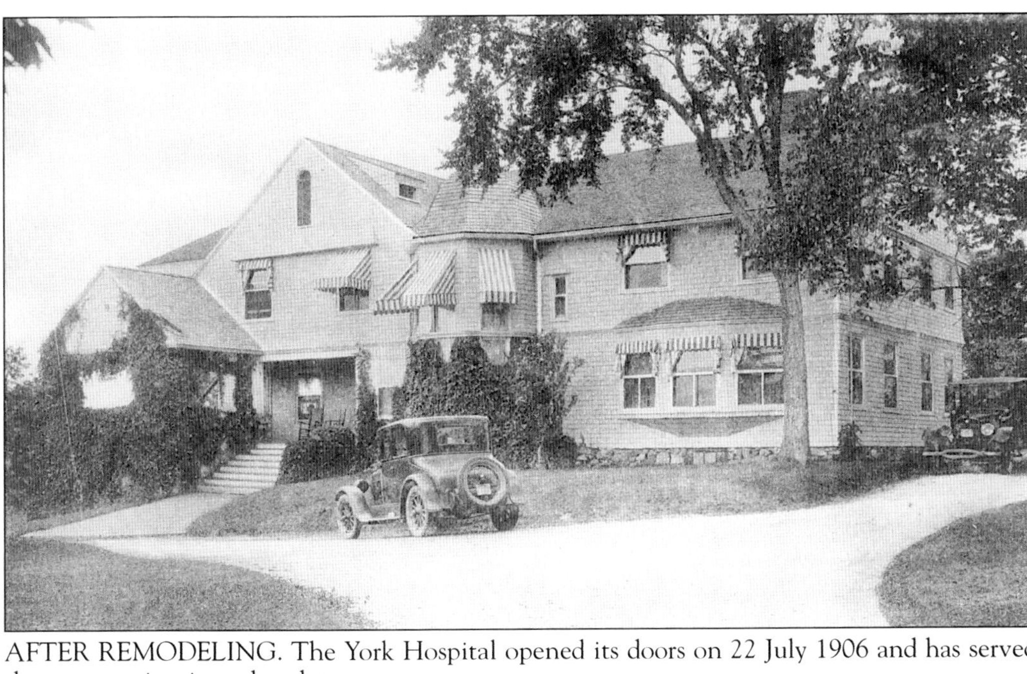

AFTER REMODELING. The York Hospital opened its doors on 22 July 1906 and has served the community since that date.

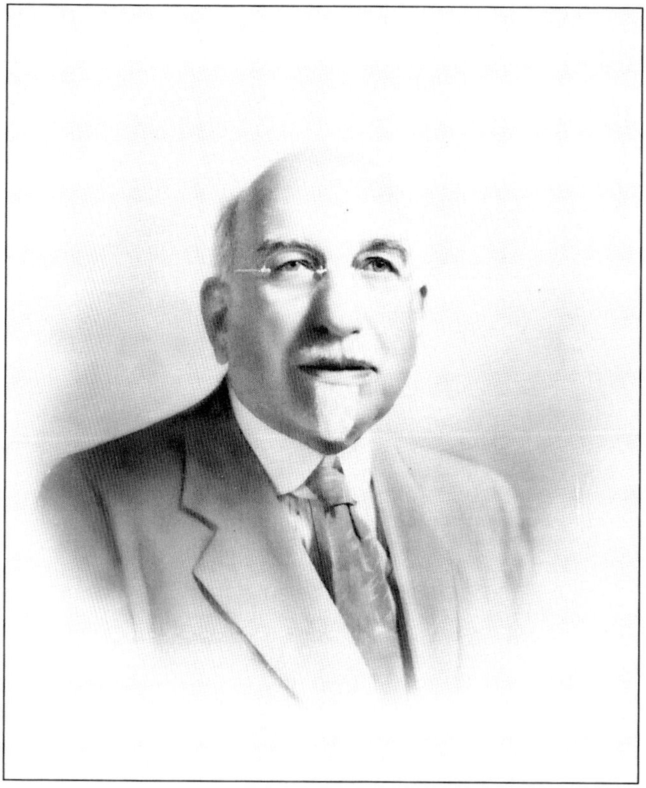

DR. EDWARD CHASE COOK, the husband of Sally Moody Cook and father of Dr. Edward Moody Cook. The elder Dr. Cook came to York in 1895 to practice medicine. In 1904, he and his wife helped to incorporate York Hospital which opened in 1906.

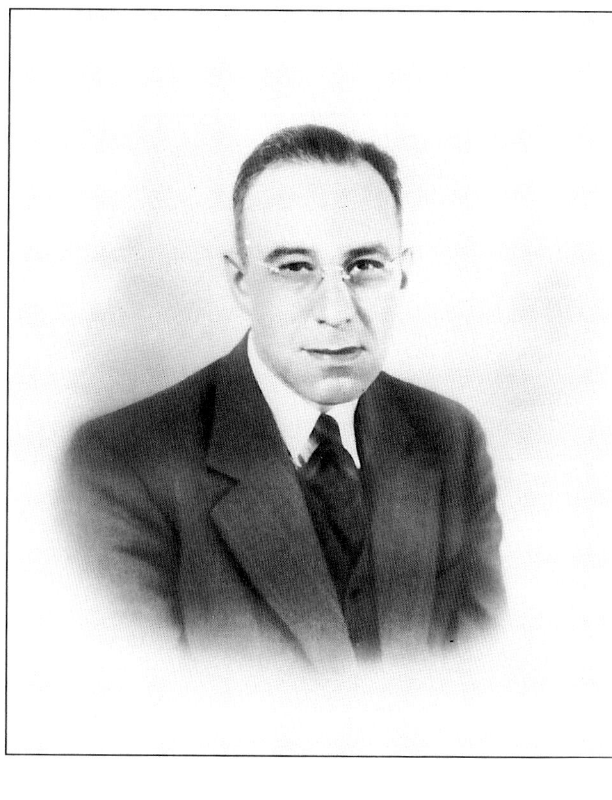

DR. EDWARD MOODY COOK also practiced medicine in York. Residents called him "young Dr. Cook" and his father "old Dr. Cook." They practiced at the same time and both used the facilities of York Hospital.

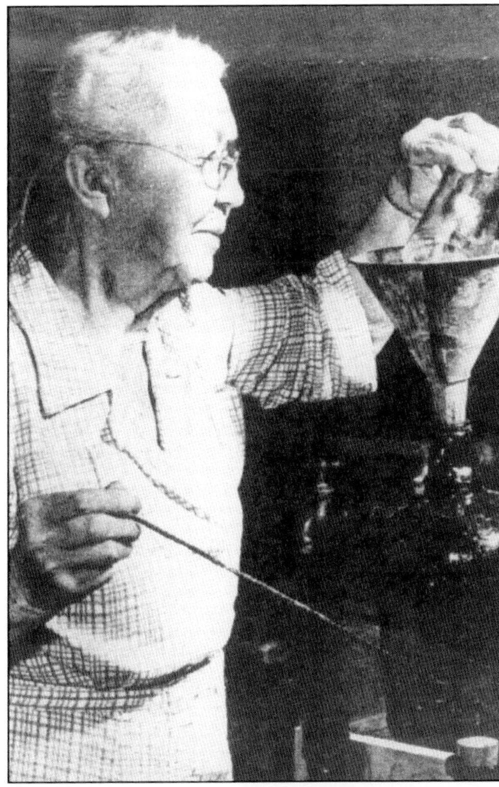

SALLY MOODY COOK was an eighty-one-year-old widow when she was pictured mixing spray for poison ivy. She became actively involved in the poison ivy control program and personally mixed about 1,000 gallons of ammate spray solution.

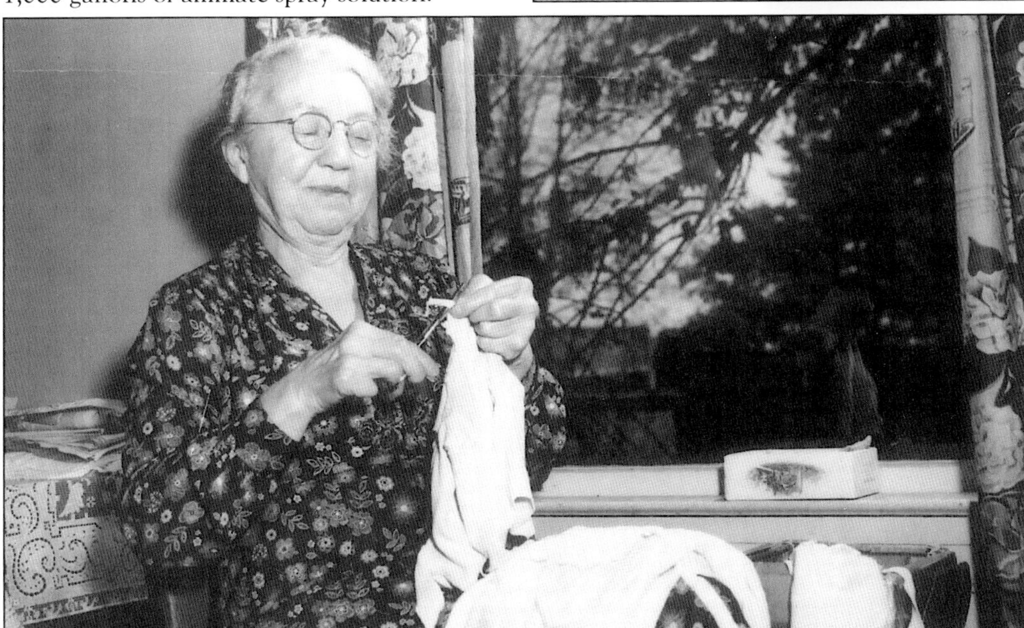

MRS. COOK WAS THE WIFE OF DR. EDWARD CHASE COOK AND THE MOTHER OF DR. EDWARD MOODY COOK. She made the first bed for the first patient at York Hospital and founded the first Medical Association Auxiliary in the country. She was mending linens for the hospital when this picture was taken.

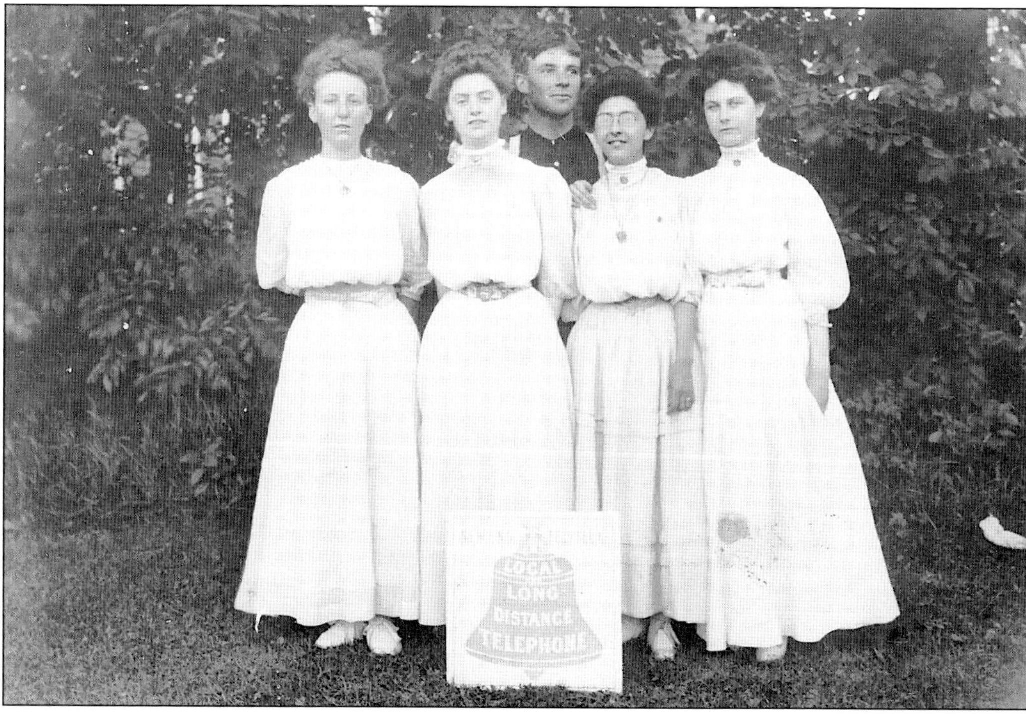

YORK TELEPHONE OPERATORS. Left to right: Sue Bridges, Flossie Martin, Cora Williams, and Mary Hanson, with Joe Martin in the rear. During the 1905 peace conference between Russia and Japan, the summer office in the Albracca Hotel averaged six hundred toll calls per day. Mary Hanson was the chief operator and she had seven operators under her supervision.

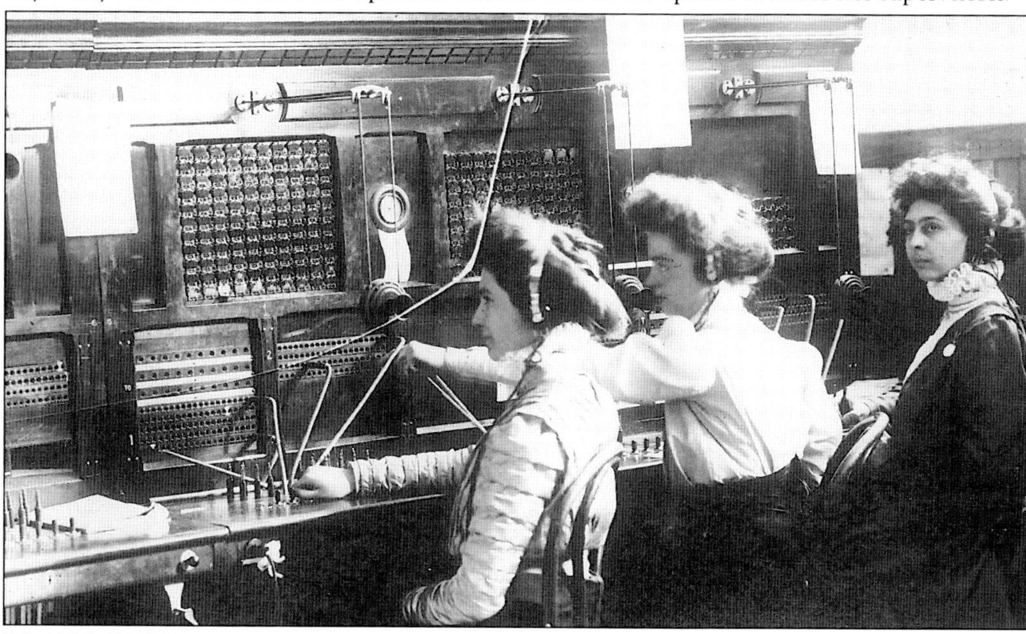

IN 1895, THERE WERE TWELVE TELEPHONE SUBSCRIBERS and the switchboard was located in Walker's general store. By 1911, the office had moved to the Realty building and was servicing 287 phones, including pay stations and extensions.

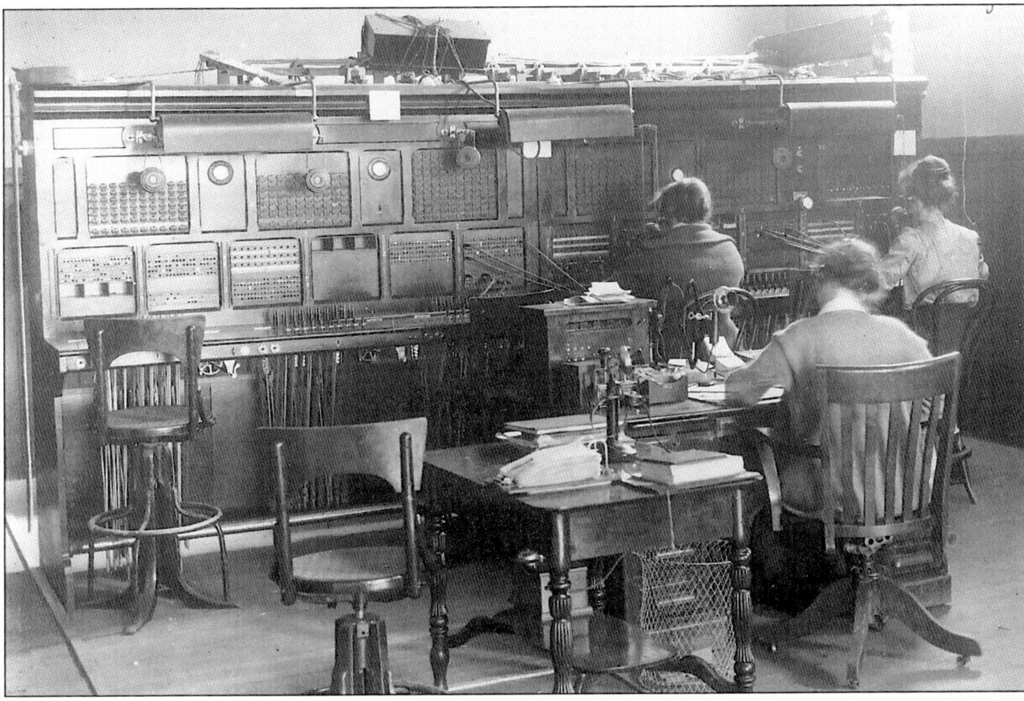

THE SWITCHBOARD AT THE TELEPHONE OFFICE. Miss Ida Starkey became the chief operator, Miss Marion Banks was senior operator, and Priscilla Craig was an operator. The old magneto system was replaced with a battery system at a cost of $25,000. At this time, the telephone exchange occupied one entire side of the Realty building.

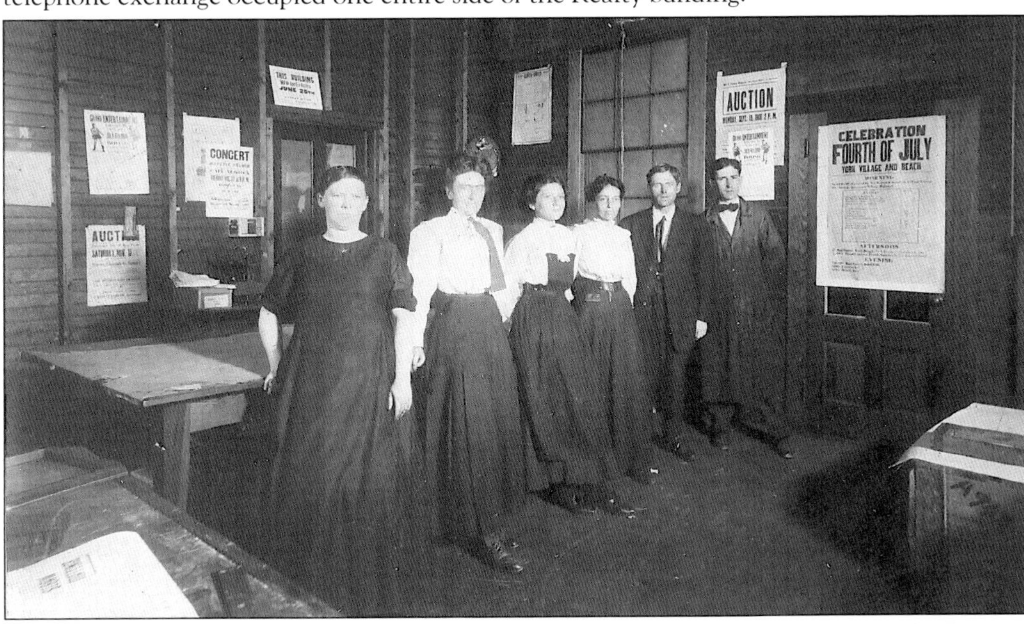

THE YORK PRESS WAS ALSO LOCATED IN THE REALTY BUILDING. Pictured here is the staff of the local newspaper when it was published by Myron Cox (second from right). Mr. Cox came to York from Meredith, New Hampshire and became an active member of the community.

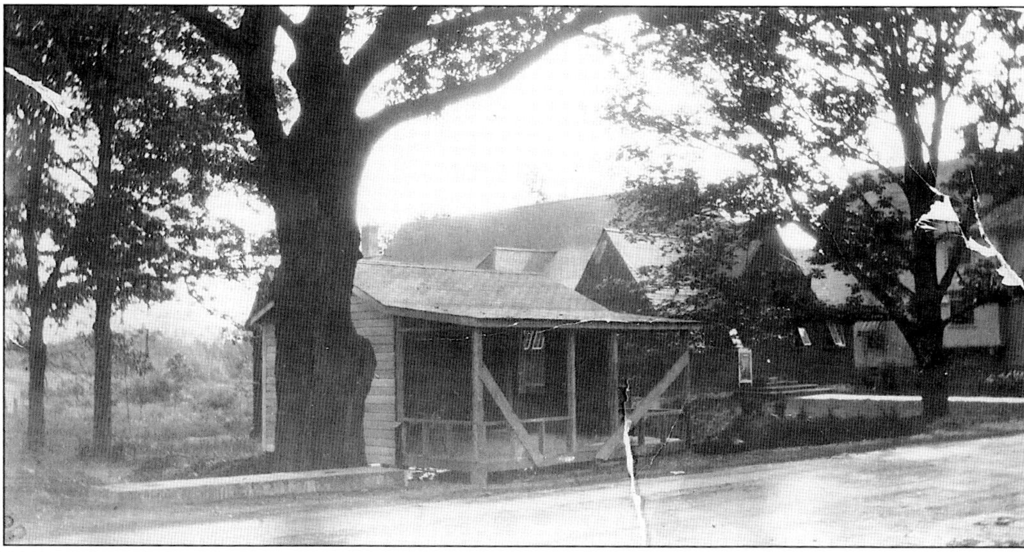

BILL GALLAGHER'S STORE as it appeared in 1930.

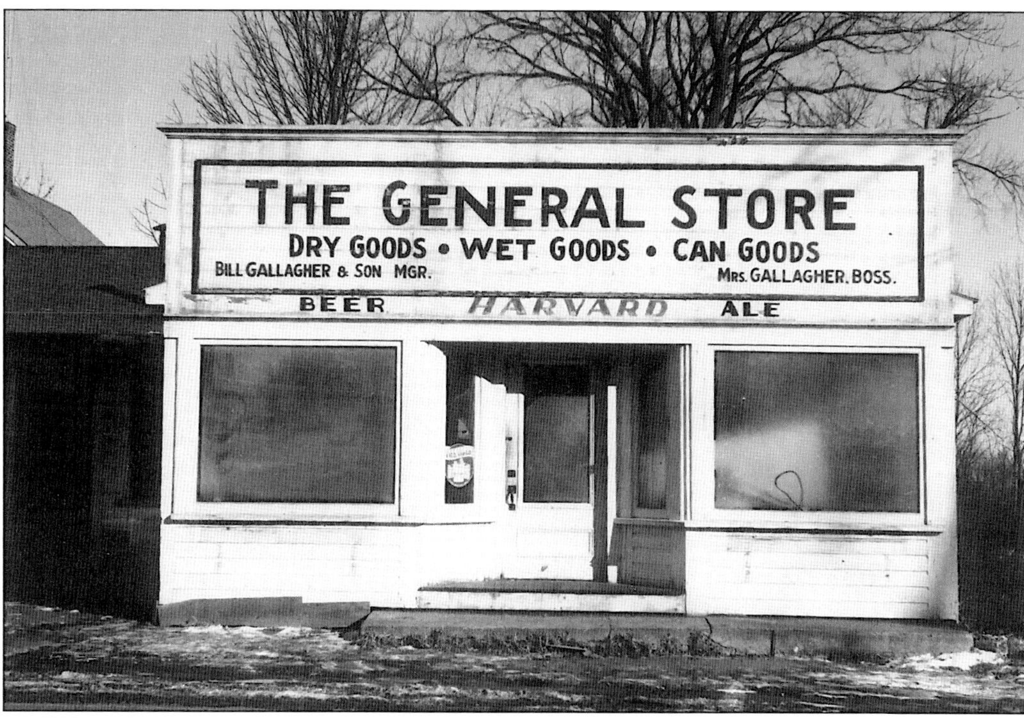

THE FAMOUS SIGN ON BILL GALLAGHER'S STORE reflected his sense of humor. There is reason to believe that he sold more wet goods than dry goods. Otherwise, it was a typical small town grocery store.

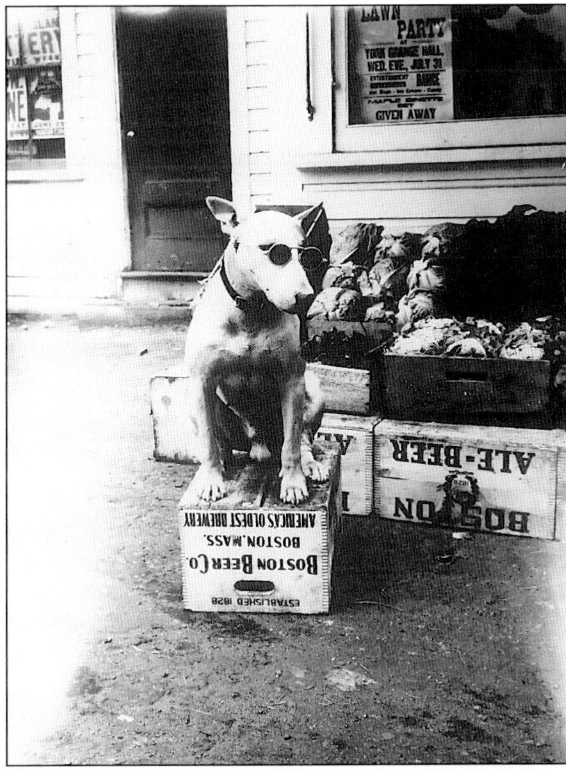

"PEPPER" THE BOSTON PIT BULL TERRIER posed for Bill Gallagher's ads in the local newspaper. Pepper would ignore customers until Bill assured him that they were acceptable playmates. With Bill's approval, he could become as playful as any dog in the neighborhood.

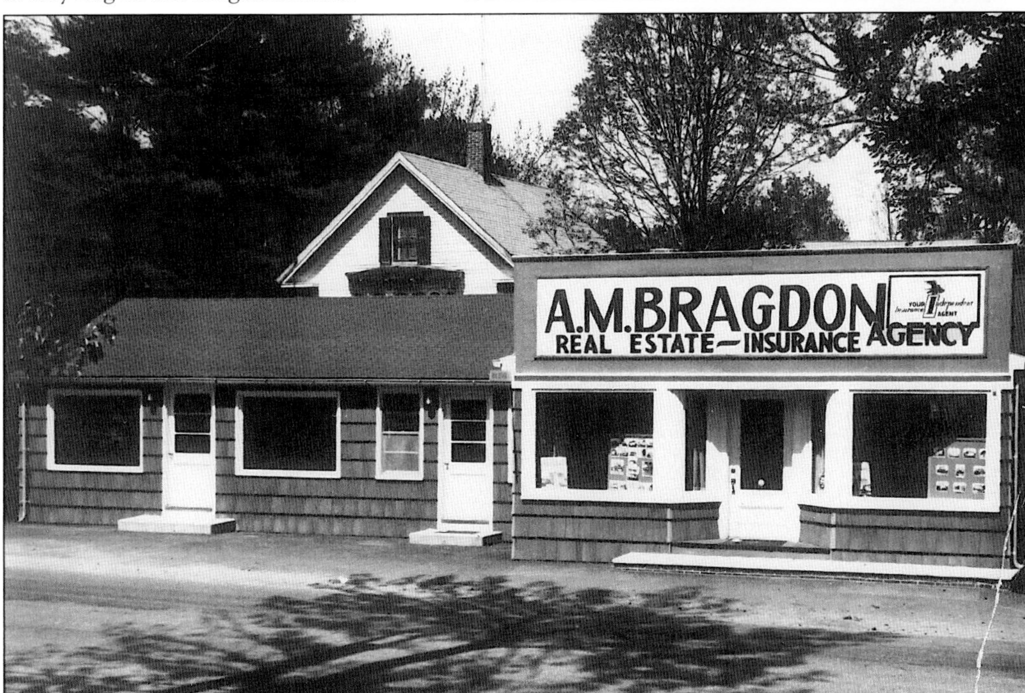

THE A.M. BRAGDON AGENCY PURCHASED THE BUILDING and converted it into an insurance and real estate office.

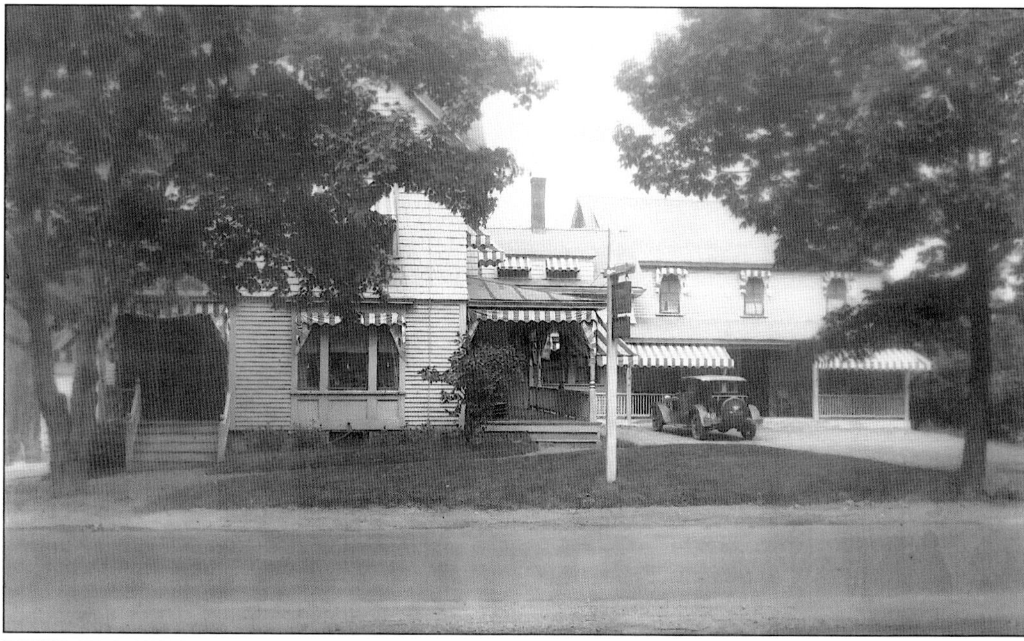

THE LITTLEFIELD INN was known for its Down East hospitality, comfortable beds, and home-cooked food. Built by Lyman Littlefield, the inn on York Street was a center of community activity. Lyman ran a blacksmith shop in the rear while his wife, Mary Abigail, supervised the cooking and the housekeeping. The inn was sold in the early 1930s.

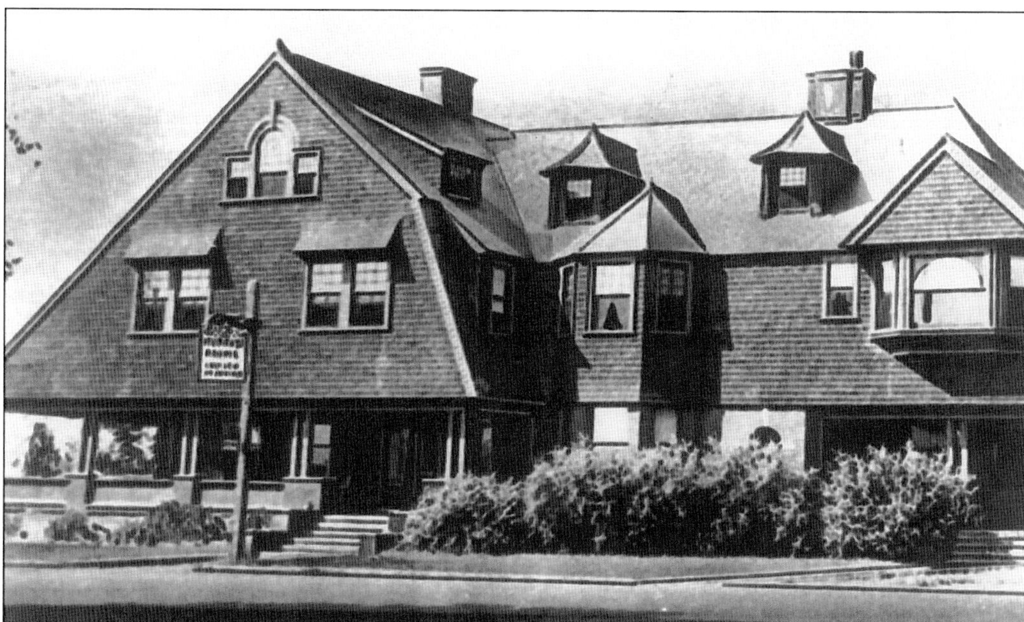

JOTHAM NORTON BUILT THIS FINE RESIDENCE with a view of Barrell's Mill Pond in 1896. After his death, it was used as a lodge and became the Norton Inn. A later owner renamed it Murray's Inn. It was purchased by members of the Catholic Church who held services in the building until it was razed so that St. Christopher's-By-The-Sea could be erected on the site.

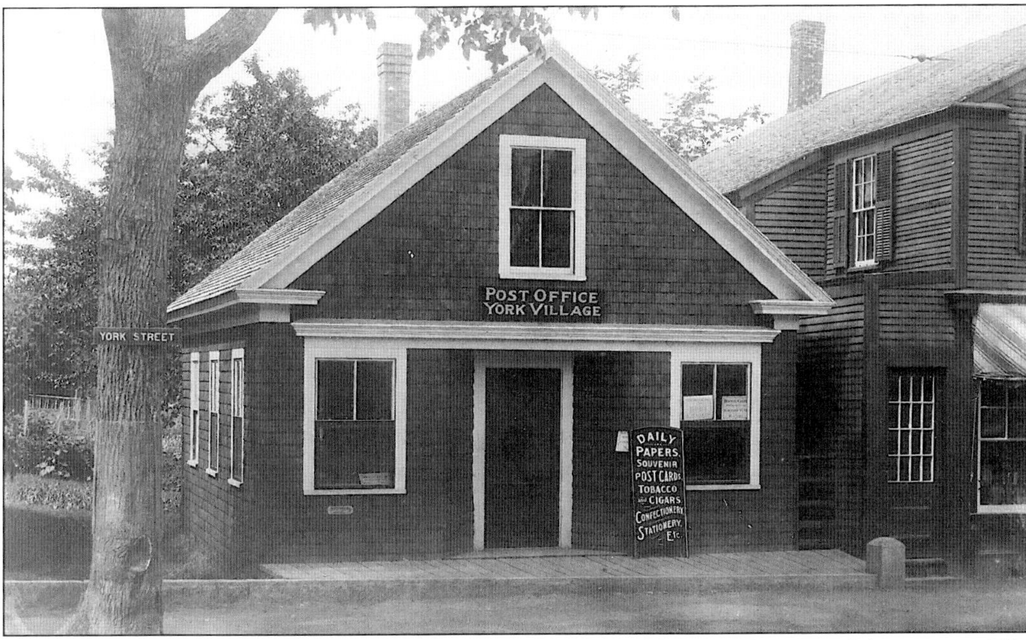

THE VILLAGE POST OFFICE was once housed in a building on the site of the present Ellis Agency office building. This is how it looked in the 1920s before it was moved back from the street and used for the storage of hardware and plumbing supplies. When the Baker buildings were razed and replaced by a bank, the old post office was rebuilt for use as a bookstore and a real estate office.

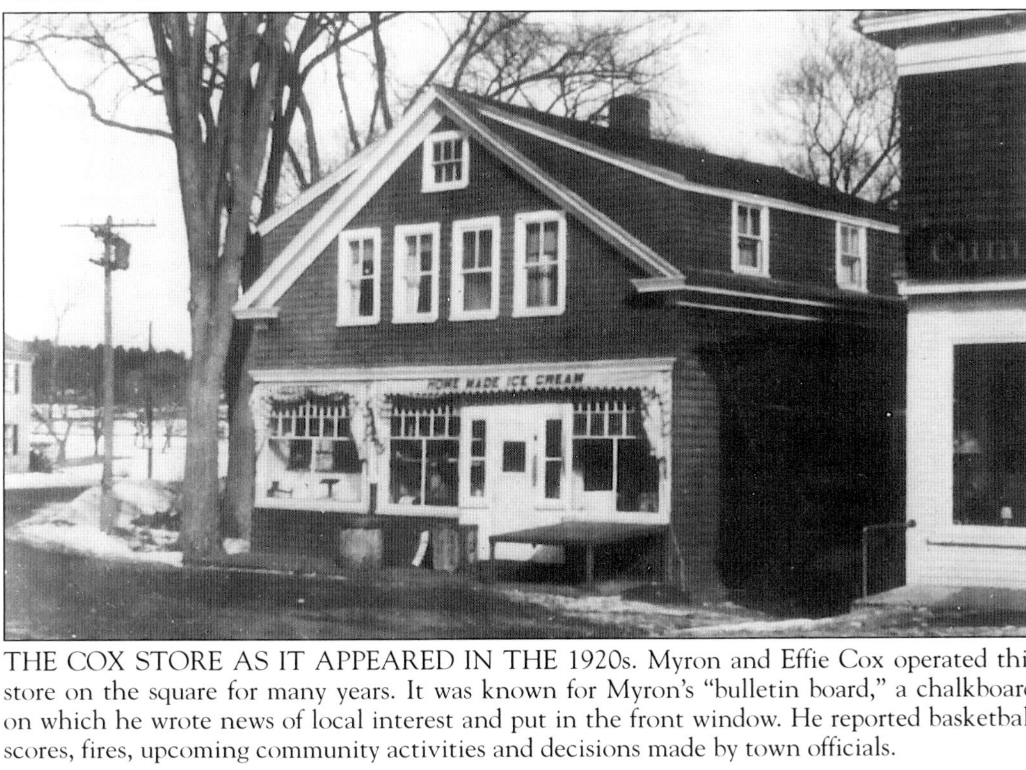

THE COX STORE AS IT APPEARED IN THE 1920s. Myron and Effie Cox operated this store on the square for many years. It was known for Myron's "bulletin board," a chalkboard on which he wrote news of local interest and put in the front window. He reported basketball scores, fires, upcoming community activities and decisions made by town officials.

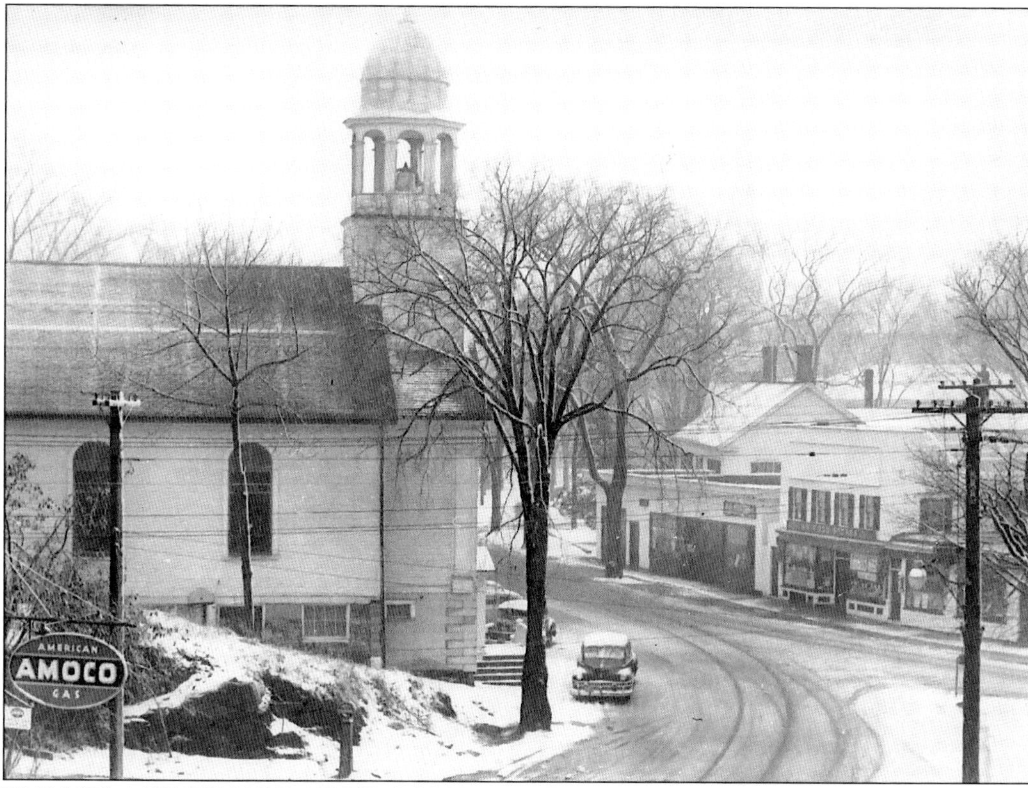

THE VILLAGE SQUARE AFTER A LIGHT SNOWSTORM. In the lower left is an "Amoco" sign indicating the location of a filling station that was operated by John Stover for many years. The Methodist Church is on the left. Grocery stores, a hardware store and the post office are on the right.

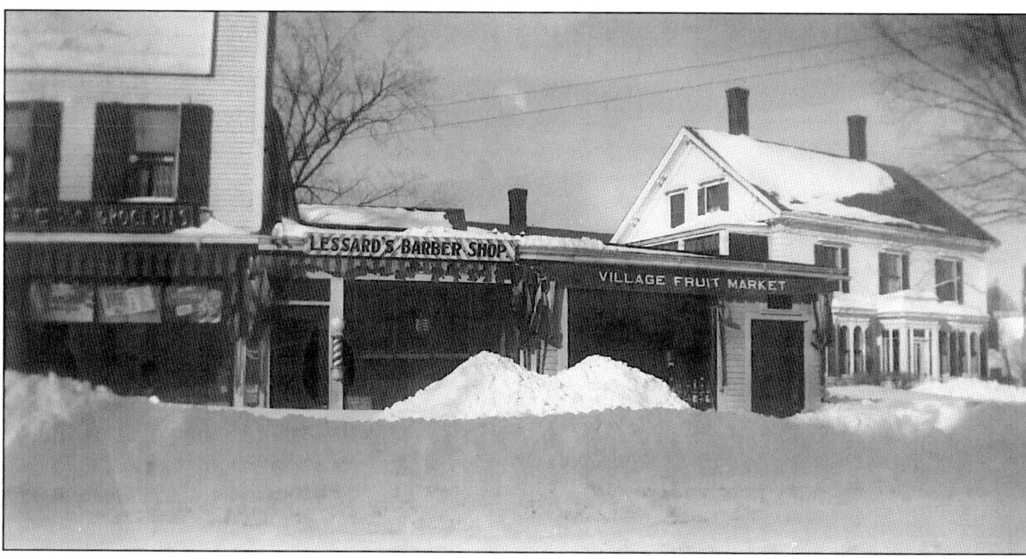

LESSARD'S BARBERSHOP AND THE VILLAGE FRUIT MARKET after a heavy snowstorm. All of these stores and the house on the right were razed to clear the site for the new bank.

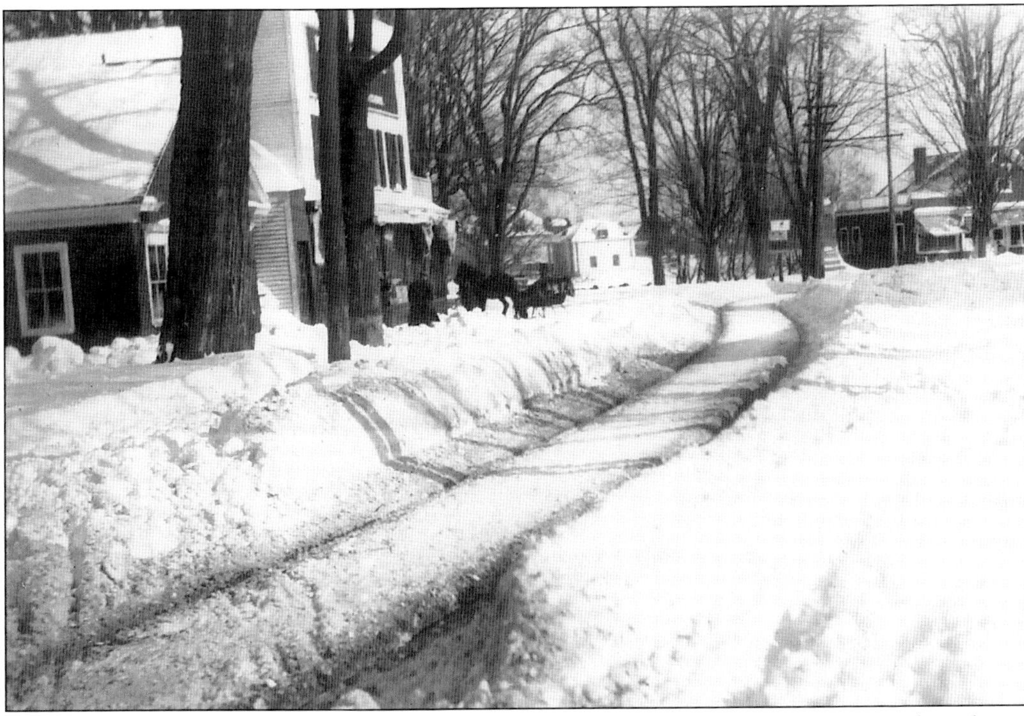

TROLLEY TRACKS IN THE SNOW were made by the plow on an electric car that cleared the tracks and enabled cars to operate during the winter months.

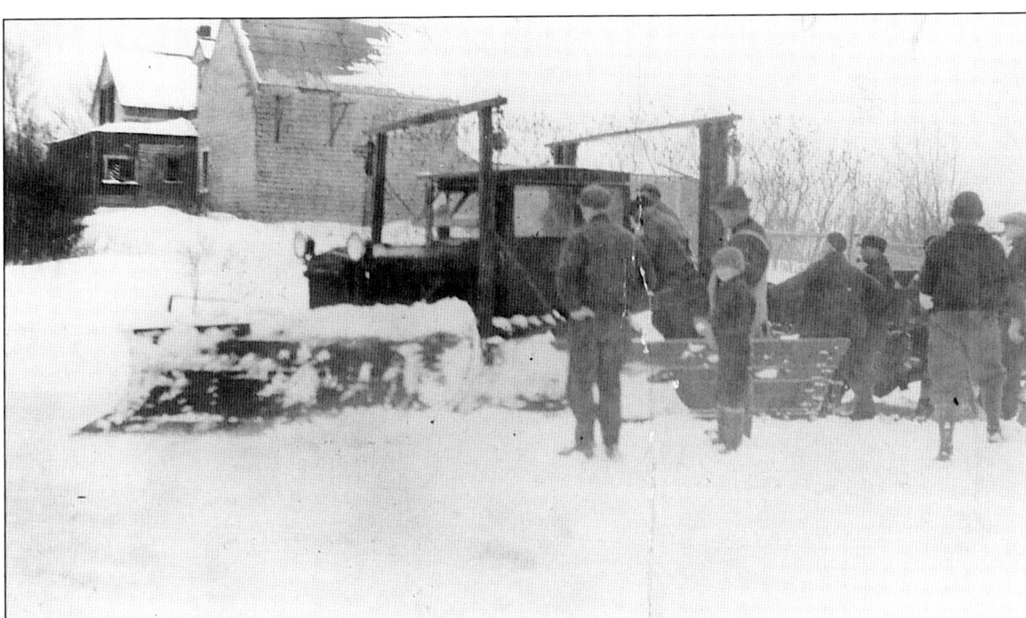

AN EARLY SNOWPLOW being carefully examined by a group of curious onlookers.

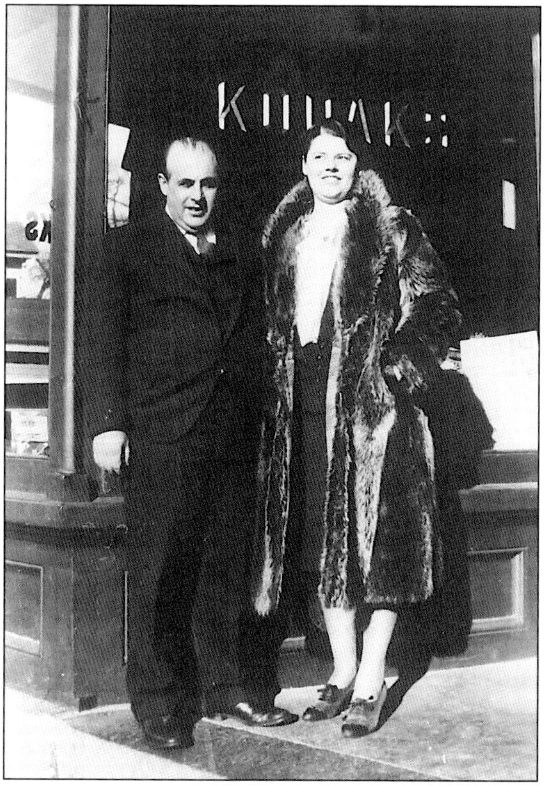

MORTON AND ELEANOR FRY in front of the village drug store. Fry purchased "Dr. Hawkes Pharmacies" in York Village, York Harbor and York Beach. The village store was open all year and was his base of operations.

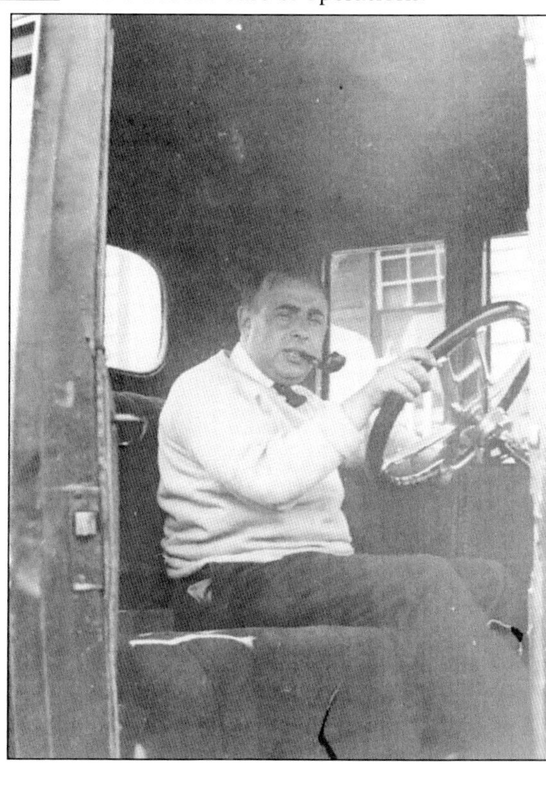

MORTON FRY operated the York Harbor movie theater in Lancaster Hall. He also operated a summer theater in Ogunquit. During the winter months, movies were shown in the York Village Fire Station.

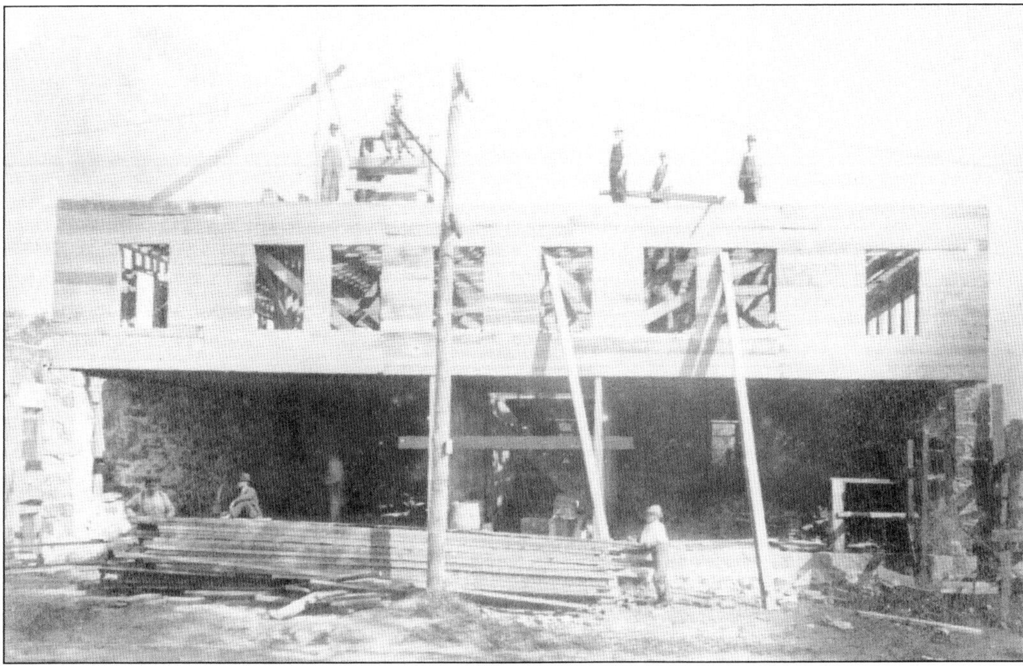

THE AUSTIN BLOCK UNDER CONSTRUCTION IN 1912. It was constructed by Frank Austin who sold it to Earl Baker in 1936. Baker operated a shoe store in the building until his death in 1946.

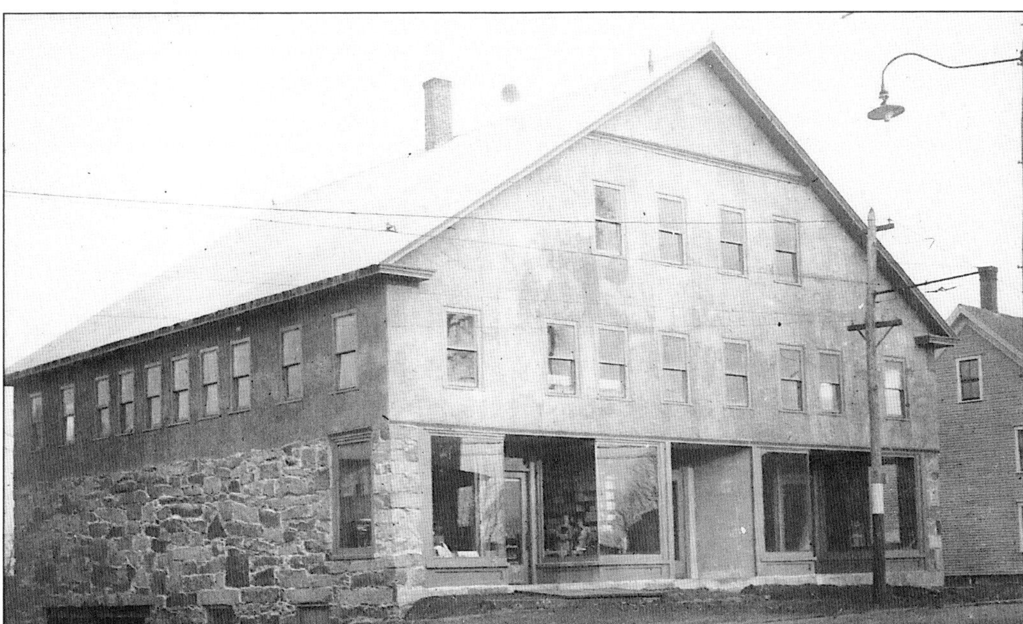

PAUL A. WILLIAMS PURCHASED THE PROPERTY IN 1947 and operated a dry goods business in one half of the store. Mr. Weaver operated a grocery store and meat market in the other half. When Weaver retired, Williams expanded his business to include the whole store. The property was acquired by Donald Williams in 1966. Don and his son Jim conducted business on the site for nearly thirty years.

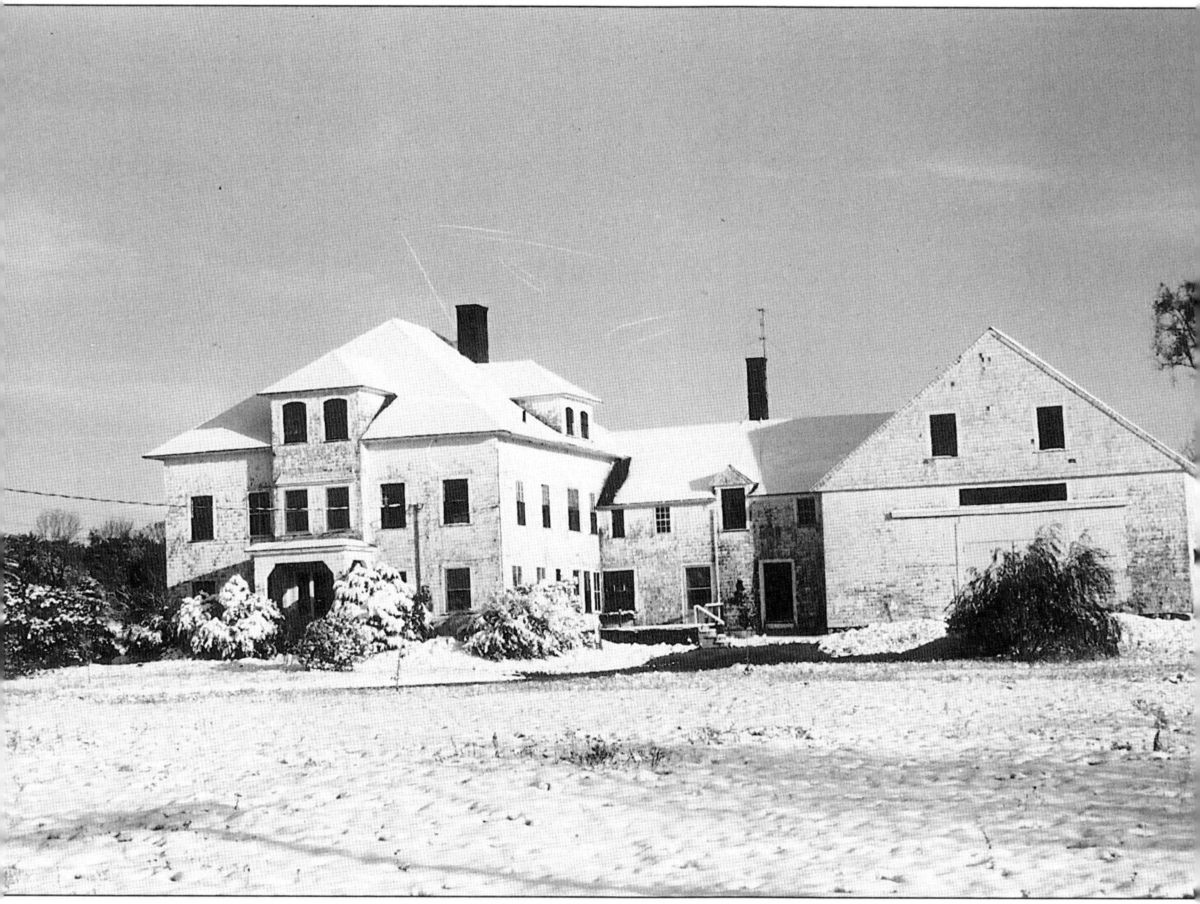

THE TOWN FARM OR "NEW HOME" was built in 1891 by E.B. Blaisdell to replace a dilapidated facility that was built in 1838. The new building had separate quarters for the superintendent, a large dining room for inmates, a strong room for the violent, and a locked and barred room for violent tramps. In 1892, the average number of inmates was fourteen and lodging was provided for sixty-one tramps who were served two meals per day.

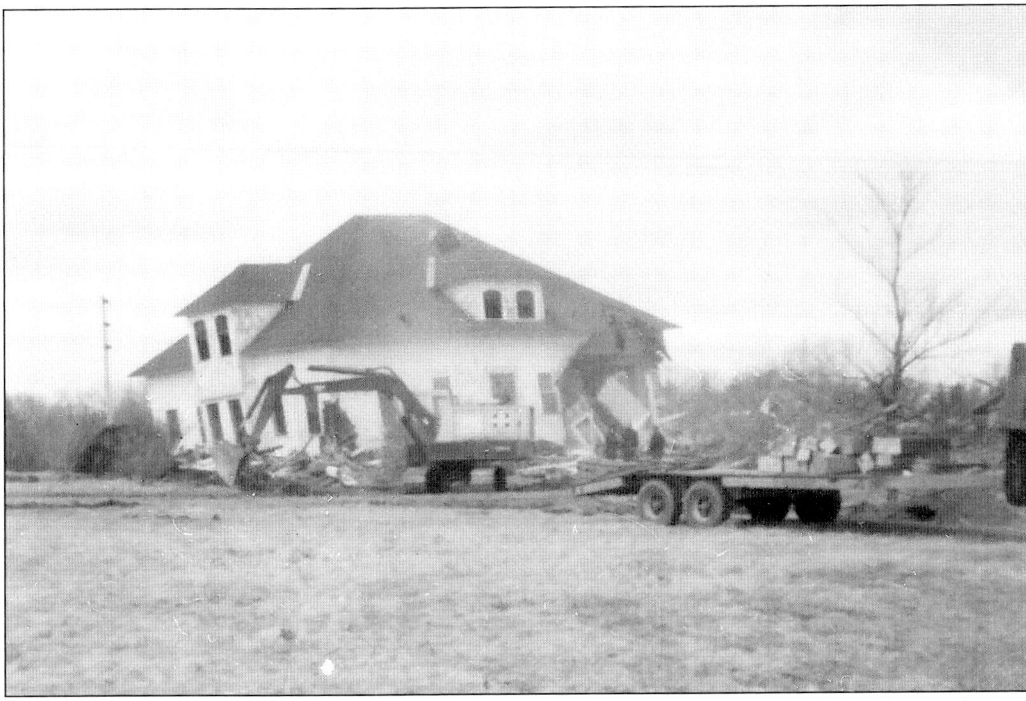

THE TOWN FARM EVENTUALLY BECAME A NURSING HOME for elderly people with limited resources. It was rented by the town to private individuals who operated it as a business.

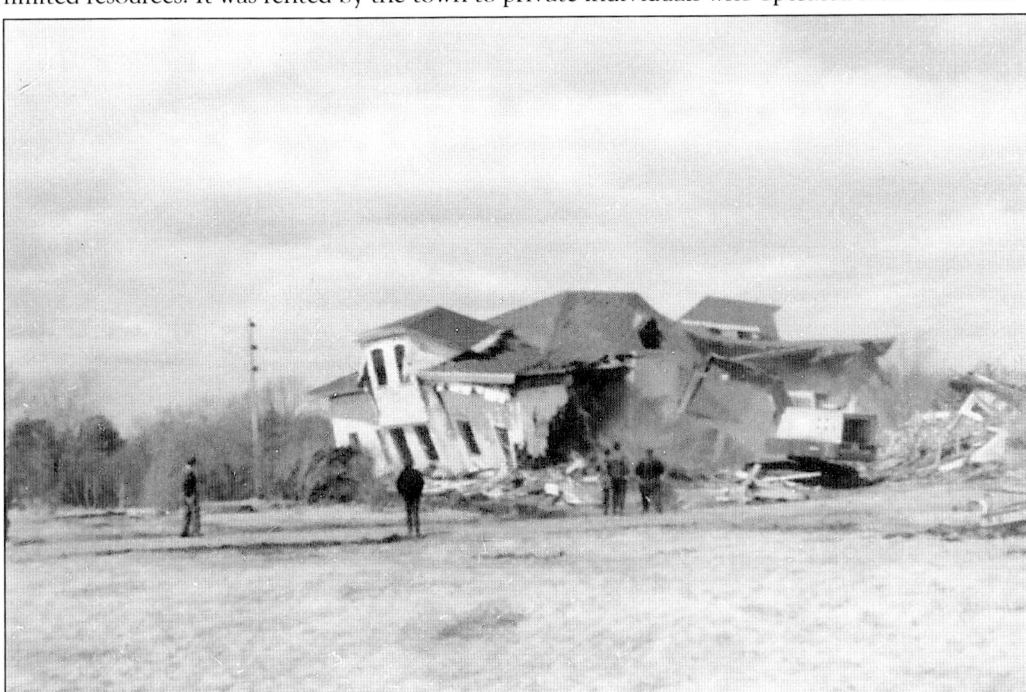

THE BUILDINGS BECAME DILAPIDATED IN THE LATE 1960s and voters at the 1970 town meeting authorized the selectmen to "raze the town farm buildings." They were torn down that spring.

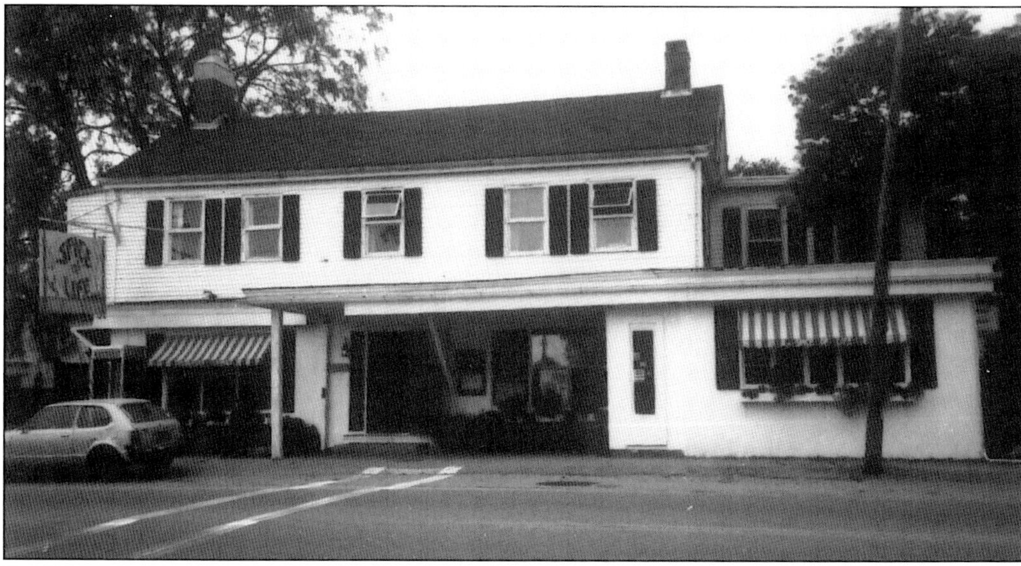

THE SPICE OF LIFE RESTAURANT as it appeared in 1986 before the exterior was restored to resemble a residence. It is now known as the Grant House and is used as an office building.

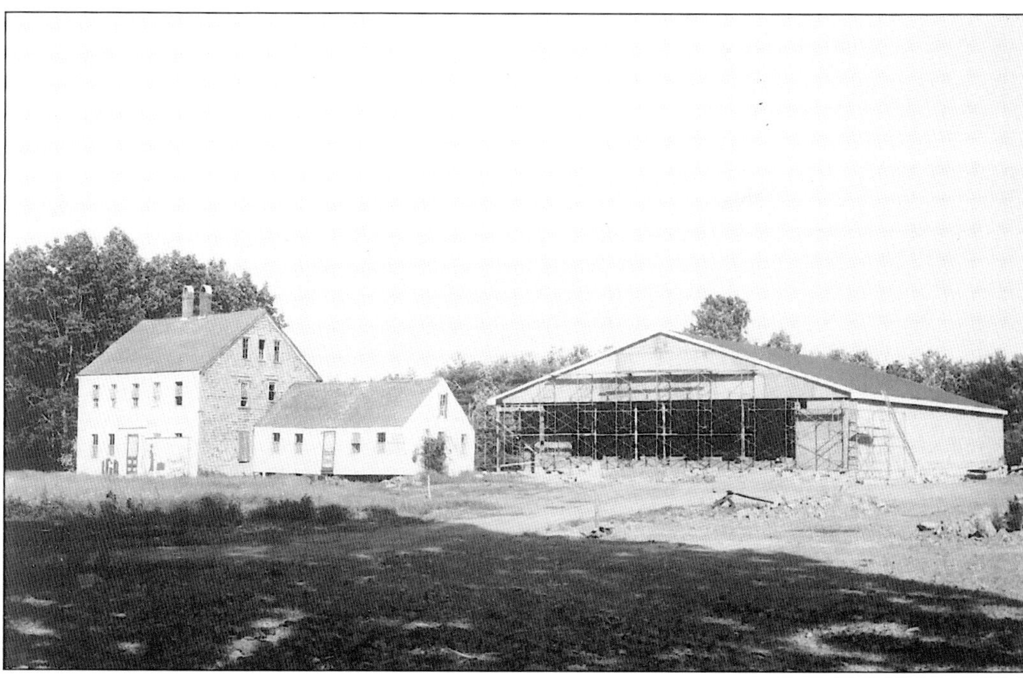

THE HUTCHINS FARM ON LONG SANDS ROAD was demolished to make room for the Village Shopping Center. The construction of the IGA was well under way when this photograph was taken. The ell was preserved by David Strater who had it moved to a new location overlooking the York River.

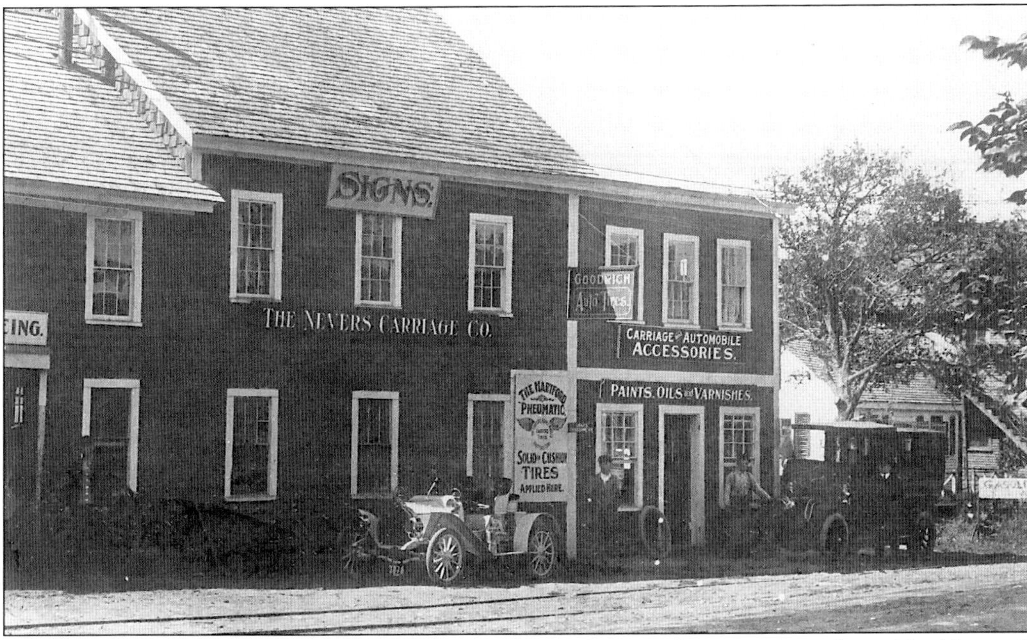

THE NEVERS CARRIAGE COMPANY was located across the street from the public library. It was here that Frank Nevers repaired and repainted carriages. Lyman Littlefield had a blacksmith shop where he shoed horses and oxen and forged parts for carriages. When automobiles became popular, Wil Bone and Elmer Young opened an auto repair service on the right side of the first floor. Most people in town owned Fords, so that is what they repaired.

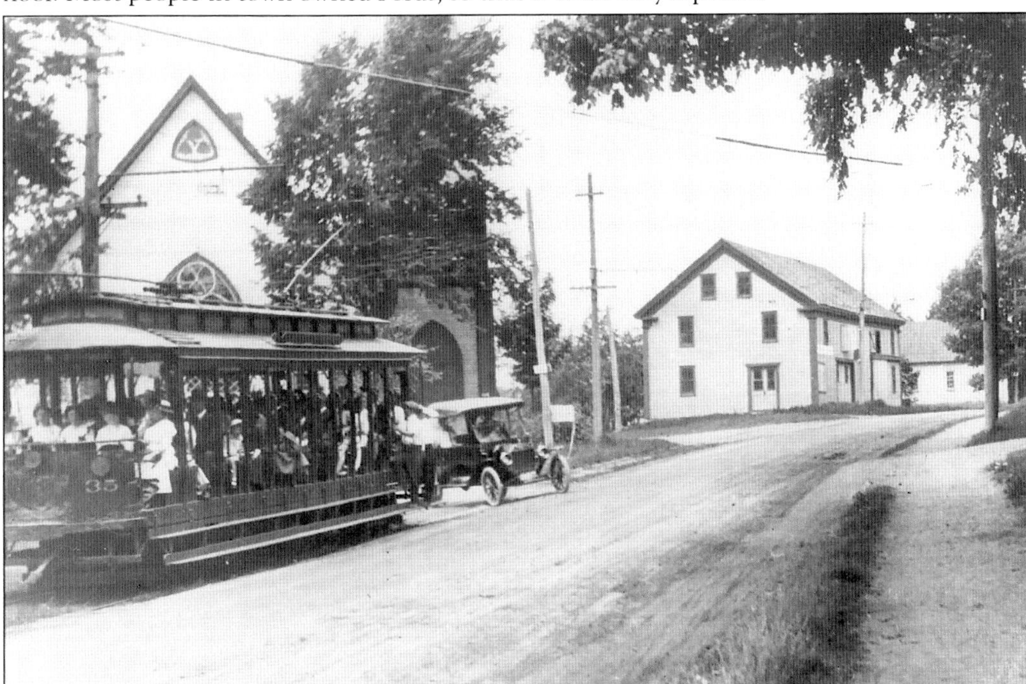

A TROLLEY CAR AT YORK CORNER JUNCTION. This Laconia 13 bench open car was used during the summer season.

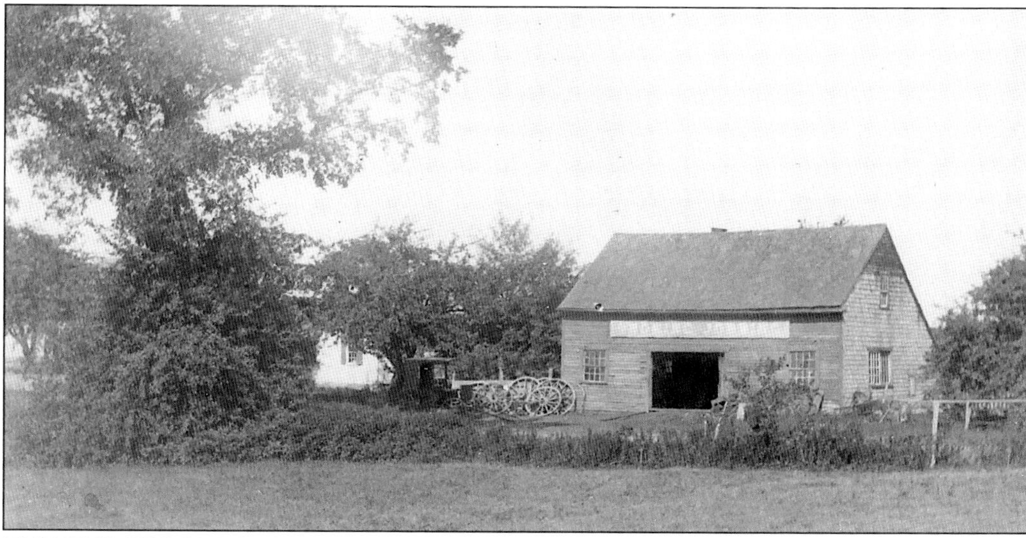

THE DURGIN BLACKSMITH SHOP AT YORK CORNER IN 1900. It was located on old Route 1 near the entrance to the Chase Pond Road. Durgin operated the shop until the late 1920s or the early 1930s. When he retired, the building remained empty for many years.

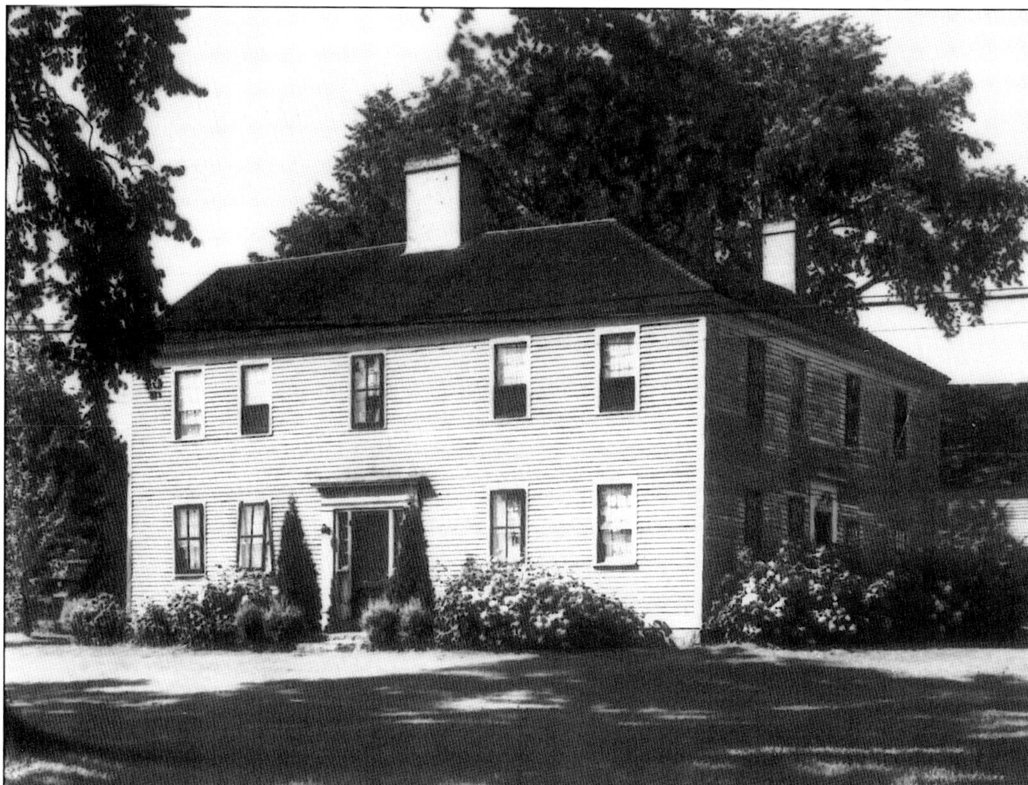

THE LEWIS BANE HOUSE was built in 1721. It stood on the north side of Route 1 near Route 91 until it was destroyed by fire in 1990. Bane was the coroner for the District of Maine. He tried to send help to the men shipwrecked on Boon Island in 1710. This story is told in Kenneth Robert's novel Boon Island.

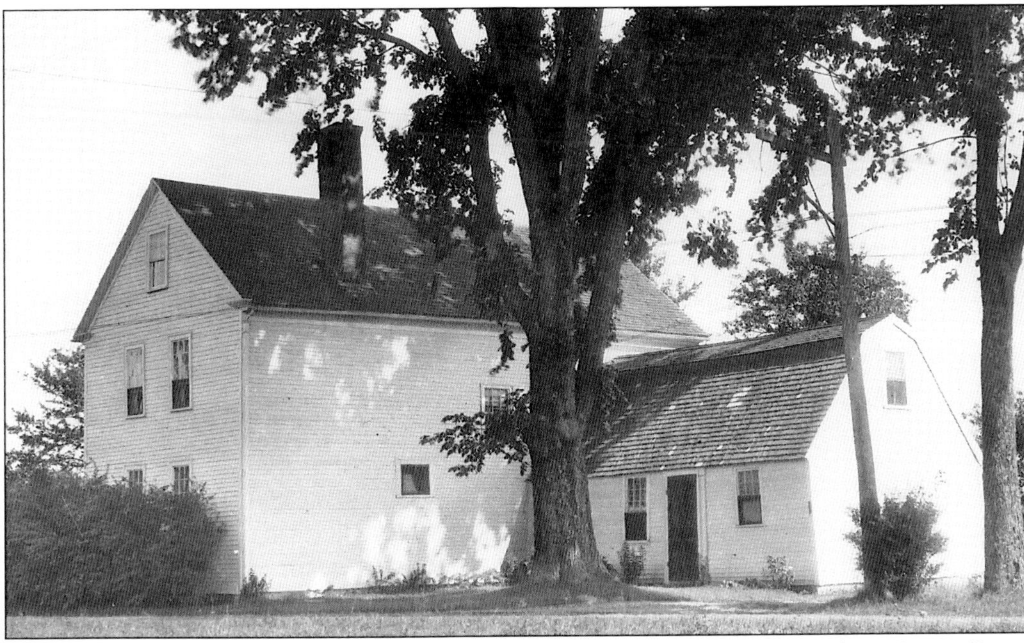

THE BRAGDON FARM AT YORK CORNER stood across the street from Lewis Bane's residence. It was built in 1732 and was known as the Jeremiah Bumstead House. The house was moved to a new location on Route 1 and converted for commercial use. The site was then used as a business park.

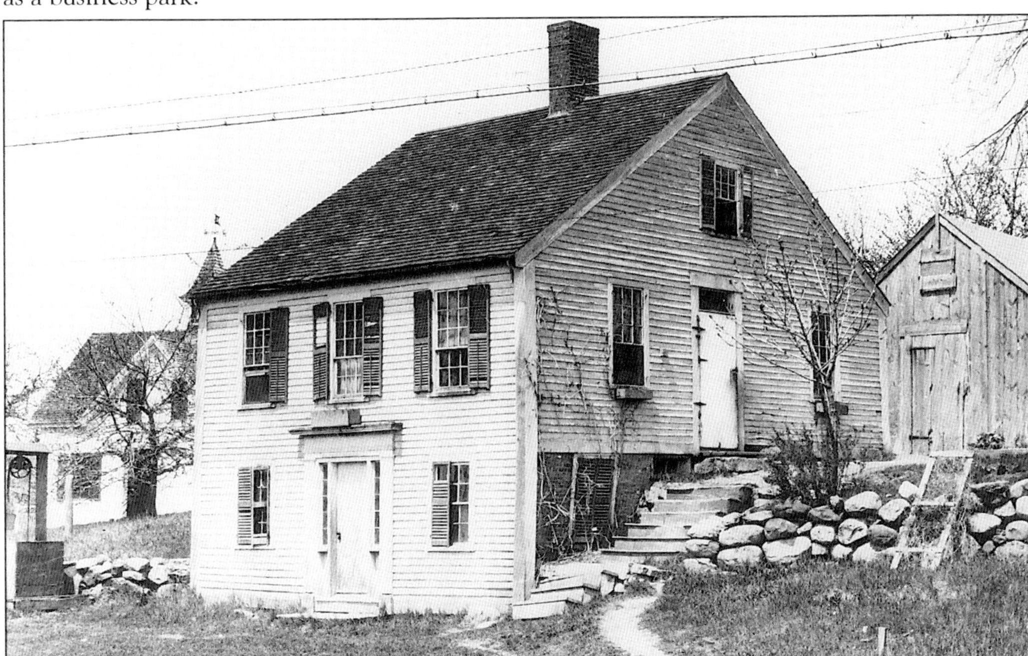

THE OLD FORT AT YORK CORNER was the home of Will Ray and his family for many years. This fine old home was replaced by a Standard Oil filling station when "gasoline alley" began to evolve at the corner in the 1920s. The building may have been moved to another location nearby.

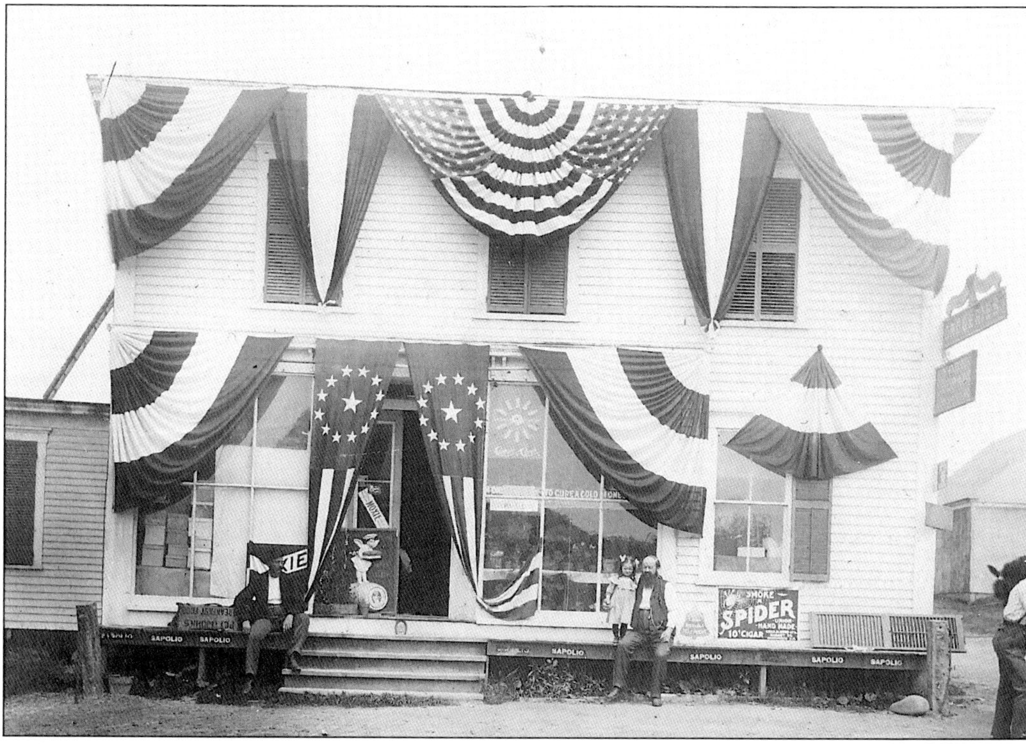

PLAISTED'S STORE WAS LOCATED ON A TRIANGLE OF LAND between Route 1 and Route 1-A. The building faced Route 1-A and the dry goods counter was on the left as you entered the front door. There were bolts of cotton, gingham, calico and oil cloth. Beyond the dry goods counter there were boots, shoes and men's stockings. On the right was a counter with penny candy. The shelves behind the counter were lined with patent medicines such as Jamaica Ginger, paregoric, peppermint and mustard.

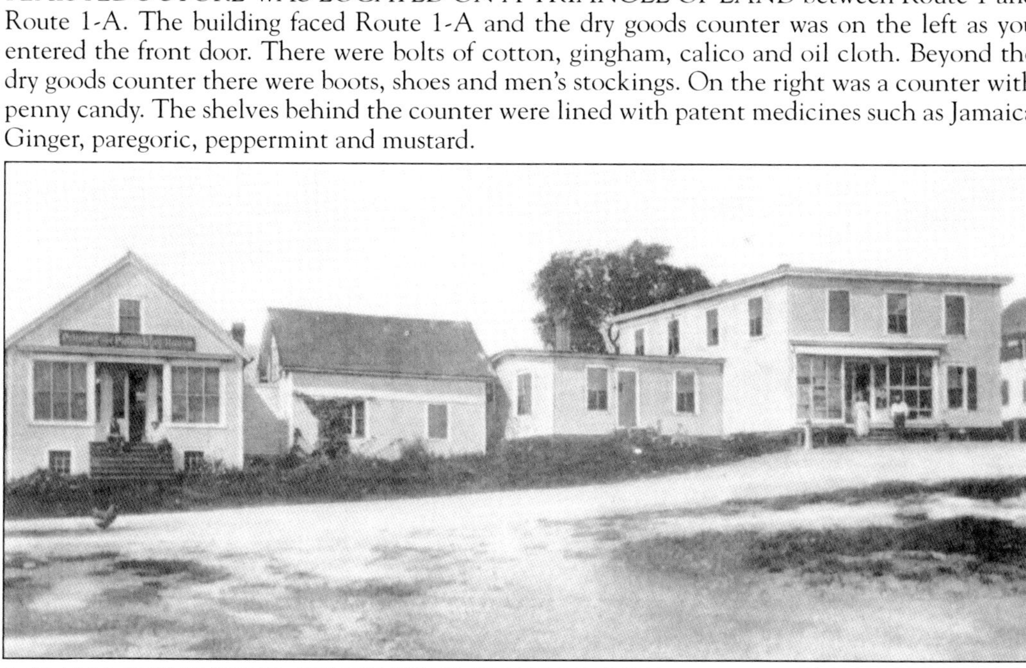

A SMALL PRINT SHOP AT THE REAR OF THE STORE was operated by George Plaisted's son, Purcell. He was a skillful printer who amazed everyone by his ability to read upside down. George was a Notary Public and had a small office where he drew up wills and deeds. He also had a large print shop where he printed the York Courant, a weekly newspaper.

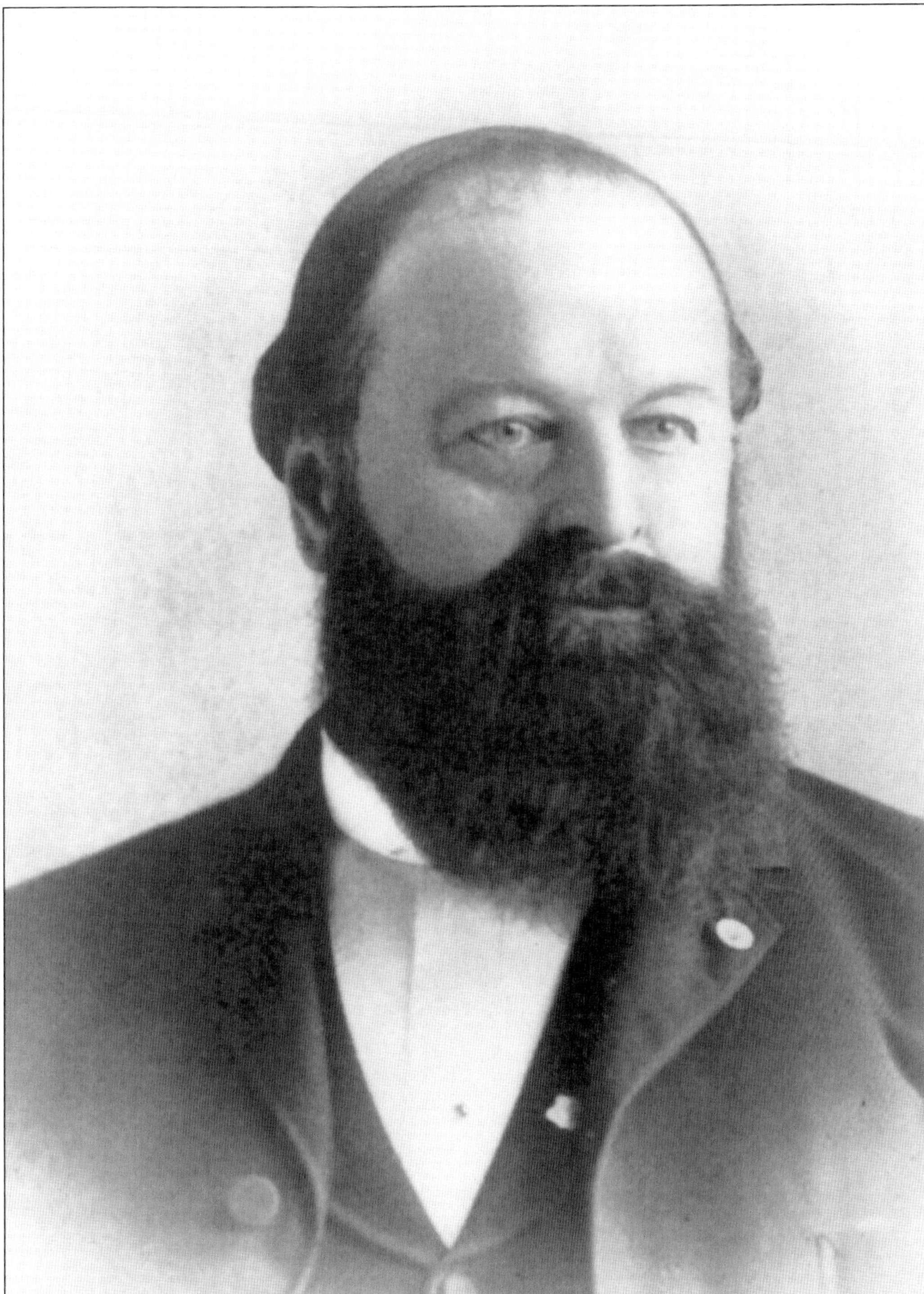

"I KNOW NOT WHAT THE TRUTH MAY BE, I'M TELLING IT TO YOU AS IT WAS TOLD TO ME," was on the masthead of the York Courant which was published by George Plaisted at York Corner.

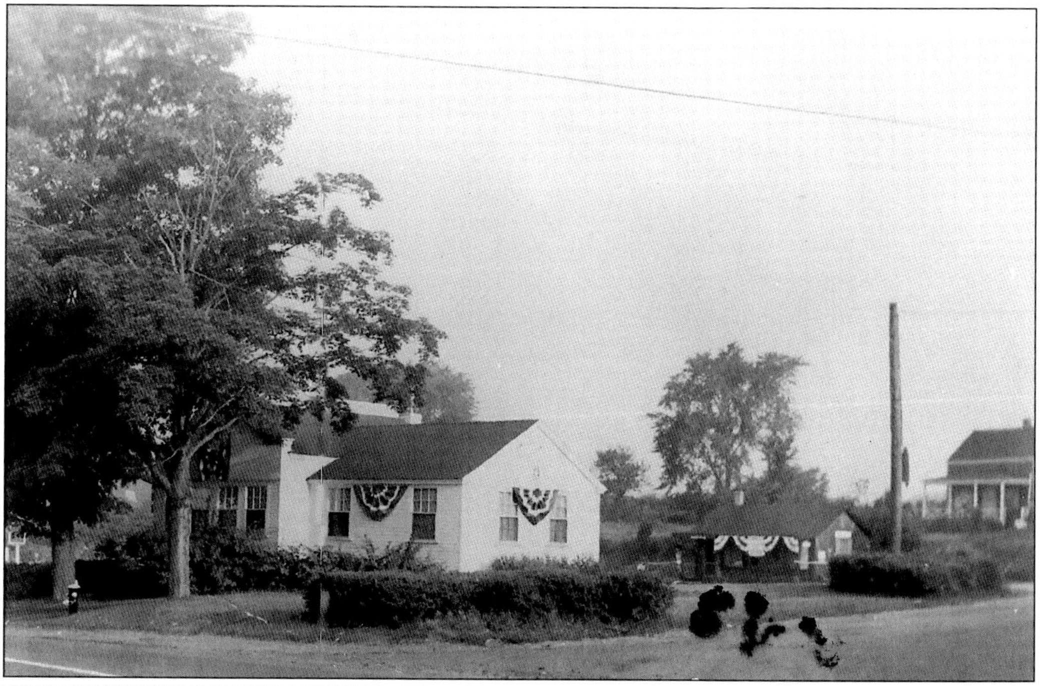

THE TOURIST INFORMATION CENTER AT YORK CORNER in the early 1950s. It was sold and moved up on Route 1 to be used as an antique shop. The Chamber of Commerce focused its efforts on York Beach where it operated from a cabin-like building on the edge of the beach.

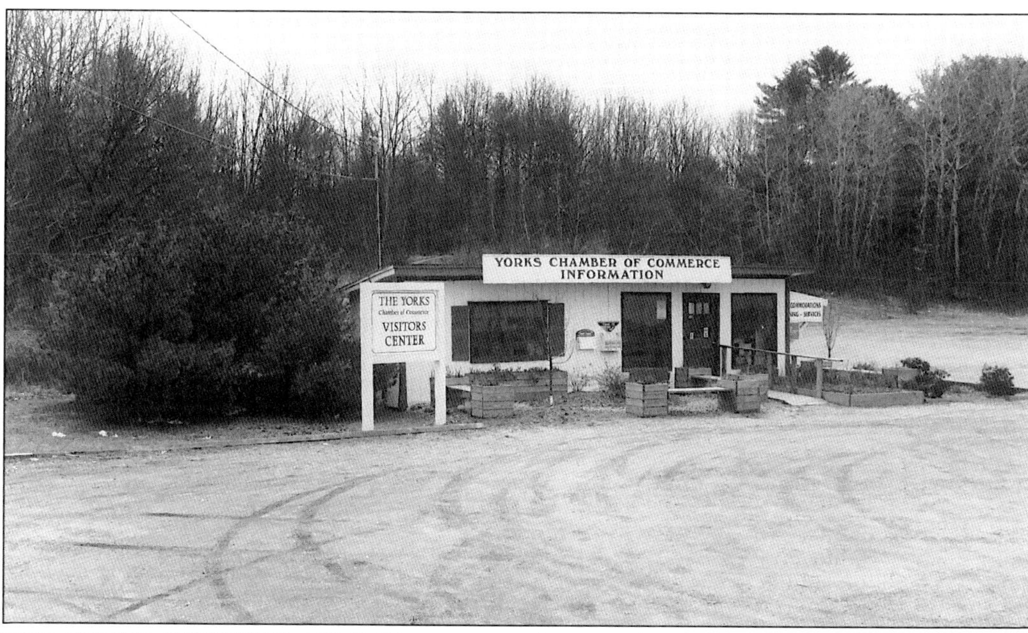

THE YORKS VISITOR'S CENTER was opened across from the Turnpike exit on Route 1. The makeshift facility made a poor impression on visitors and was replaced by a beautiful new facility that was opened in 1994. This new facility is only a short distance from the original information center that was abandoned in the 1950s.

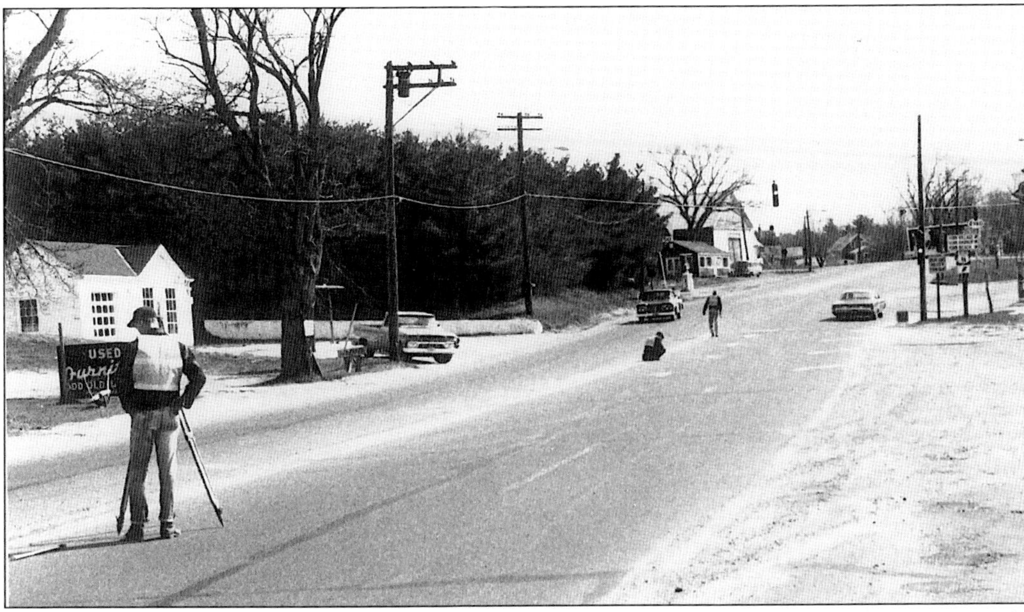

SURVEYING ROUTE 1 AT YORK CORNER in preparation for widening it to four lanes. The triangle of land at York Corner was created in 1827 when the road between the Corner and the Post Road, or Nason Road, was built. The road was widened as far as Cape Neddick, but the construction of the Maine Turnpike brought an end to the Route 1 project.

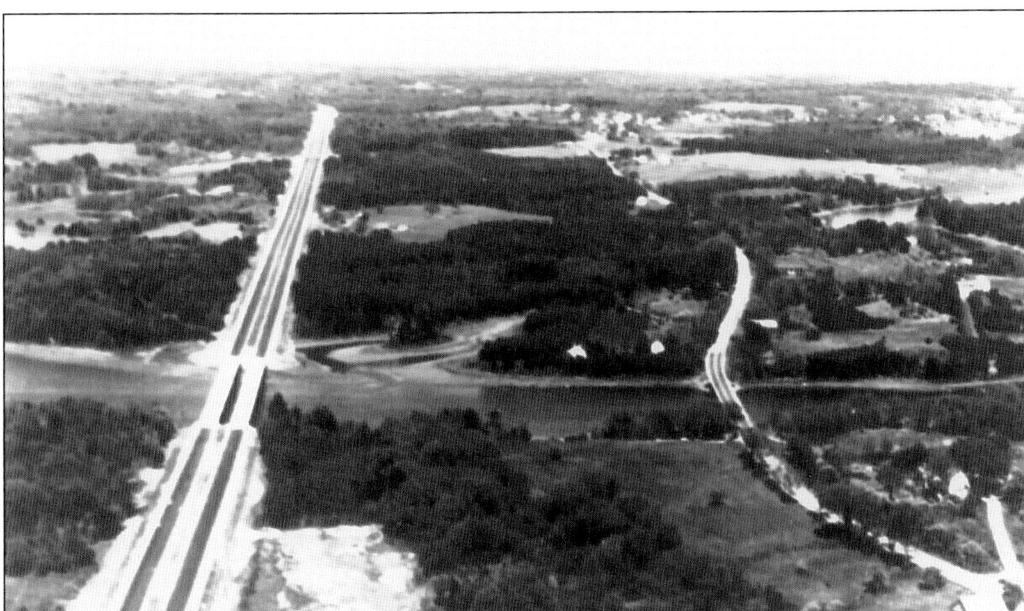

THE MAINE TURNPIKE AND ROUTE 1 can be seen in this aerial photograph. The Maine Turnpike was opened to the public on May 15, 1947. The 47-mile toll road was built from scratch in about a year and a half and was the first postwar highway constructed in the country. The road cost $20 million to build and was expected to pay for itself in twenty-five or thirty years.

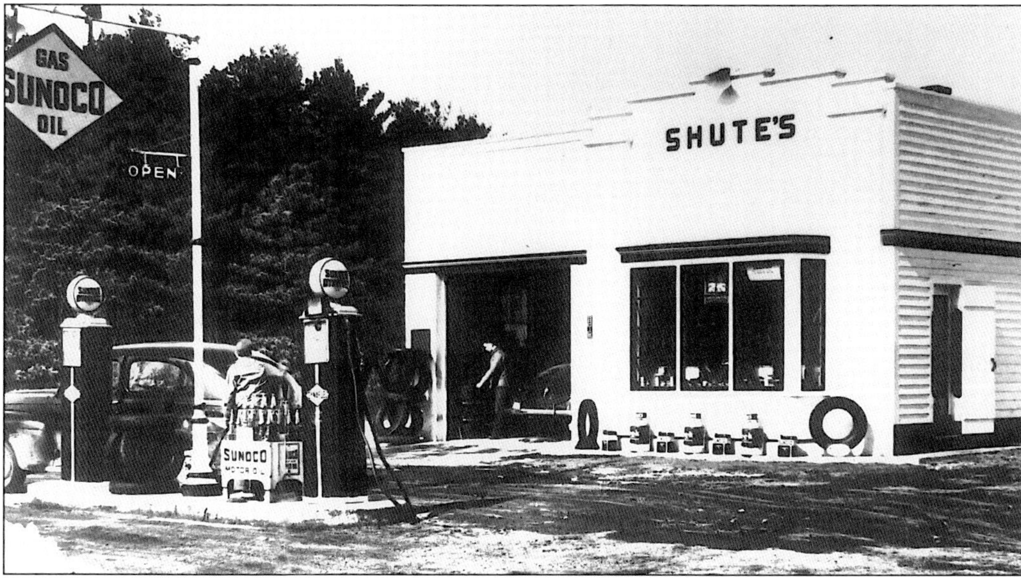

SHUTE'S SUNOCO STATION was located near the present site of Starkey Ford at York Corner. It was part of the "gasoline alley" of busy filling stations. A few survived but this one closed and fell into disrepair. The owner did nothing to prevent it from falling apart.

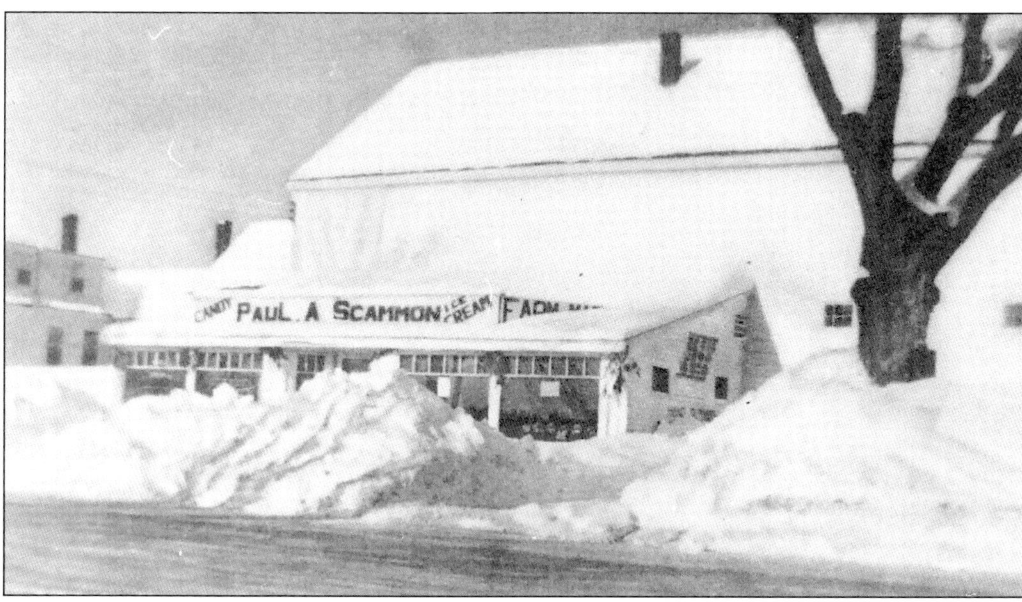

FARM-MADE CANDY WAS PRODUCED IN THIS ROUTE 1 BUSINESS when Paul A. Scammon converted Will Thompson's barn into a candy store and ice cream shop. Ice cream sales were slow at this time of year but the workers were busy making and packaging the candy.

Two

Preserving York's Past

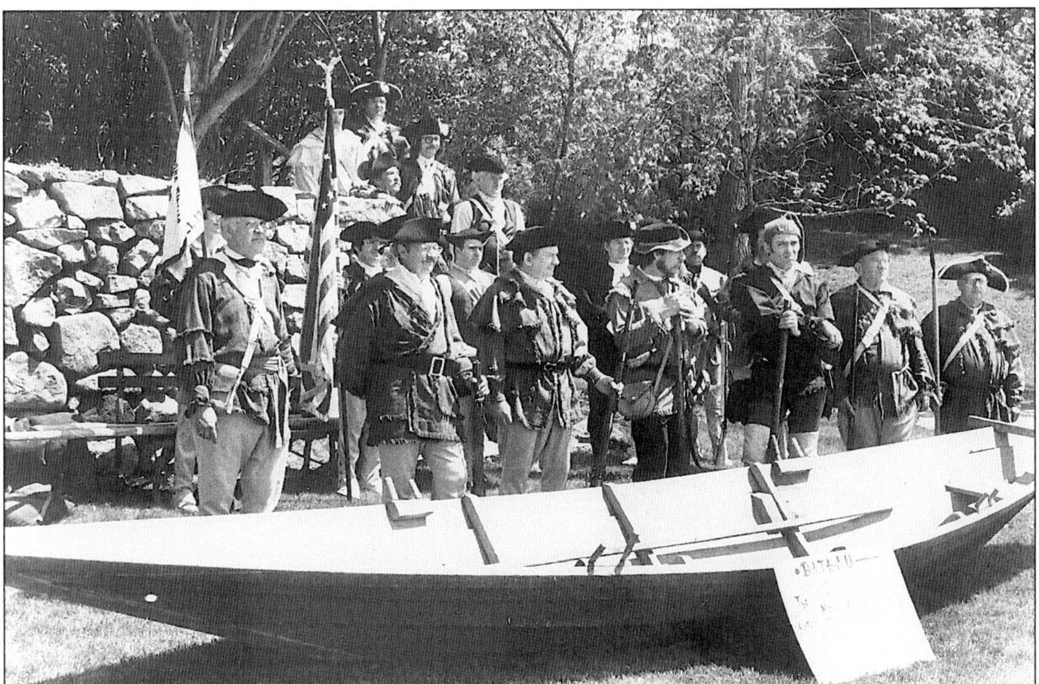

THE BATTEAU OF THE YORK MILITIA COMPANY used in 1975 for the re-creation of Arnold's march to Quebec. One of the most dramatic re-enactments during the bicentennial period was that of Benedict Arnold's march through Maine and Canada in an unsuccessful attempt to capture Quebec from the British. The York Militia Company financed the construction of a batteau and fifty-six men joined Captain Roger Shorey of the Goodrich Company. The expedition drew large crowds as it moved through Maine and Canada.

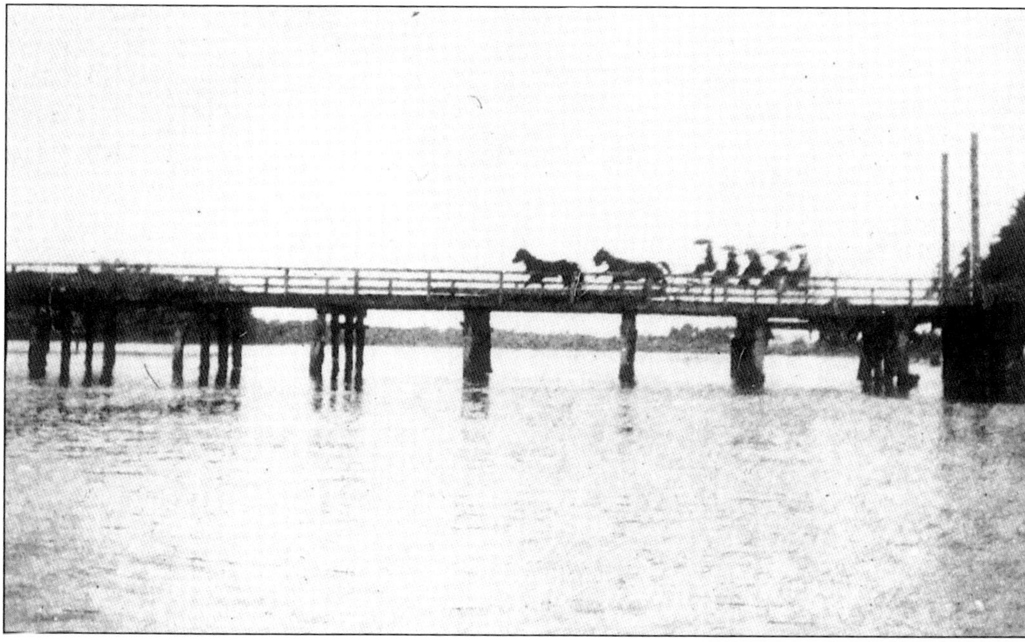

CROSSING SEWALL'S BRIDGE. In 1742, it was voted at the town meeting to allow any combination of persons to build a bridge in the vicinity of Sewall's Ferry, but at no expense to the town and with the stipulation that the citizens of York would not be charged for crossing the bridge. The bridge was not open to traffic until 1761. However, the "Way to the River," now Lindsay Road, was laid out in 1745.

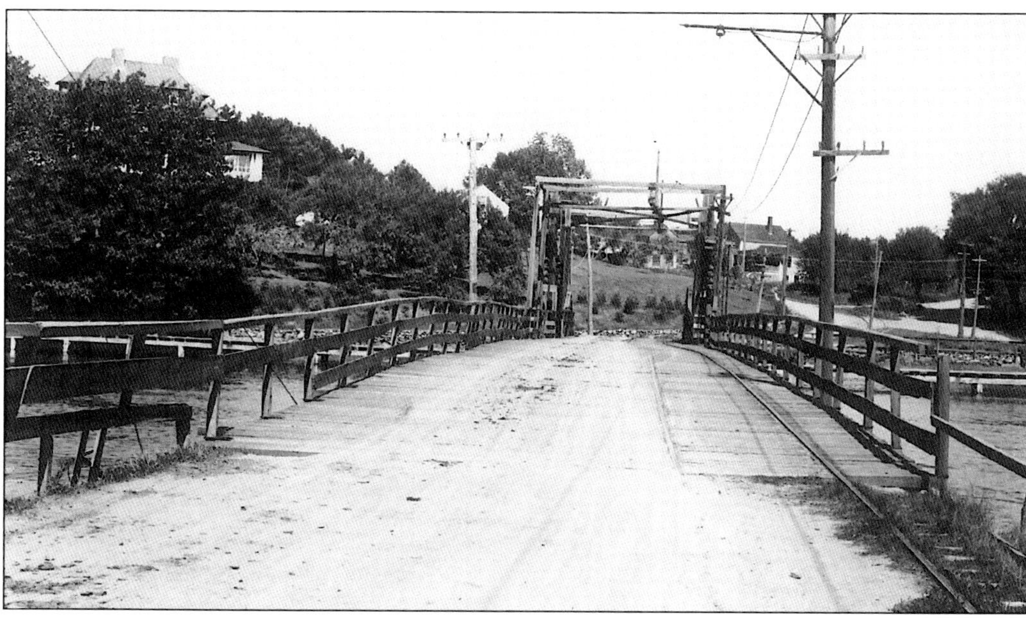

SAMUEL SEWALL INVENTED A BRIDGE STRUCTURE consisting of multiple piles bound in a cluster at the top with iron bands. He also contrived a crude pile driver with a trip hammer that would release a heavy log endways upon the caps. This view of the bridge was taken in 1912 when it had been widened and strengthened to accommodate the passage of trolley cars.

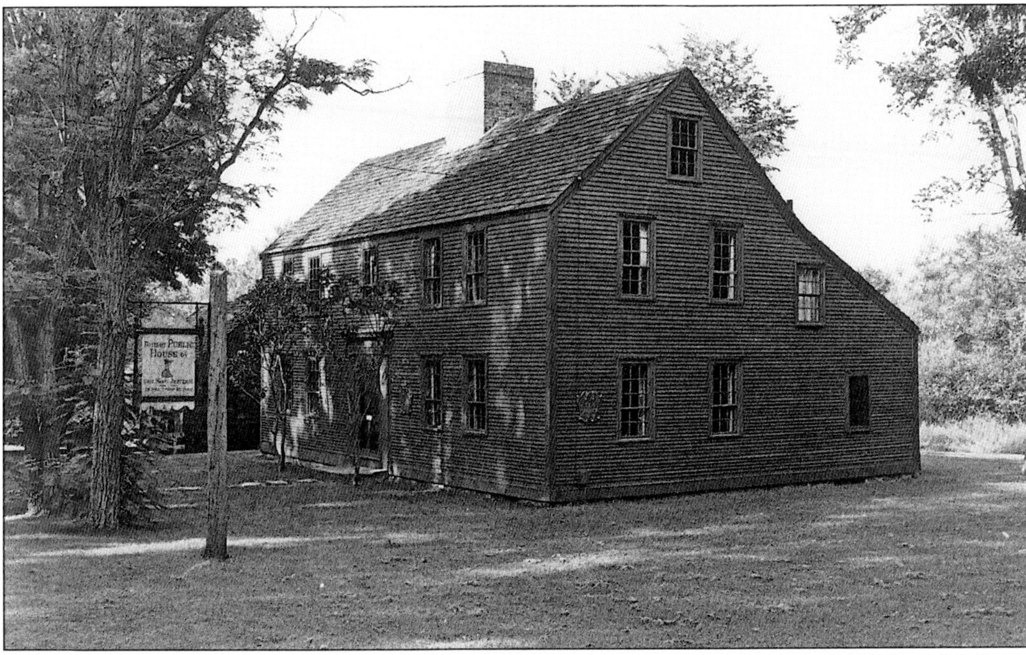

JEFFERDS TAVERN WAS MOVED FROM WELLS BY ELIZABETH PERKINS UNDER THE GUIDANCE OF ARCHITECT HOWARD PECK. In 1939, the dilapidated building was moved piece by piece and gradually assembled near what is now the entrance to Raydon Road. It was later moved to its present location across from the Old Burying Ground in the village.

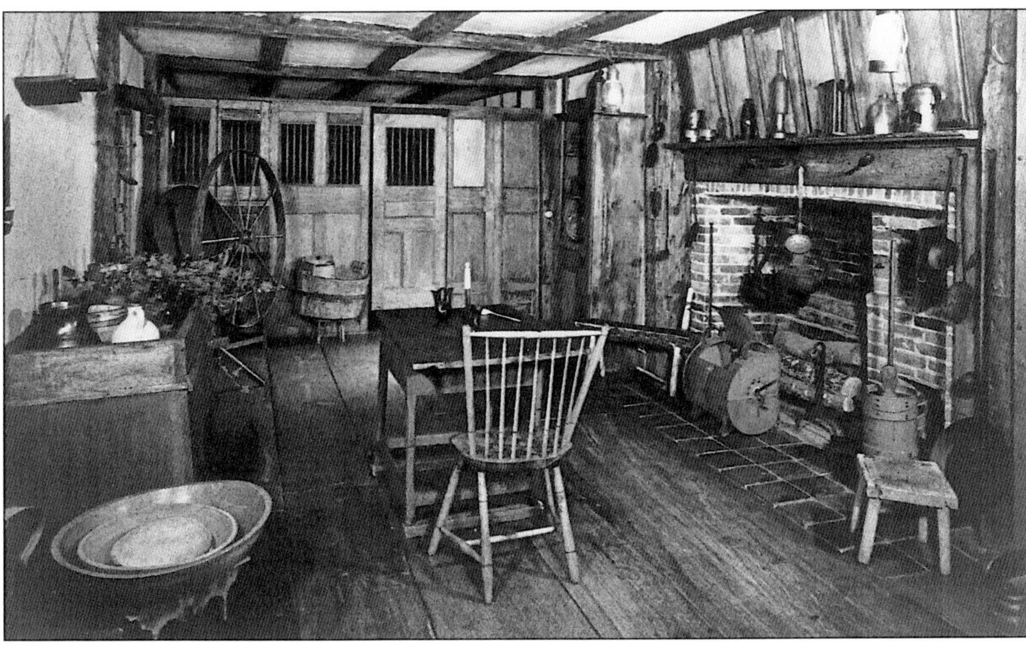

THE KITCHEN OR KEEPING ROOM IN JEFFERDS TAVERN is nearly the same as it was in the original tavern. The only exception is the east end which has been made into a modern working kitchen. The grill was copied from a small swinging door which was found in the tavern.

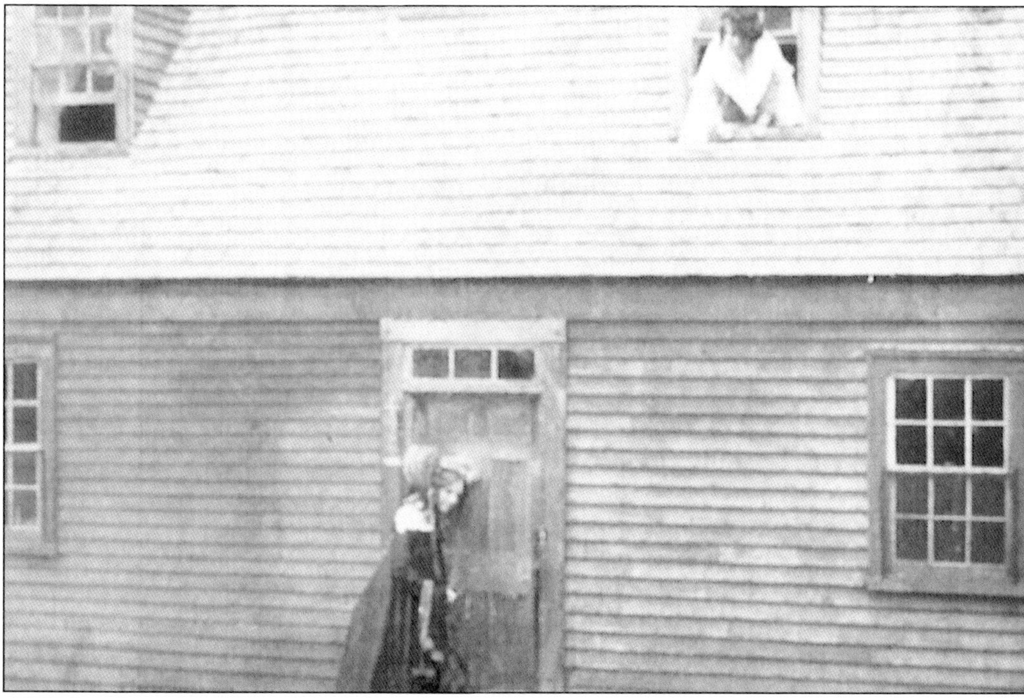

YORK'S OLD GAOL was probably started by a court order in April 1707 directing "that a small prison be erected in York forthwith." In 1737 the court ordered the construction of a wooden addition to the stone dungeon. This probably consisted of a kitchen and a large room and entry over the cellar. The dungeon was called the Gaol and the wooden addition was known as the Gaol House.

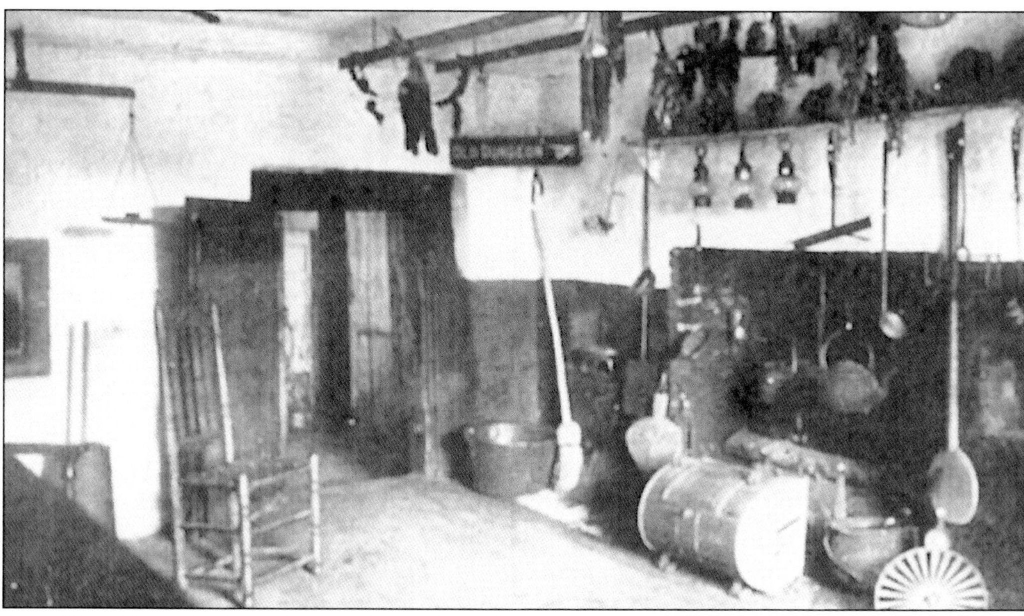

OWNERSHIP OF THE GAOL WAS VESTED IN THE COUNTY but the land on which it stands has always been church property. In 1868 the county sold its interest in the land and building to Washington Junkins, and in 1869 he conveyed the property to the town.

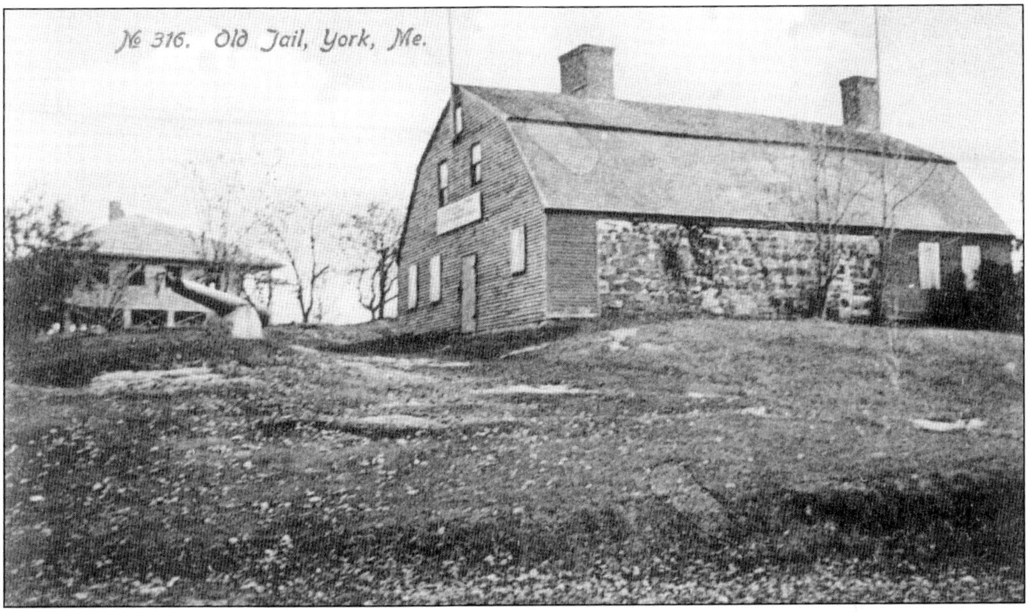

THE RE-OPENING OF THE GAOL TOOK PLACE ON 4 JULY 1900, with a large gathering present. The first stone gaol in Maine was repaired and restored. It is generally conceded that is the oldest remaining English municipal building in the country.

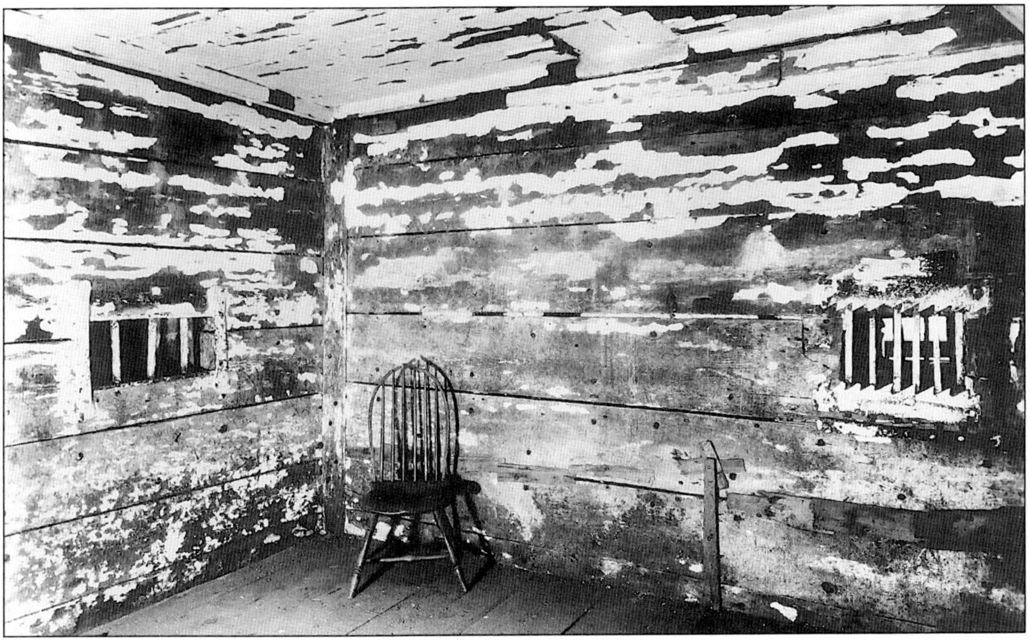

THE OLD GAOL DUNGEON. William Dean Howells, editor of the Atlantic Monthly, and a York Harbor summer resident, was one of the first to propose that the historic building should be restored and preserved as a museum. Under the leadership of President James T. Davidson of the Old York Historical Society, funds were solicited for this purpose.

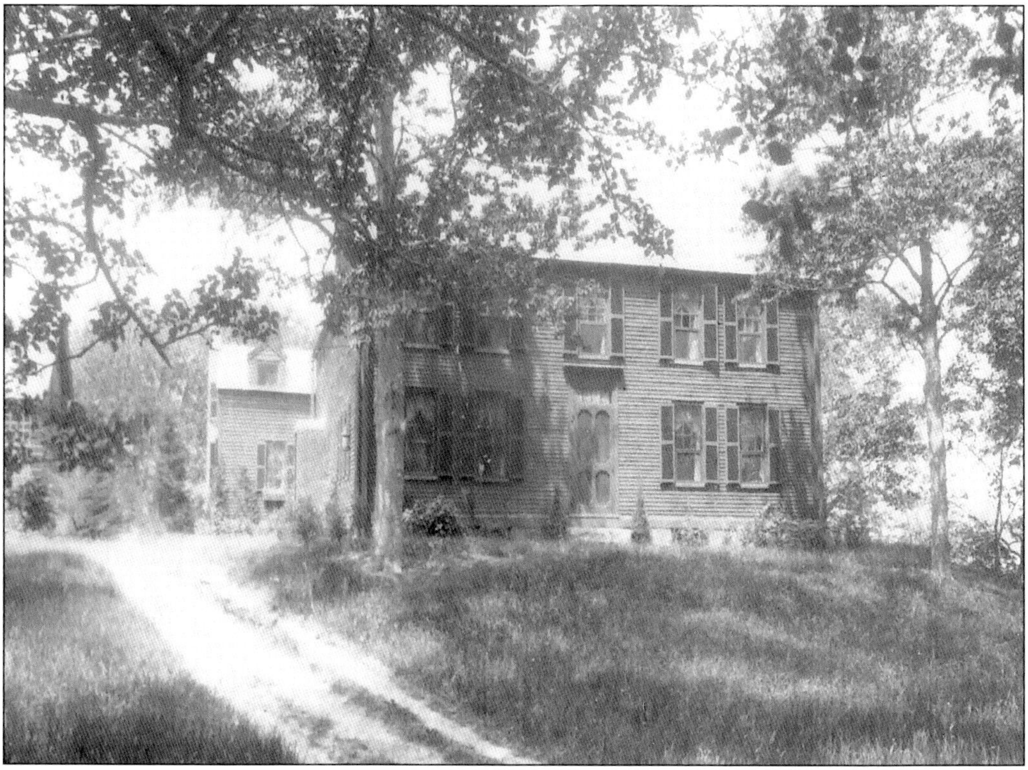

THE ELIZABETH PERKINS HOUSE. Captain Joseph Holt built this house on the south side of the York River in 1731. It came into the possession of Holt's stepson, John Pell, and was acquired by the descendents of Samuel Sewall after Pell's death.

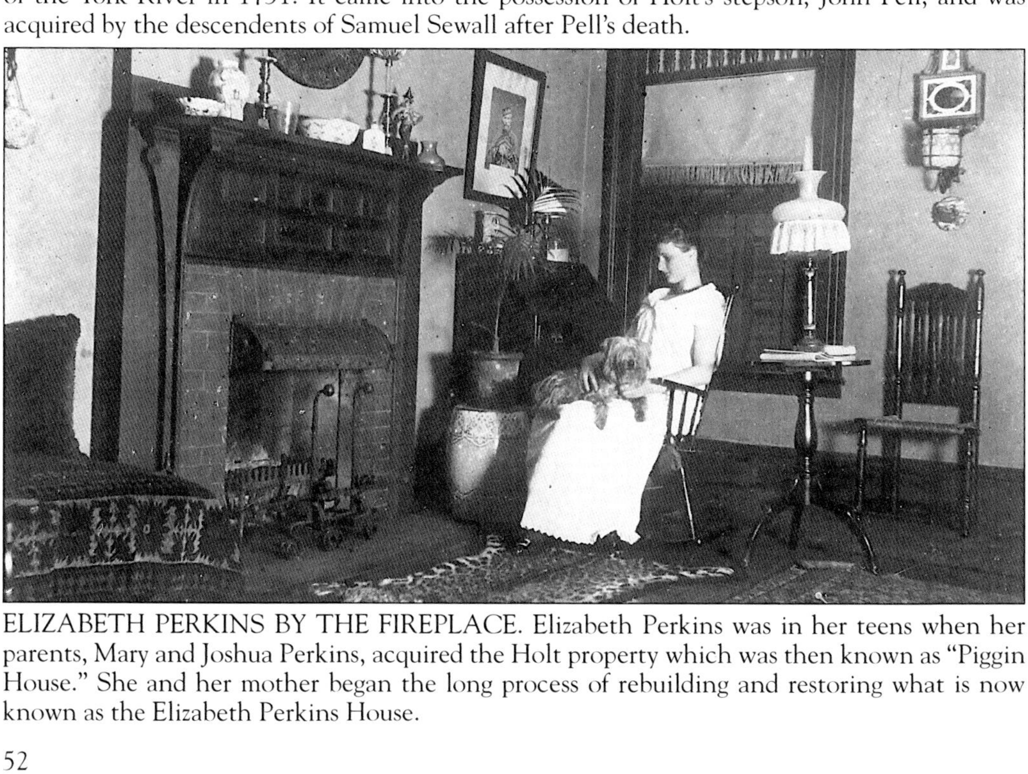

ELIZABETH PERKINS BY THE FIREPLACE. Elizabeth Perkins was in her teens when her parents, Mary and Joshua Perkins, acquired the Holt property which was then known as "Piggin House." She and her mother began the long process of rebuilding and restoring what is now known as the Elizabeth Perkins House.

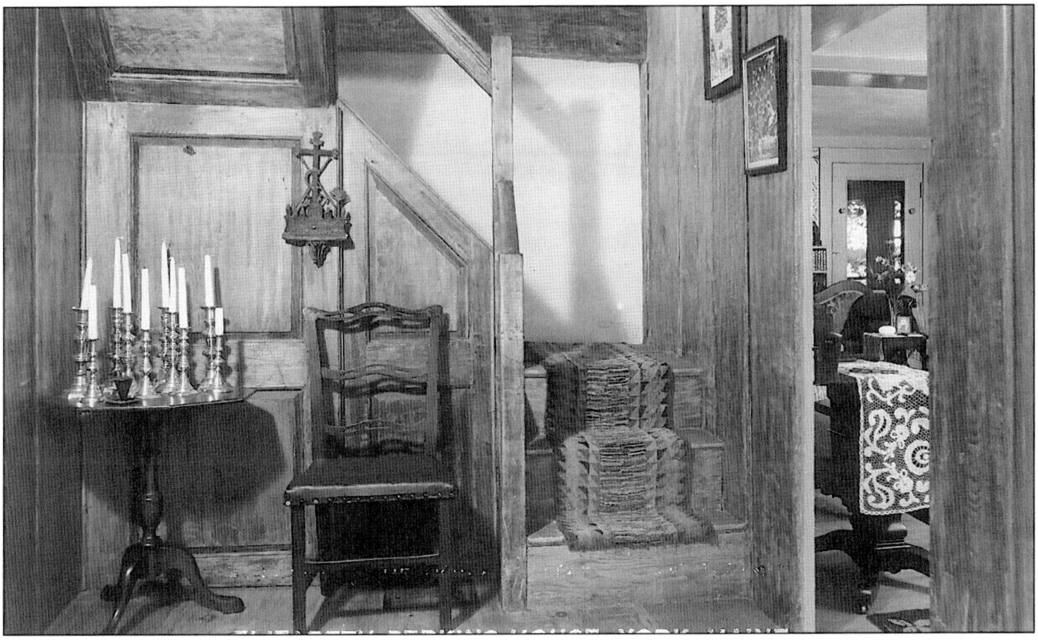

THIS IS THE COLONIAL HOUSE as it was lived in as a summer residence by the Perkins family. Miss Perkins left the house to the Society for the Preservation of Historic Landmarks, which she founded in 1939. It is now administered by the Old York Historical Society.

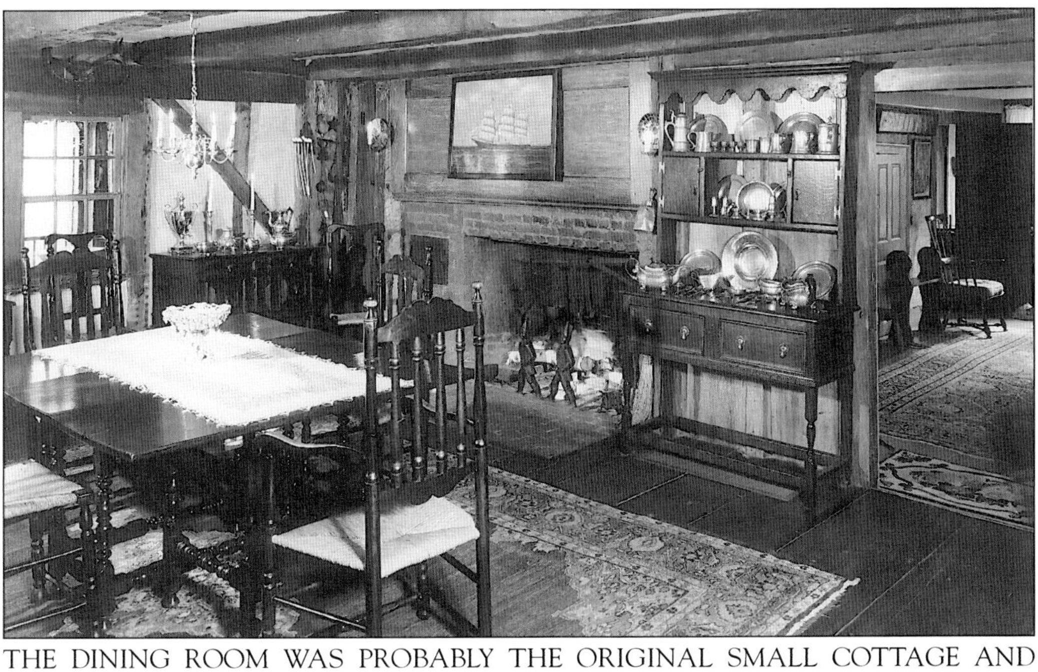

THE DINING ROOM WAS PROBABLY THE ORIGINAL SMALL COTTAGE AND CHIMNEY. There is evidence that Timothy Yeales had a house on the site in 1686 and also that a house there escaped destruction during the massacre of 1692 because it was located across the river.

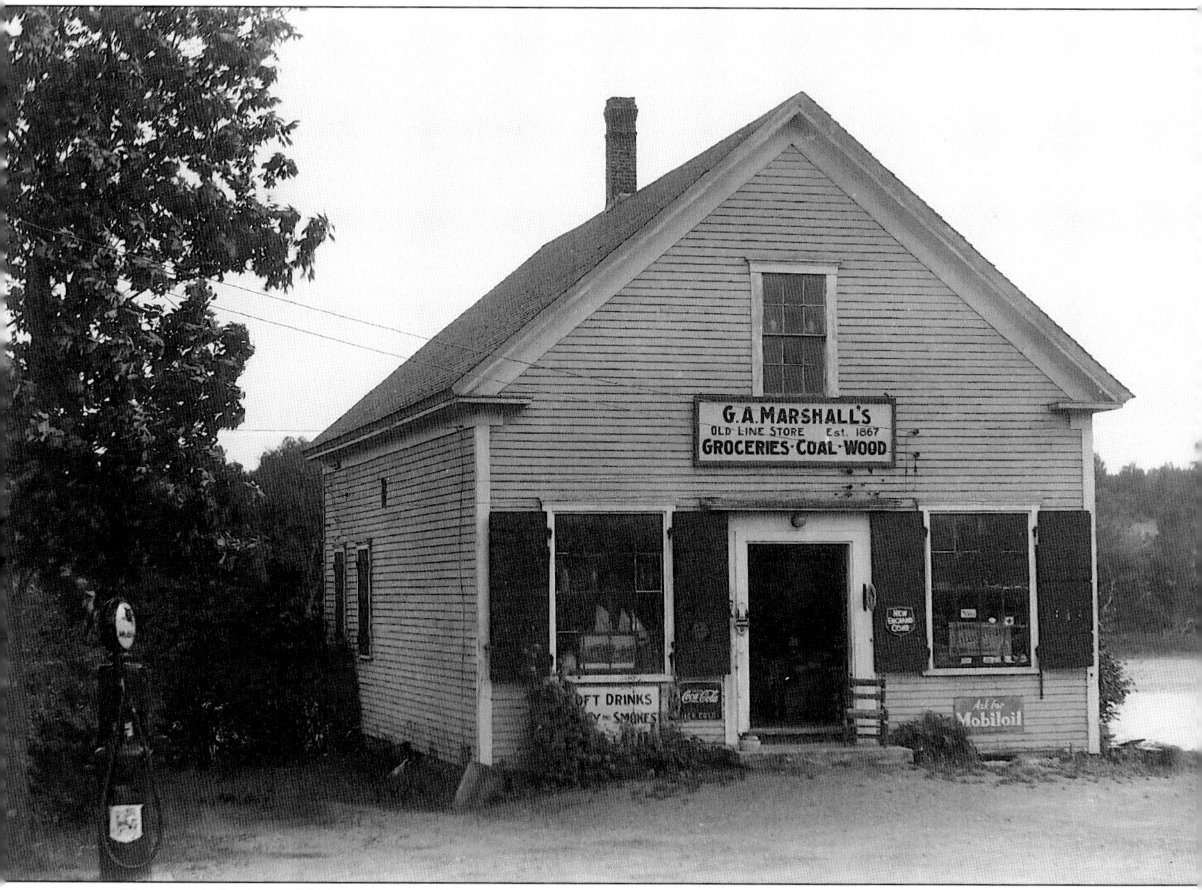

GEORGE A. MARSHALL OPENED THIS STORE IN OCTOBER 1867 and transacted business here for approximately sixty years. Located on the York River, the property was acquired by the Society for the Preservation of Historic Landmarks in 1967 and is now administered by the Old York Historical Society.

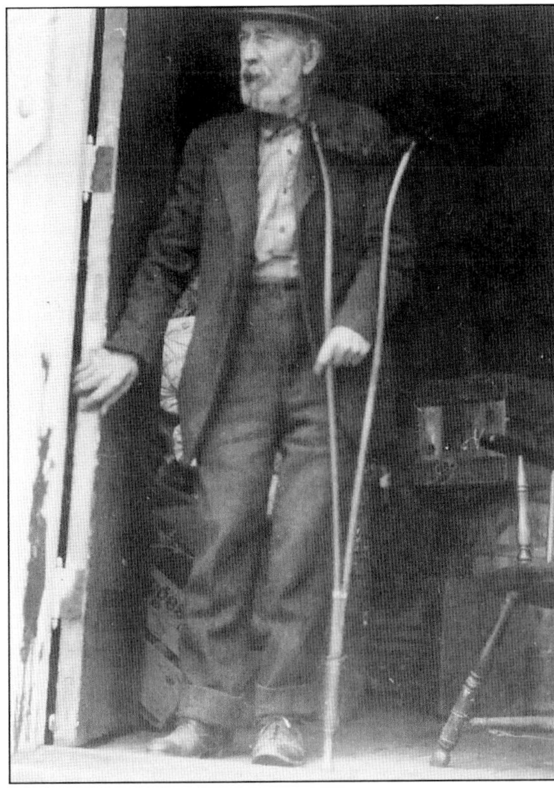

GEORGE MARSHALL CELEBRATED HIS EIGHTIETH BIRTHDAY IN 1923. He spent the day in his store, on the job as usual. He used a crutch to compensate for slight lameness, but was otherwise alert and vigorous.

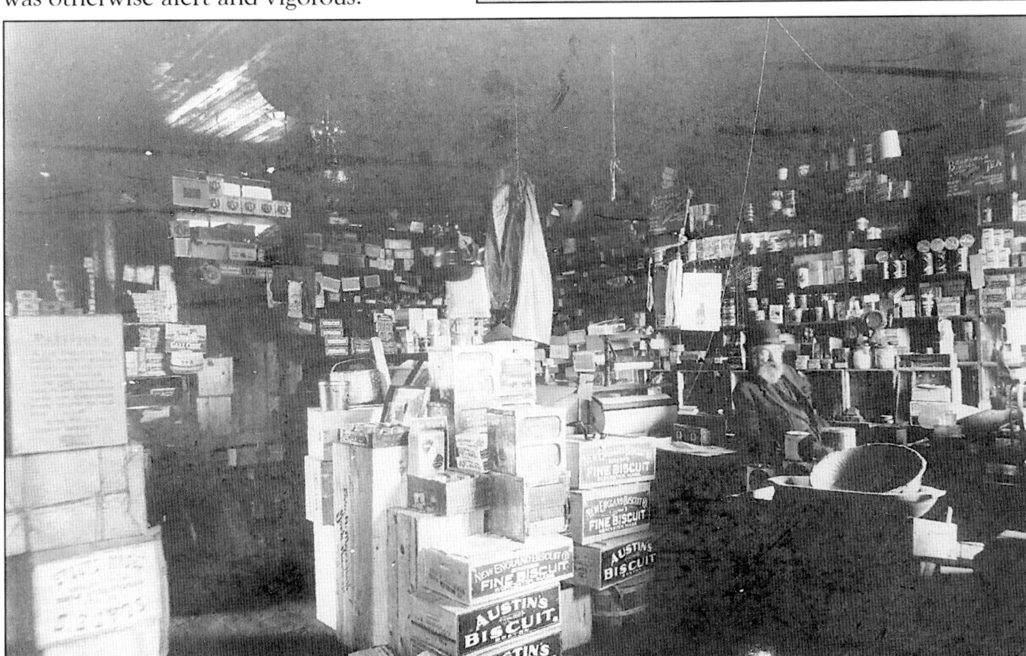

ONE COULD PURCHASE ANYTHING FROM FROM MARSHALL'S STORE. From a toothpick to a ton of coal; a plug of tobacco to a cut of cloth. George is shown here surrounded by his merchandise.

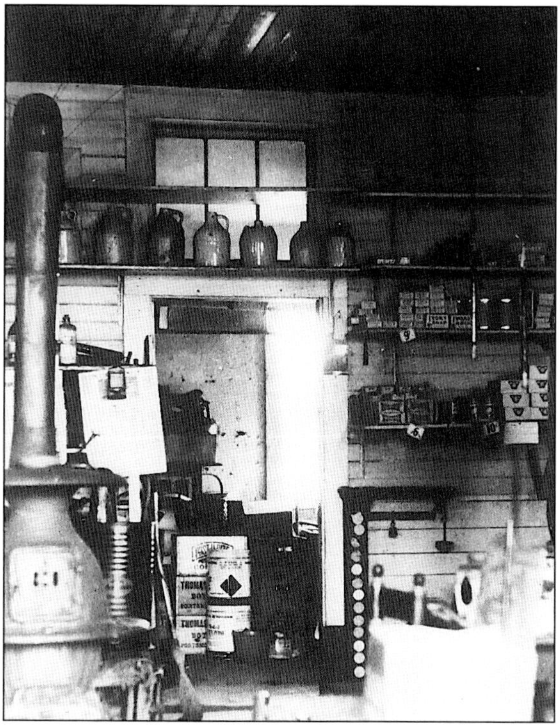

MARSHALL'S STORE WAS ONE OF THE FEW OF ITS KIND and his motto was "a square deal for the customer." This interior, photographed in the 1940s, shows a coal stove, scales and goods.

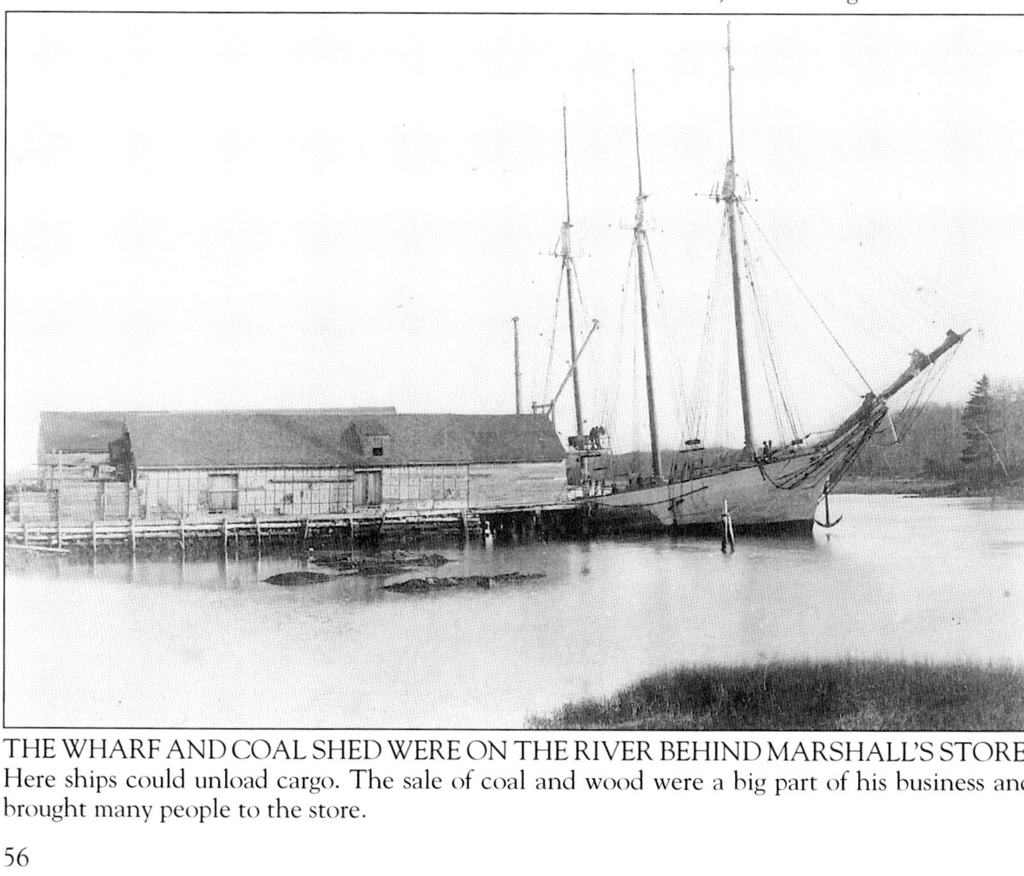

THE WHARF AND COAL SHED WERE ON THE RIVER BEHIND MARSHALL'S STORE. Here ships could unload cargo. The sale of coal and wood were a big part of his business and brought many people to the store.

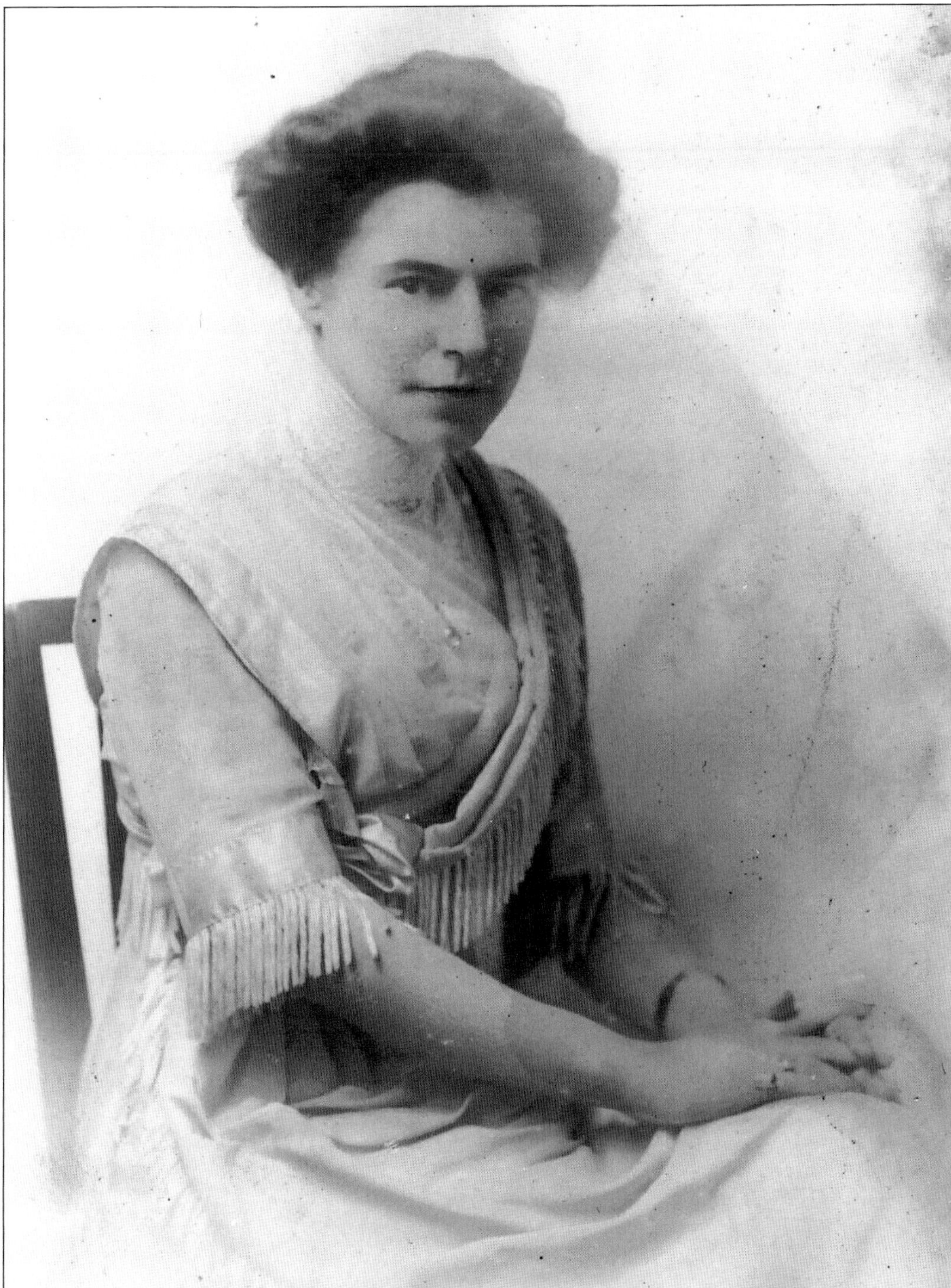

KATHERINE EASTMAN MARSHALL was the daughter of George A. Marshall and the last proprietor of Marshall's Store.

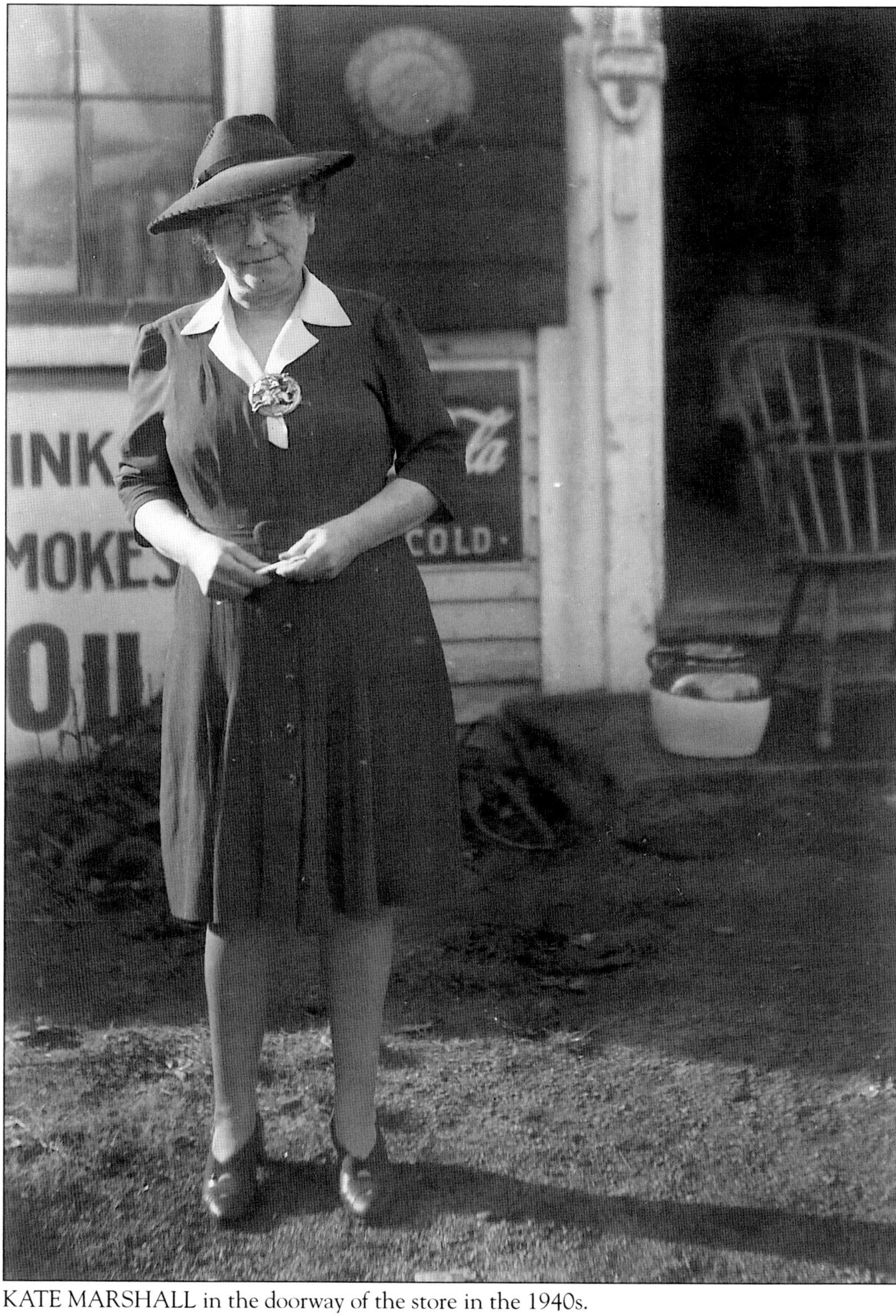

KATE MARSHALL in the doorway of the store in the 1940s.

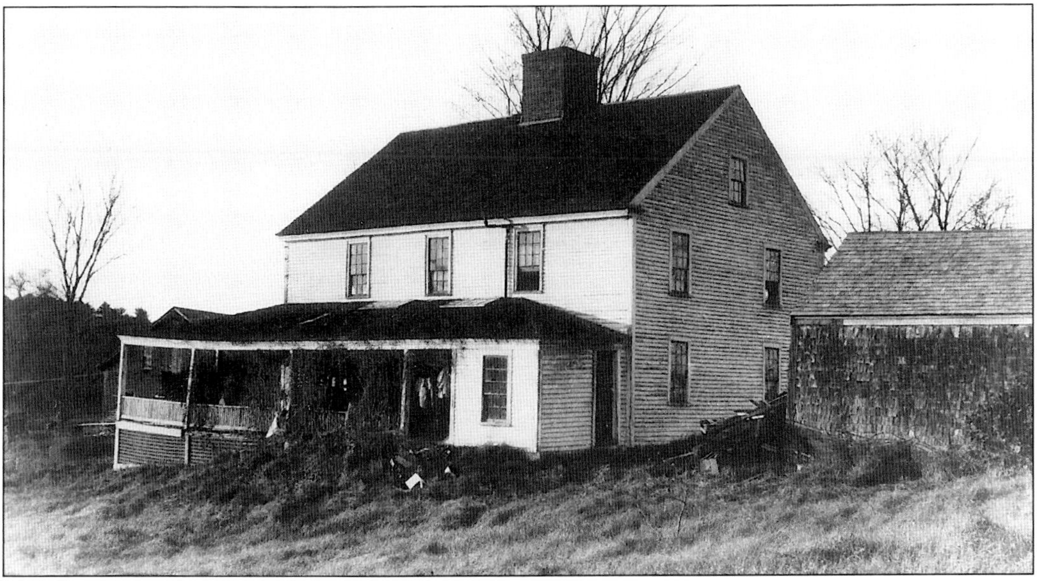

THE CAPTAIN SAMUEL LINDSAY HOUSE WAS BUILT IN 1795 on the hill above the Hancock warehouse. It was the home of both George Marshall and Katherine Marshall while they operated the store.

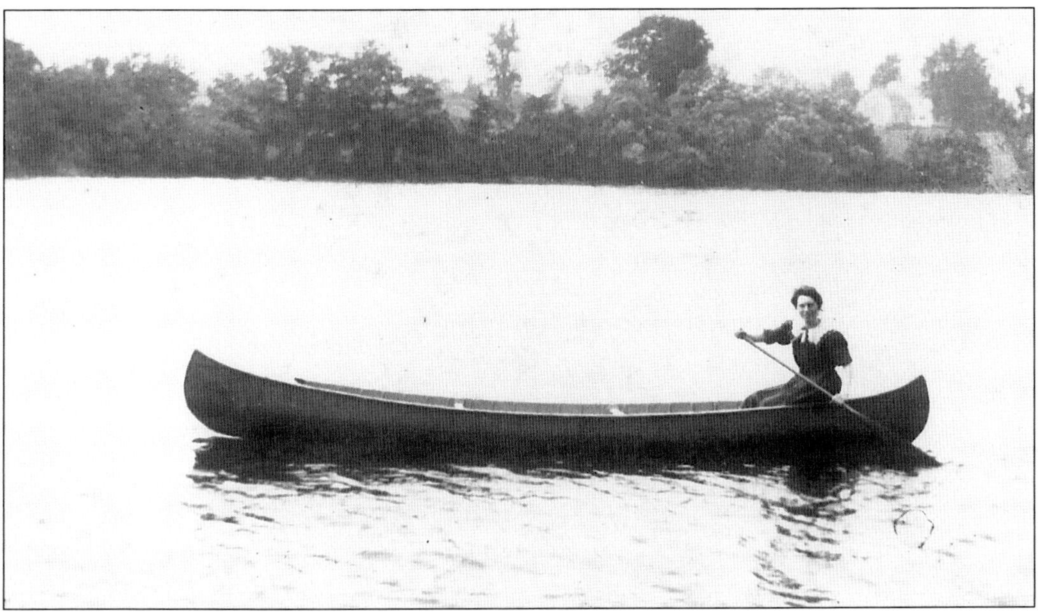

KATHERINE MARSHALL ON THE YORK RIVER. The opening of the Country Club in 1901 contributed to an increase in boats and canoes on the river. A dock was built near the club and Millard Sewall tended the water craft for the golfers and tennis players. Kate Marshall had her own dock.

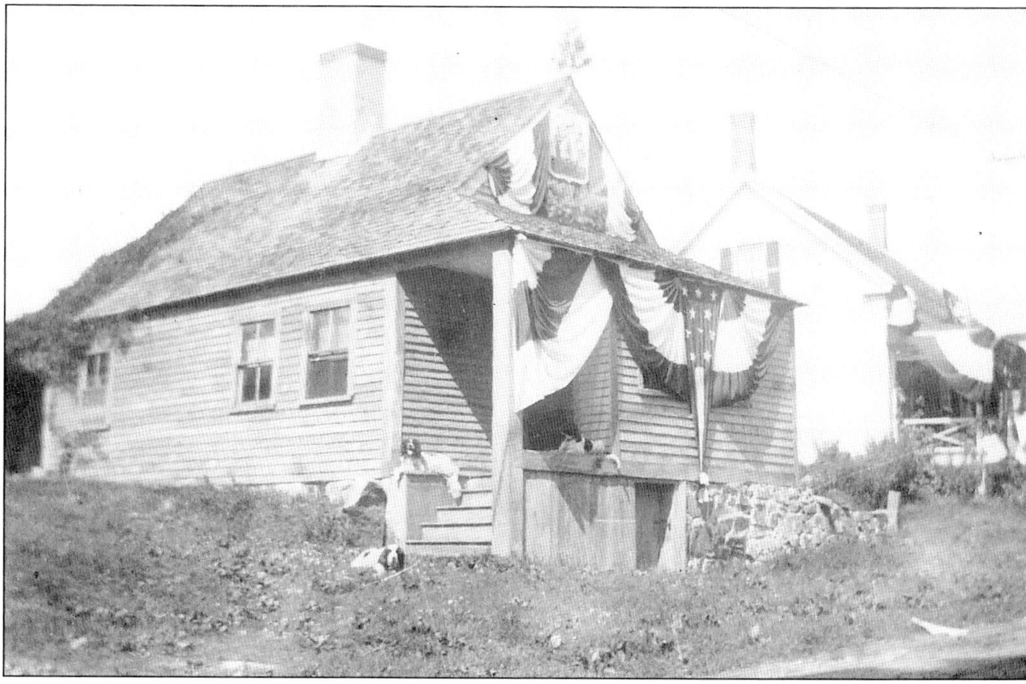

ALL RESIDENTS WERE ORDERED TO LEAVE THE ISLES OF SHOALS DURING THE AMERICAN REVOLUTION. Many families took their houses apart and floated them to the mainland to be reassembled. Twenty-two Shoals houses reached York and most of them were rebuilt on Stage Neck. This one reached the village where it was rebuilt near the fire station. This is how it appeared in 1952. In 1959 it was torn down to make room for a more modern structure.

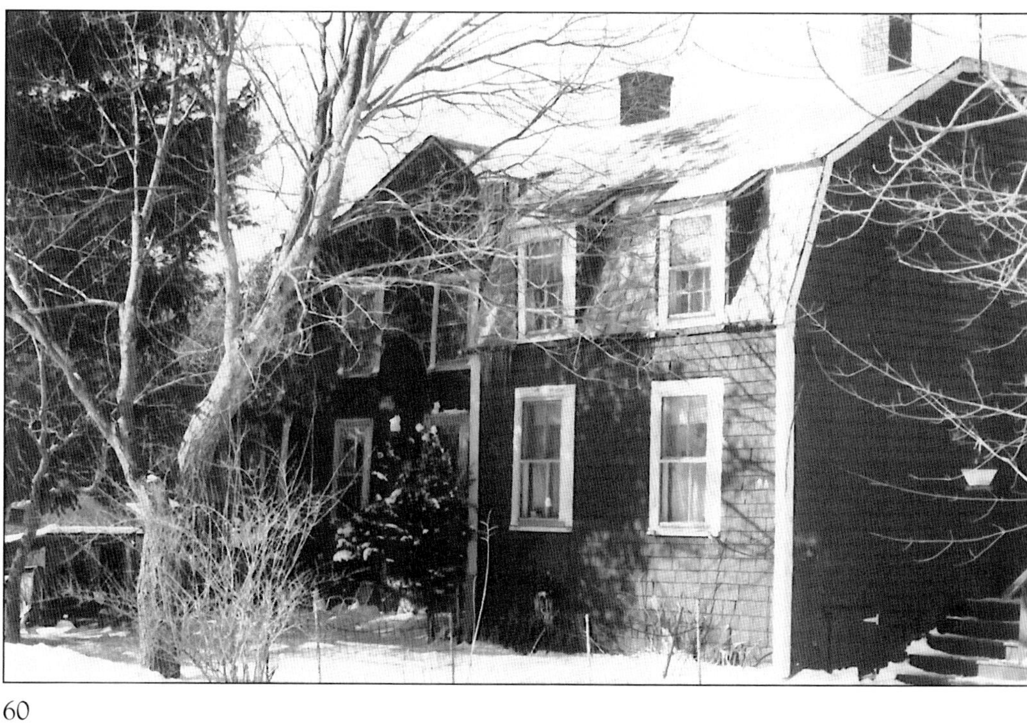

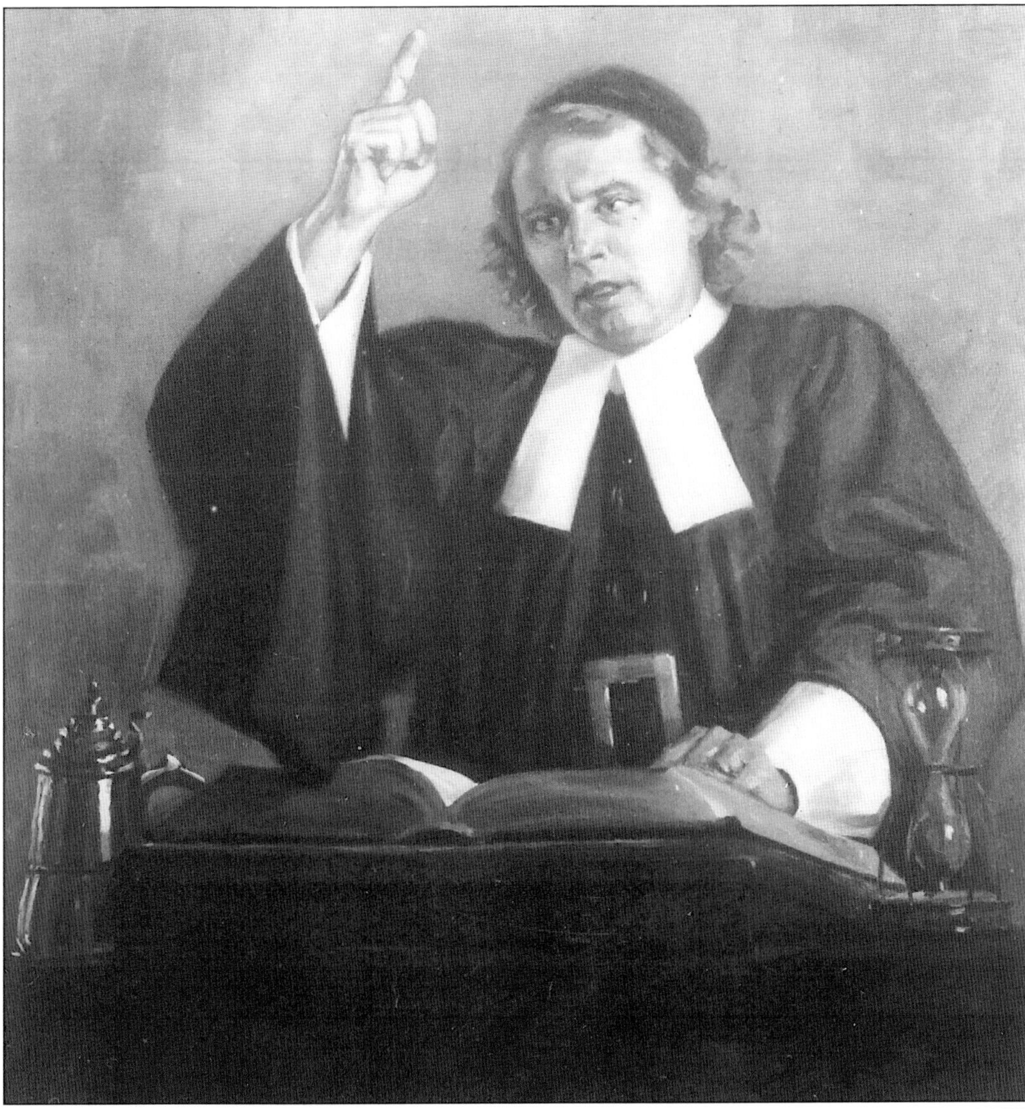

THE SUSAN RICKER KNOX PAINTING OF REVEREND HAROLD MILLINGER delivering his "Parson Moody" sermon. Moody came to York after the massacre of 1692 and served as the community's religious leader for fifty years.

OPPOSITE: THE FRED DONNELL HOUSE WAS ONE OF THE SHOALS HOUSES THAT SURVIVED. It was moved from Dinah's Hill to a lane off the south side of Woodbridge Road.

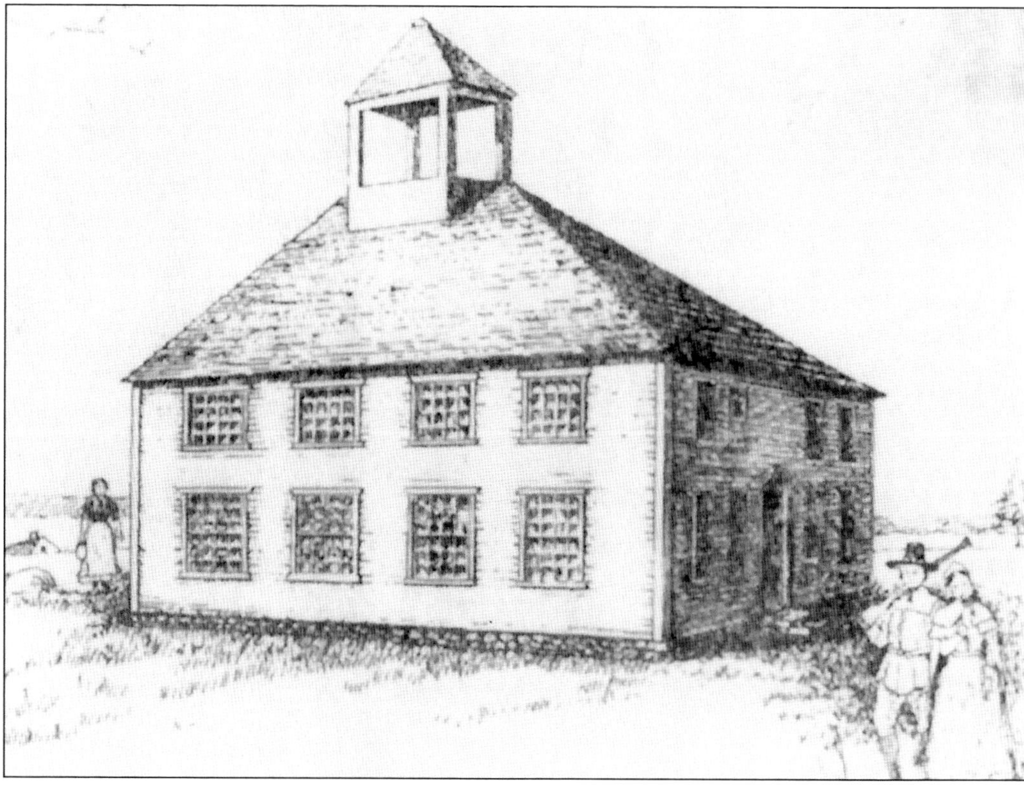

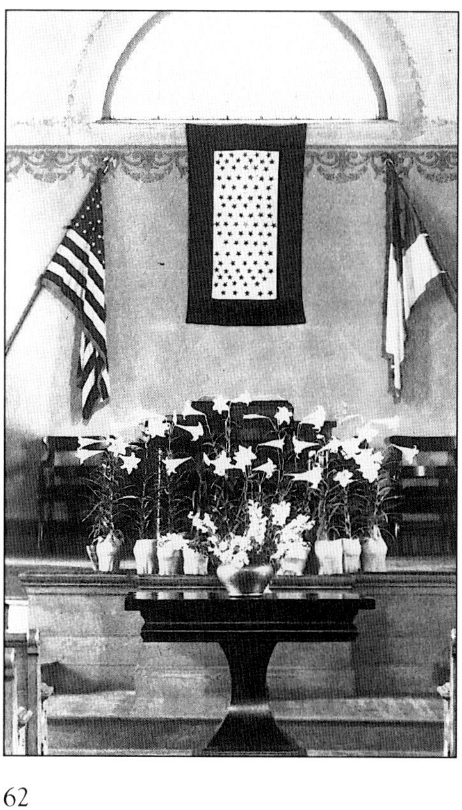

A SKETCH OF THE SECOND MEETING HOUSE built by Henry Sayward in 1667. The first had been built between Sentry Hill and the York River in 1636; the second was built beside a path which in 1900 was named Lindsay Road. The stream in the valley below was called Meeting House Creek.

THE CURRENT FIRST PARISH CHURCH IS THE FOURTH MEETING HOUSE AND THE OLDEST RELIGIOUS SOCIETY IN MAINE. This is the altar decorated for an Easter service in the 1940s. The stars on the service flag indicate the number of members serving in the military forces during the Second World War. The gold star in the center indicates that one of these young people had given his life for his country.

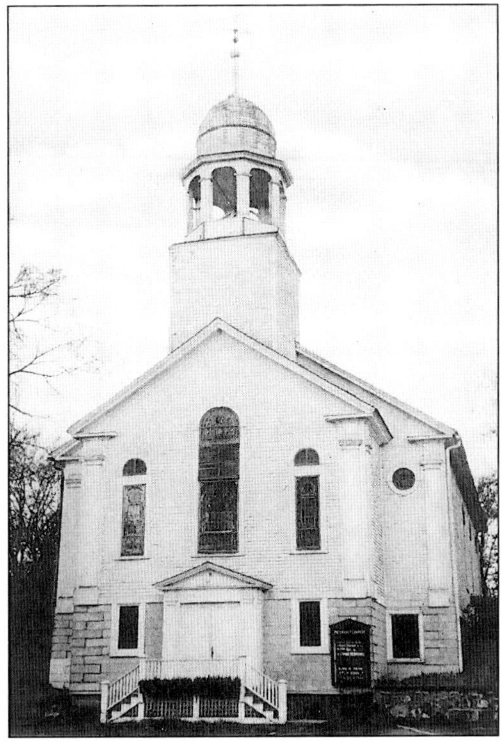

THE METHODIST SOCIETY WAS ORGANIZED IN 1829. They held services from time to time in the courthouse (now the town hall) with the permission of the First Parish. The Methodists erected this building in the village in 1833.

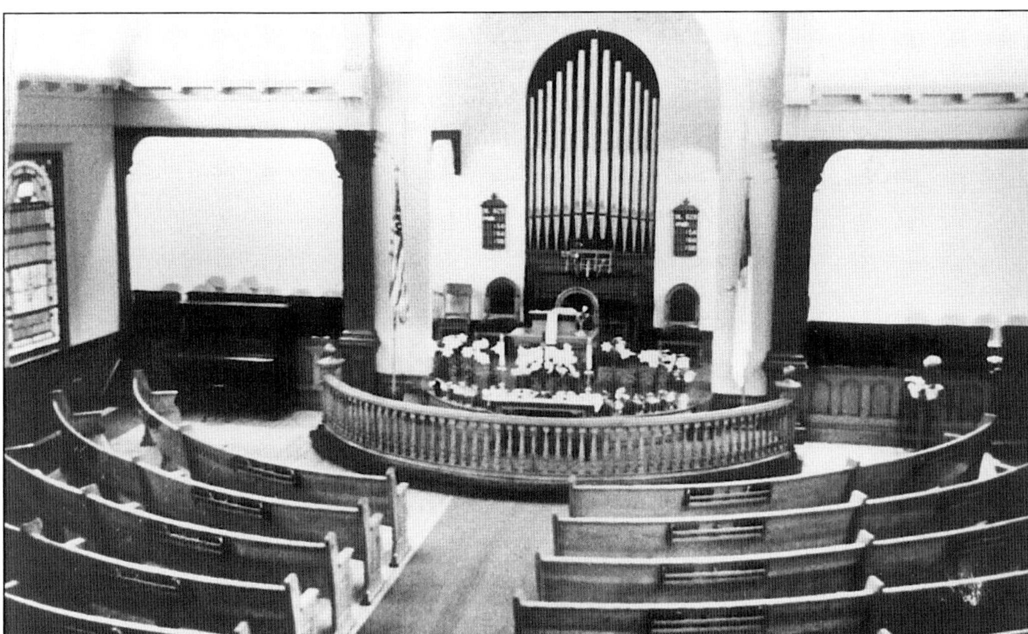

AN INTERIOR VIEW OF THE METHODIST CHURCH before it was sold by the society to move to a new building on Route 1.

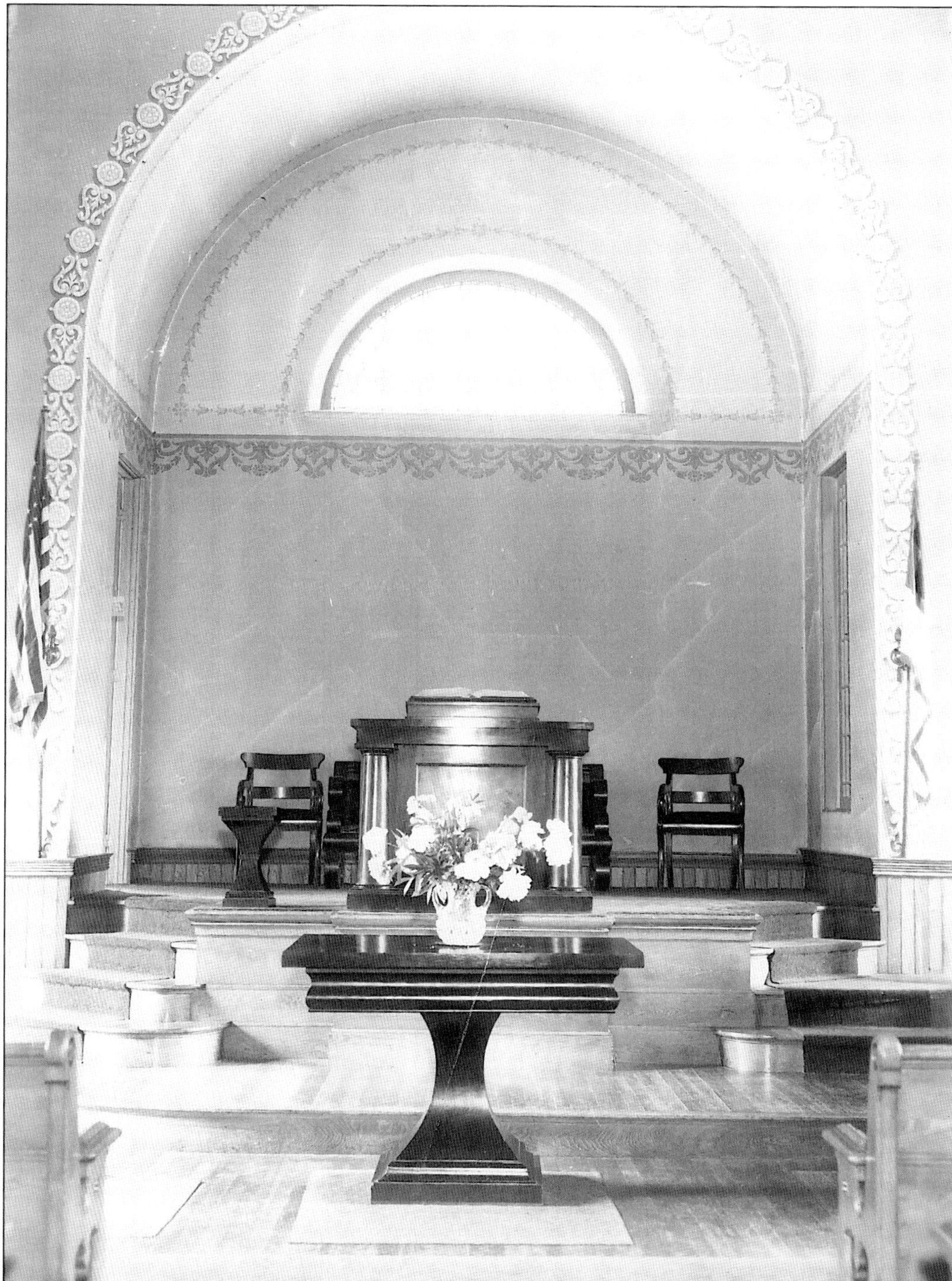

THE FIRST PARISH CHURCH BEFORE RESTORATION. In 1940, the members of the church appointed a committee to plan the restoration of the historic building.

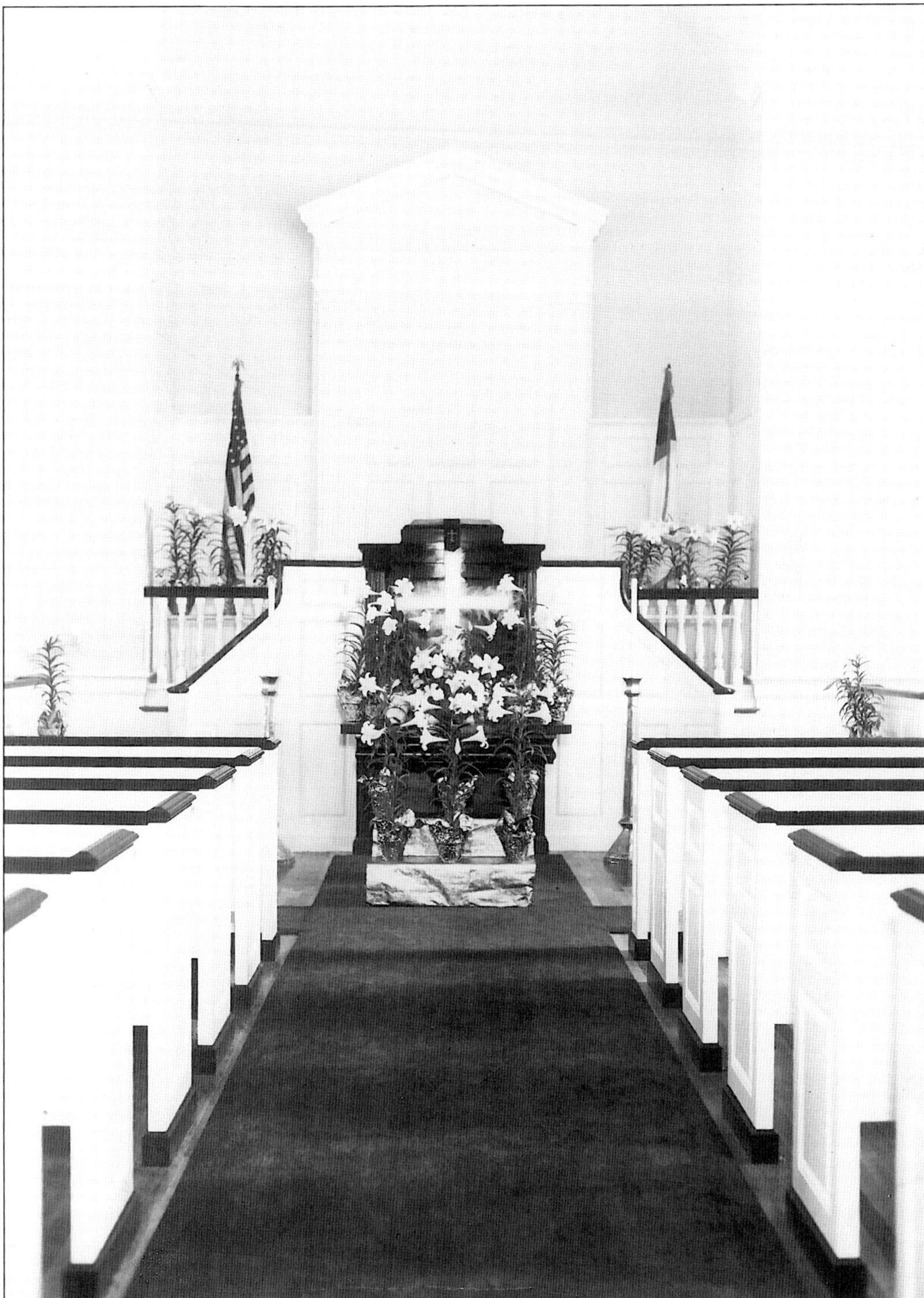

AFTER RESTORATION. Restoration efforts were interrupted by the Second World War but the project was finally completed in 1951. The work of the restoration committee lasted twelve years.

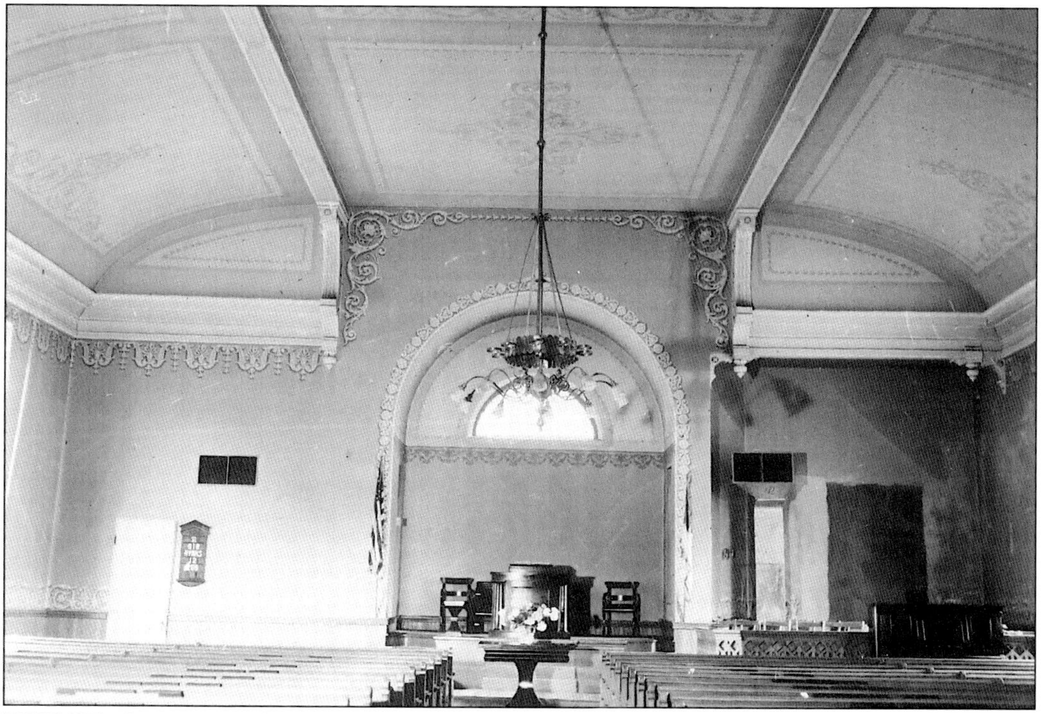

BEFORE. Committee chairperson Florence Woodward worked with architect Harold Willis whose firm had been designated the foremost ecclesiatical architectural company in the United States in 1946.

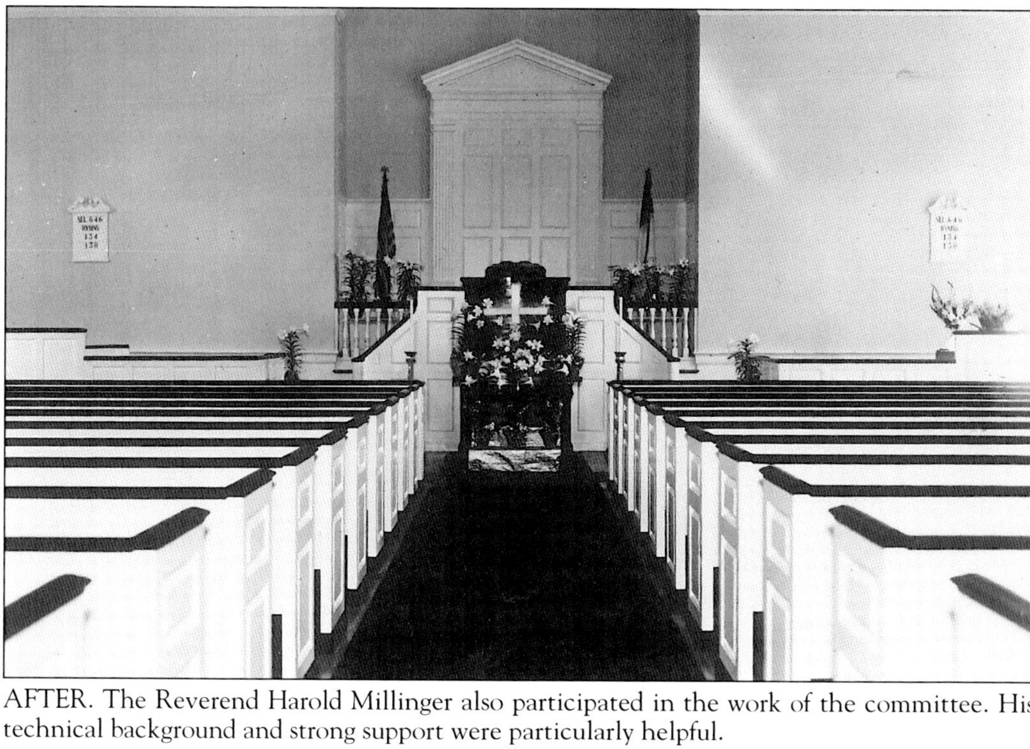

AFTER. The Reverend Harold Millinger also participated in the work of the committee. His technical background and strong support were particularly helpful.

Three

Schools and Sports

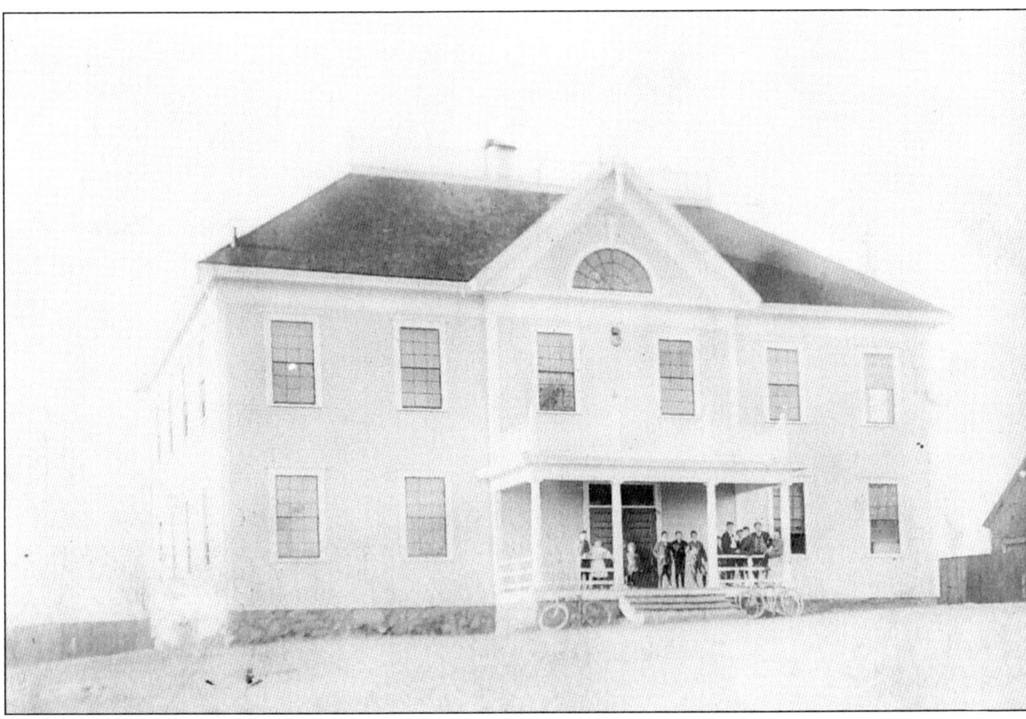

THE FIRST LARGE CENTRAL SCHOOL WAS IN THIS BUILDING located on the site now occupied by the village fire house. It housed eight grades in four rooms. A larger elementary school was built in 1915 and this building was turned over to the newly organized fire department in 1916.

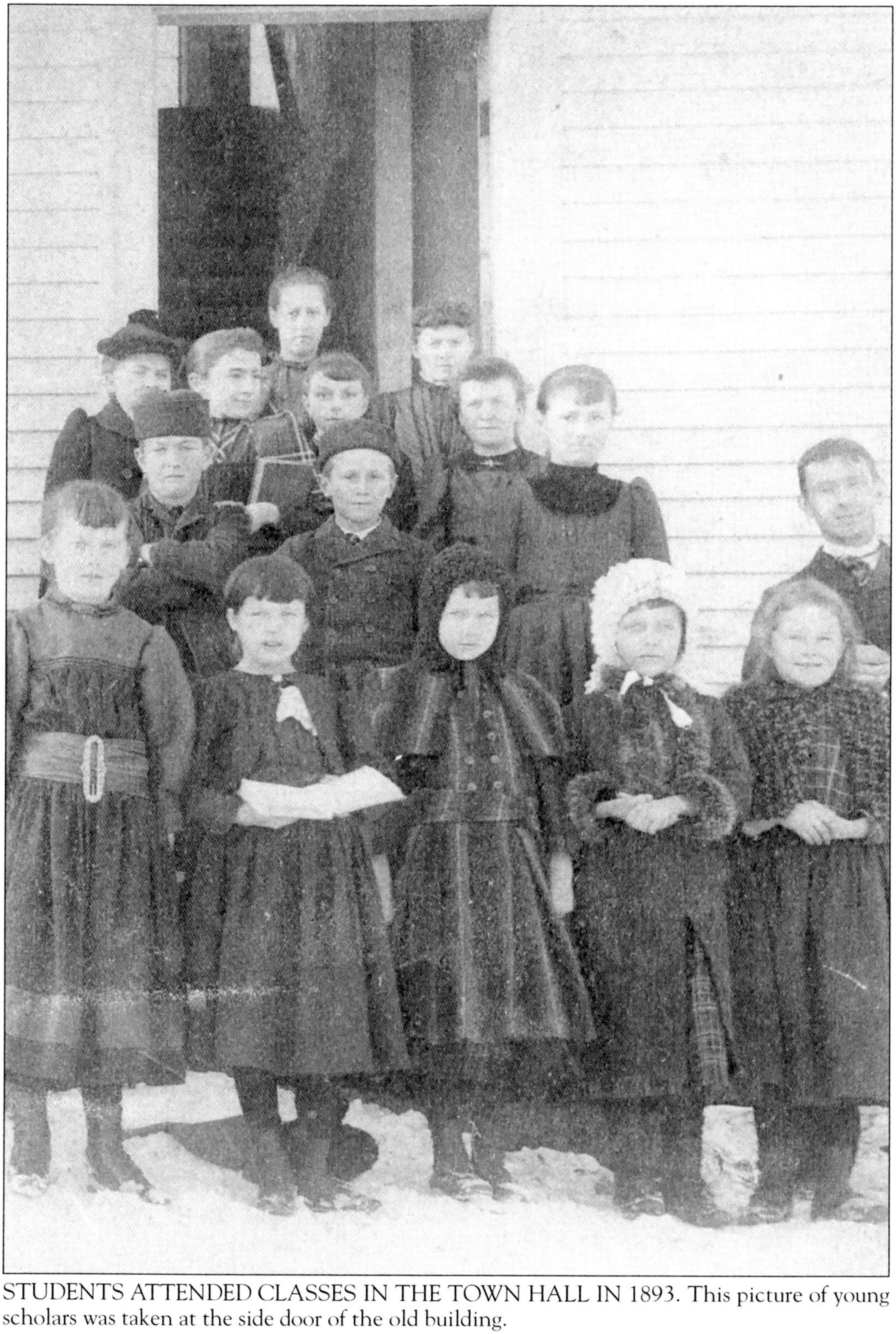

STUDENTS ATTENDED CLASSES IN THE TOWN HALL IN 1893. This picture of young scholars was taken at the side door of the old building.

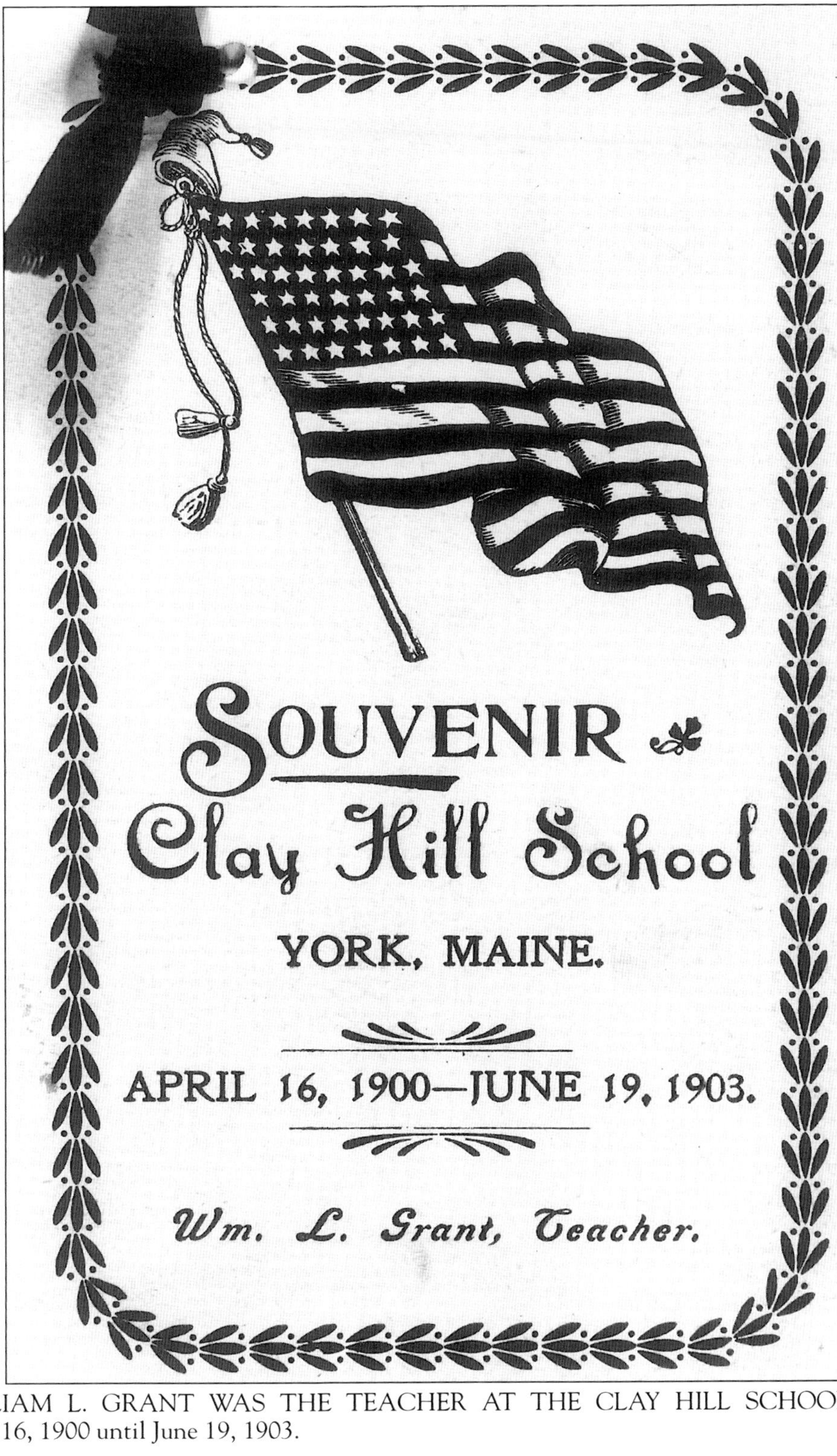

WILLIAM L. GRANT WAS THE TEACHER AT THE CLAY HILL SCHOOL from April 16, 1900 until June 19, 1903.

Names of Pupils

Carlton R. Moulton

Nellie M. Moulton

Esther B. Moulton

Edith A. Moulton

Adrian B. Moulton

Mildred O. Moulton

Hattie E. Perkins

Edna M. Perkins

Maud A. Perkins

Harold W. Perkins

Ruby O. Perkins

Margaret M. Reid

Leander A. Reid

Laura D. Reid

Hattie M. Russell

Edna E. Russell

Ada M. Taylor

THERE WERE SEVENTEEN SUCCESSFUL PUPILS at the Clay Hill School during this period. Six were from the Moulton family, five were from the Perkins family and there were three Reids, two Russells and a Taylor.

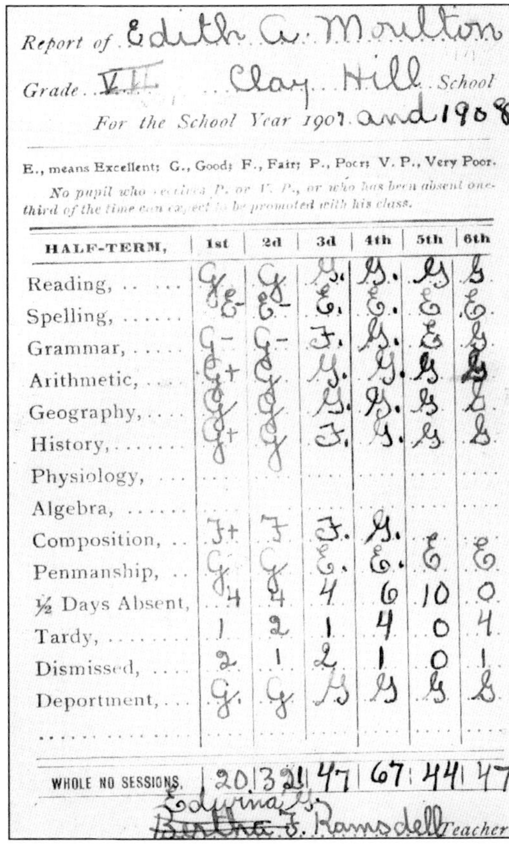

Report of Edith A. Moulton

Grade VII Clay Hill School

For the School Year 1907 and 1908

E., means Excellent; G., Good; F., Fair; P., Poor; V. P., Very Poor.

No pupil who receives P. or V. P., or who has been absent one-third of the time can expect to be promoted with his class.

HALF-TERM,	1st	2d	3d	4th	5th	6th
Reading,	G	G	G.	G.	G	G
Spelling,	E-	E-	E.	E.	E	E
Grammar,	G-	G-	F.	G.	E	G
Arithmetic,	G+	G	G.	G.	G	G
Geography,	G	G	G.	G.	G	G
History,	G+	G	F.	G.	G	G
Physiology,						
Algebra,						
Composition,	F+	F	F.	G.	E	E
Penmanship,	G	G	E.	E.	E	E
½ Days Absent,	4	4	4	6	10	0
Tardy,	1	2	1	4	0	4
Dismissed,	2	1	2	1	0	1
Deportment,	G.	G	G	G	G	G
WHOLE NO SESSIONS.	20	32	47	67	44	47

~~Bertha F.~~ Edwina G. Ramsdell Teacher

THE REPORT CARD FOR EDITH A. MOULTON for the school year 1907-08. At this time she was in grade seven. It seems that she experienced a change in the teaching staff and Bertha Ramsdell was replaced by Edwina Ramsdell after the second term.

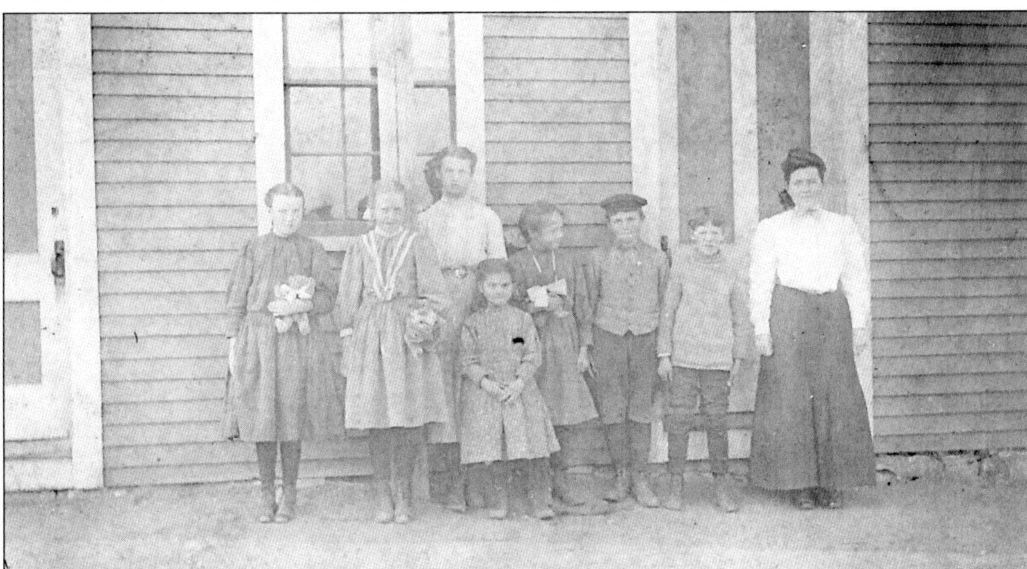

EDWINA RAMSDELL IS THE TEACHER IN THIS CLASS PICTURE. The number of pupils has been reduced to seven with the usual representation of Ramsdells, Perkins' and Moultons. Left to right: Ruby Perkins, Edna Perkins, Edith Moulton, Christine Moulton, Mildred Moulton, Adrian Moulton, Roger Perkins and teacher Edwina Ramsdell.

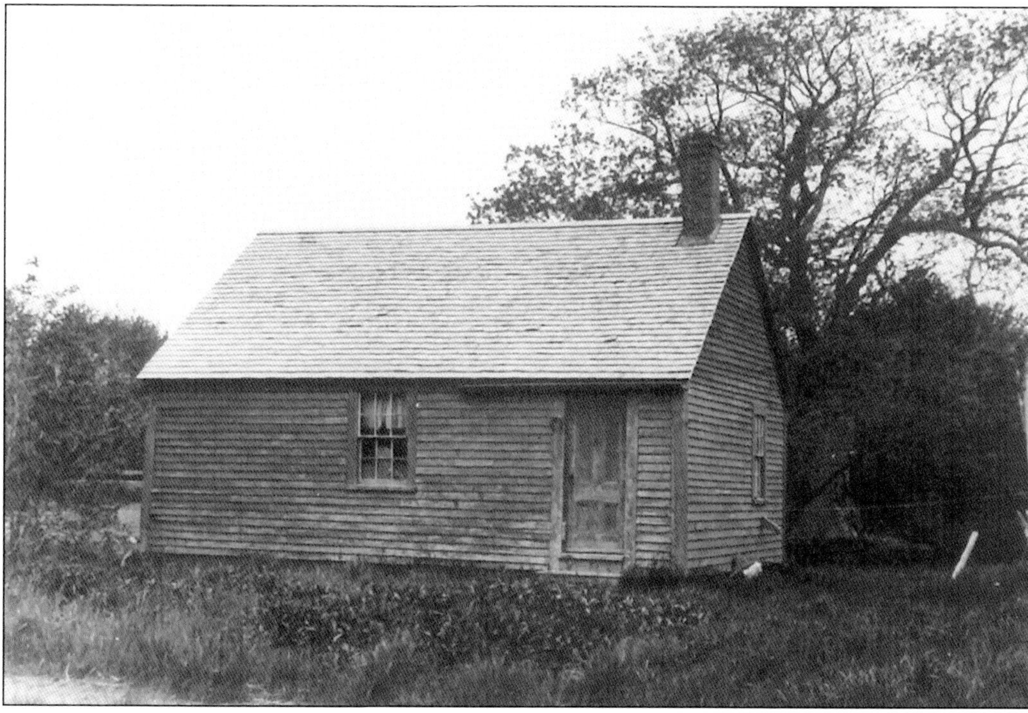

IN 1746, THE RESIDENTS OF YORK CORNER REQUESTED PERMISSION TO BUILD A SCHOOLHOUSE near the intersection of Route 1 and Route 91. In the 1850s the building was moved to this site on Organug Road and used as a home. In 1936, it was purchased by the Old York Historical Society, restored, and moved to its present site near the Old Burying Ground.

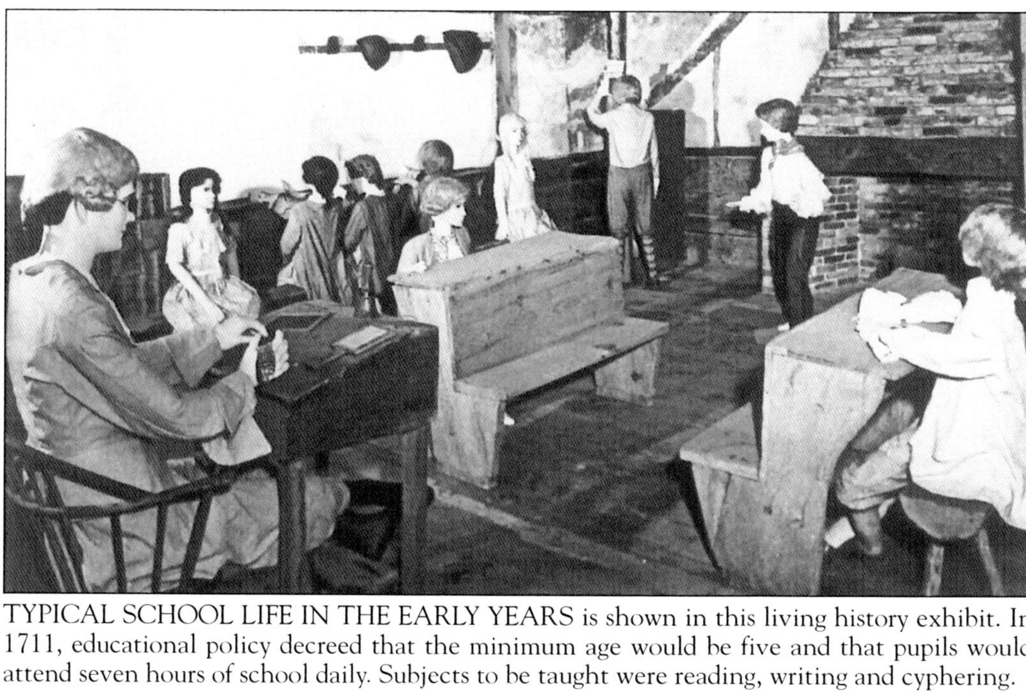

TYPICAL SCHOOL LIFE IN THE EARLY YEARS is shown in this living history exhibit. In 1711, educational policy decreed that the minimum age would be five and that pupils would attend seven hours of school daily. Subjects to be taught were reading, writing and cyphering.

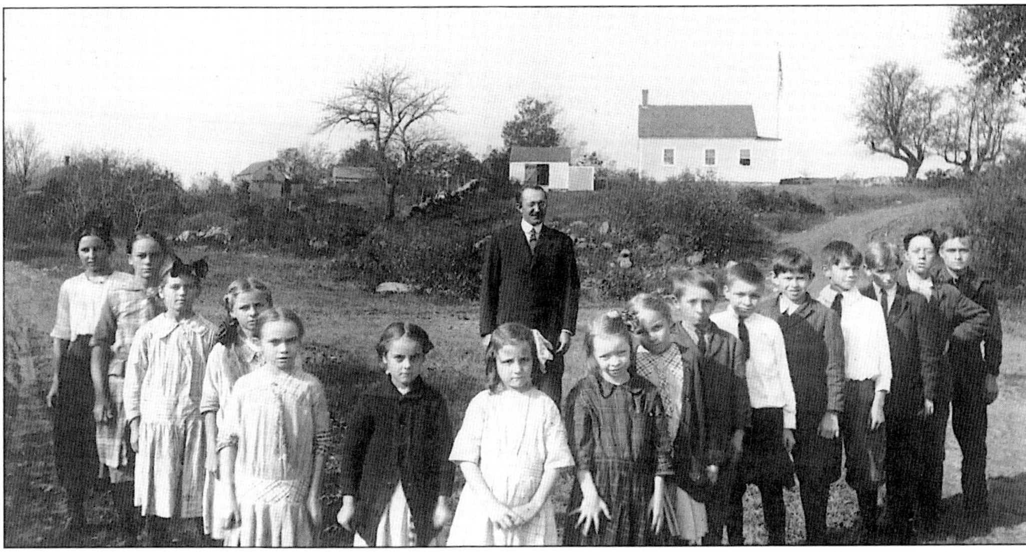

THE ONE-ROOM SCHOOL ON MOUNT AGAMENTICUS IN 1916. The site is fairly free of vegetation. The building at the rear of the school housed the woodshed and the "necessary" which was later attached to the building. Left to right: Florence Fitzgerald, Mabel Fitzgerald, Esther Fitzgerald, Annie May Parker, Beulah May Welch, Sylvia Irene Ramsdell, Carolyn Ramsdell, Elizabeth Welch, Mildred Gloria Welch, Robert Fitzgerald, Walter Gordon Welch, Ray Morris Welch, Carroll Trafton, Charles Creddiford Bracy, Elmer Frank Ramsdell and Everett Norman Welch. The teacher is William Grant.

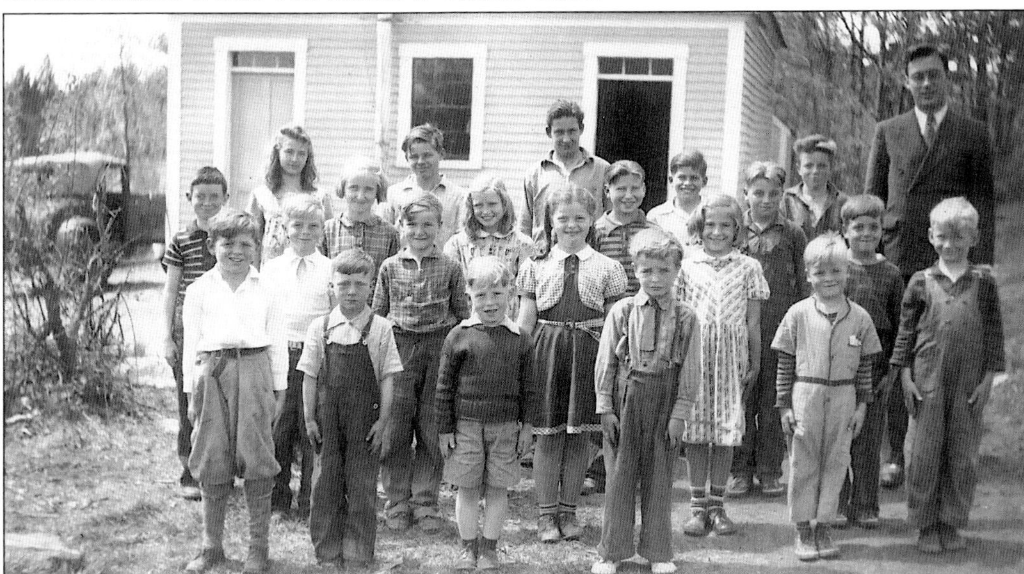

THE AGAMENTICUS SCHOOL IN 1938-39. Front, left to right: Harold Perkins, Sidney Gilchrist, Dana Hale, Danny Stevens, Clarence Perkins and Bruce Millner. Second row: Neil Ramsdell, Jack Millner, June Trafton, Margie Boston and Arthur Perkins. Third row: Eddie Ramsdell, Marion Millner, Murial Perkins, Donald Perkins and William Perkins. Fourth row: Agnes Millner, Roger Currier, Floyd Tuttle, Conrad Trafton, Gordon Ramsdell and teacher Robert Whitney.

NOTICE.

TO WHOM IT MAY CONCERN.

At an adjourned meeting held at the School House in District No. 4, in the town of York, May 3d, 1884, the report of the building committee in relation to building a school house in said District was accepted, and the committee was instructed to issue posters calling for proposals in relation to building the aforesaid house according to the following plan :

The house is to be built thirty-two feet long, twenty-four feet wide, with twelve feet posts, with the following kinds of lumber: The sills, cross sills, posts and plates to be of pine, and all the rest of the frame together with the boards used in building the house (with the exception of the trimmings inside and out, and the upper floor, which are to be pine) to be hemlock, and the building to be clapboarded with first-class spruce clapboards, and shingled with first-class cedar shingles. The building is to contain three windows on each side, two in the back end, one in the gable, and one in the front end between the doors, of nine by twelve glass, twelve lights to a window. The house is to be blinded, and painted on the outside with two coats of lead and oil, and the inside to be lathed, plastered, laid with a double floor, painted, grained, varnished, have two entries, crayon boards on each side of the room, and fully completed for the reception of the desk and seats, which will be furnished by the committee, but be put in their places by the builder.

A chimney is to be built from the foundation, and the school room to be ten feet high. The underpinning is to be granite, twenty inches deep, laid upon a solid stone foundation, and there is to be a stone step to each door. Concerning the foundation and the building to be built thereon, separate proposals will be received, which are to specify for how much the whole material will be furnished, and the foundation and house built.

Proposals from any and all persons will be received until May 30th, at ten o'clock in the forenoon, when said proposals will be opened and the contract given to the lowest bidder, who will be required to sign a written agreement for the completion of the house according to the foregoing plan.

Further particulars may be obtained from the building Committee.

YORK, ME., May 10th, 1884.

CHAS. W. JUNKINS,
GEORGE E. GRANT, } **Building Committee.**
JAMES A. BRAGDON,

SPECIFICATIONS FOR THE NEW SCHOOLHOUSE IN DISTRICT NUMBER 4 were posted in 1884 and the building committee called for proposals from builders.

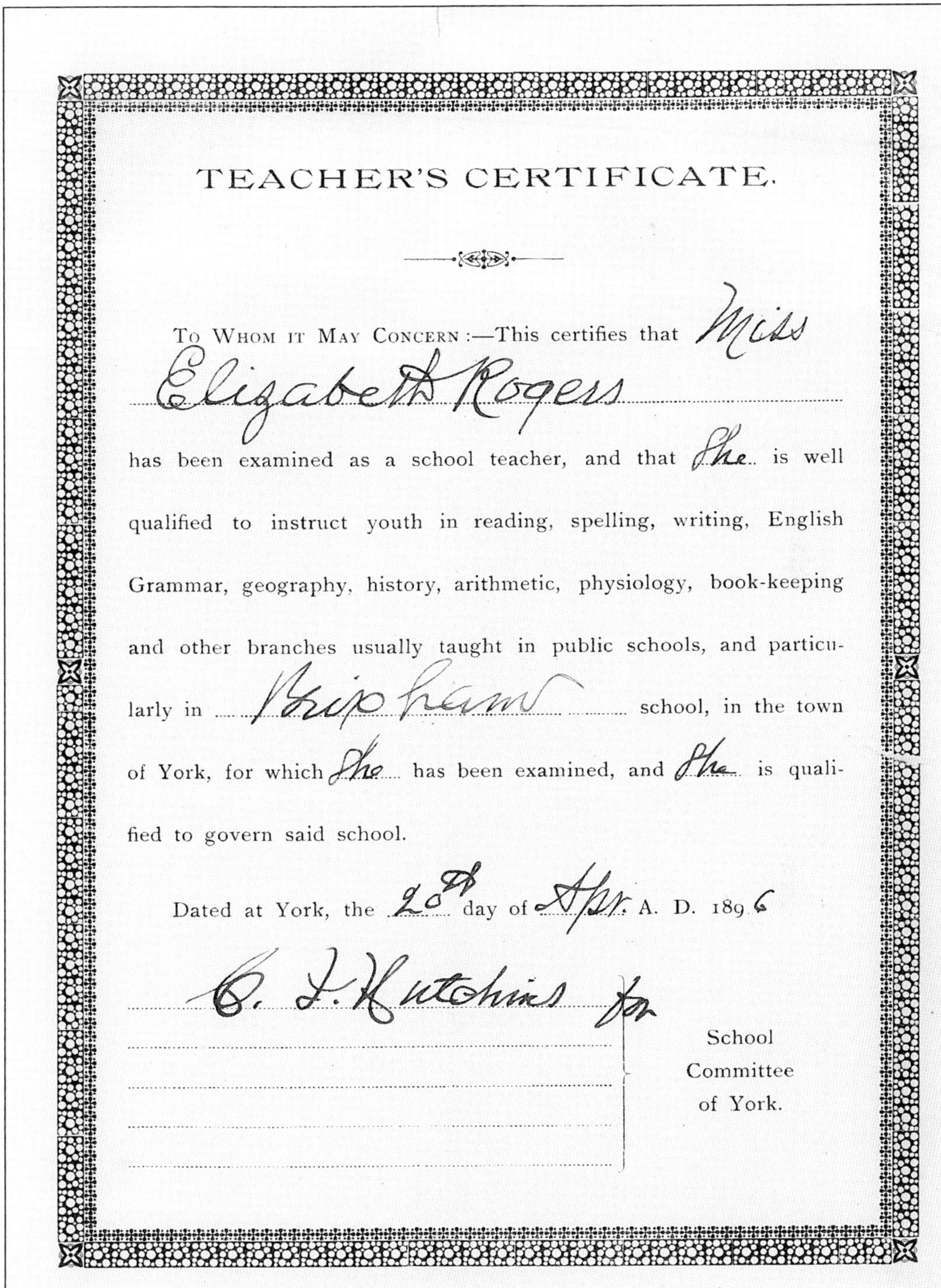

TEACHER'S CERTIFICATE.

TO WHOM IT MAY CONCERN:—This certifies that Miss Elizabeth Rogers has been examined as a school teacher, and that She is well qualified to instruct youth in reading, spelling, writing, English Grammar, geography, history, arithmetic, physiology, book-keeping and other branches usually taught in public schools, and particularly in Brixham school, in the town of York, for which She has been examined, and She is qualified to govern said school.

Dated at York, the 20th day of Apr. A. D. 1896

C. L. Hutchins for

School Committee of York.

ELIZABETH ROGERS WAS EXAMINED BY MR. HUTCHINS OF THE SCHOOL COMMITTEE and received this certificate of approval in 1896.

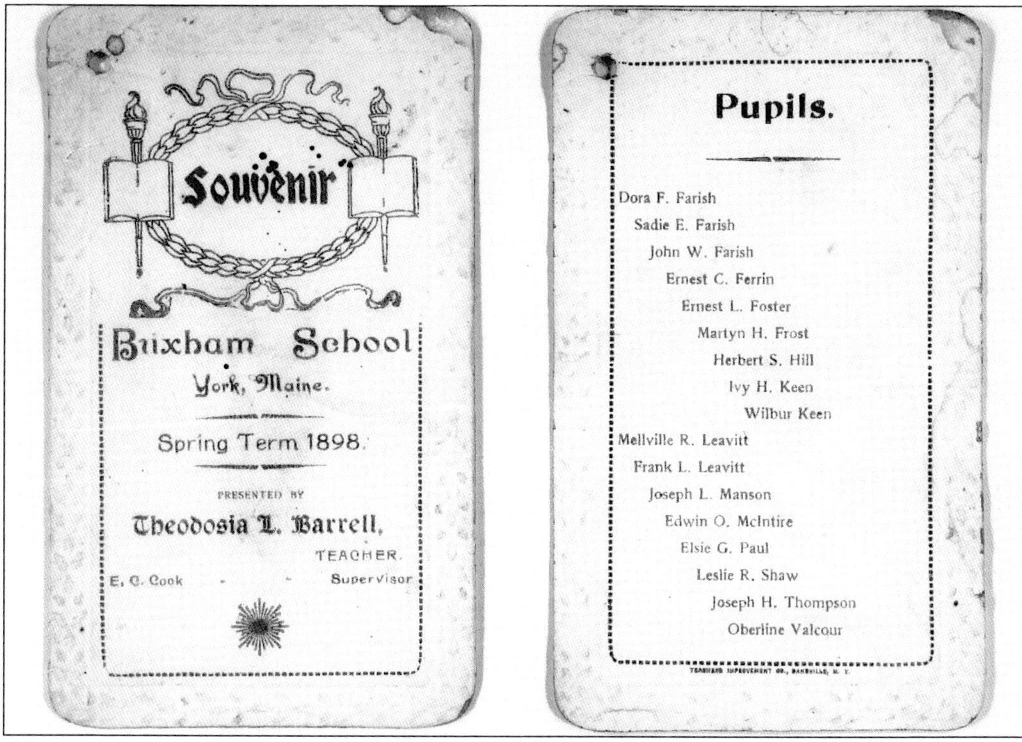

Souvenir

Brixham School

York, Maine.

Spring Term 1898.

PRESENTED BY

Theodosia L. Barrell,

TEACHER.

E. C. Cook - - Supervisor

Pupils.

Dora F. Farish
Sadie E. Farish
John W. Farish
Ernest C. Ferrin
Ernest L. Foster
Martyn H. Frost
Herbert S. Hill
Ivy H. Keen
Wilbur Keen
Mellville R. Leavitt
Frank L. Leavitt
Joseph L. Manson
Edwin O. McIntire
Elsie G. Paul
Leslie R. Shaw
Joseph H. Thompson
Oberline Valcour

THEODOSIA BARRELL TAUGHT AT THE BRIXHAM SCHOOL during the spring, fall and winter terms of 1898. She was paid eighty-eight dollars per term. Teachers traditionally changed schools each term but Theodosia spent the entire school year in Brixham.

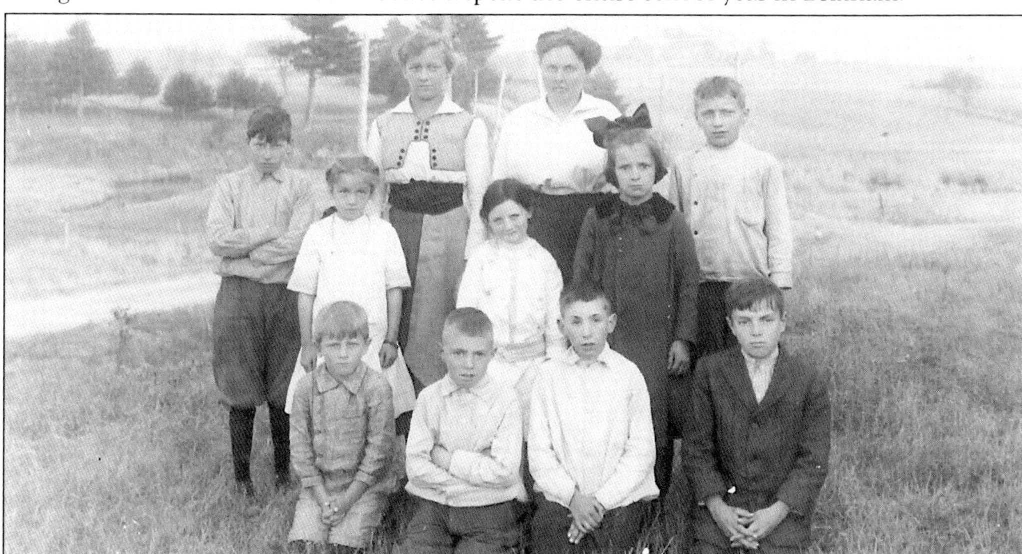

PUPILS AT THE BRIXHAM SCHOOL IN 1915. Located at Brixham Four Corners, it was one of the fifteen or more district schools that dotted the community before improved transportation led to consolidation. Front, left to right: James McIntire, Albert Ferrin, Center Ferrin and Willis Manson. Middle row: Raymond Staples, Helen McIntire, Evelyn Day, Alice Parsons and Frank Parsons. Back row: Mildred McIntire and teacher Etta McIntire.

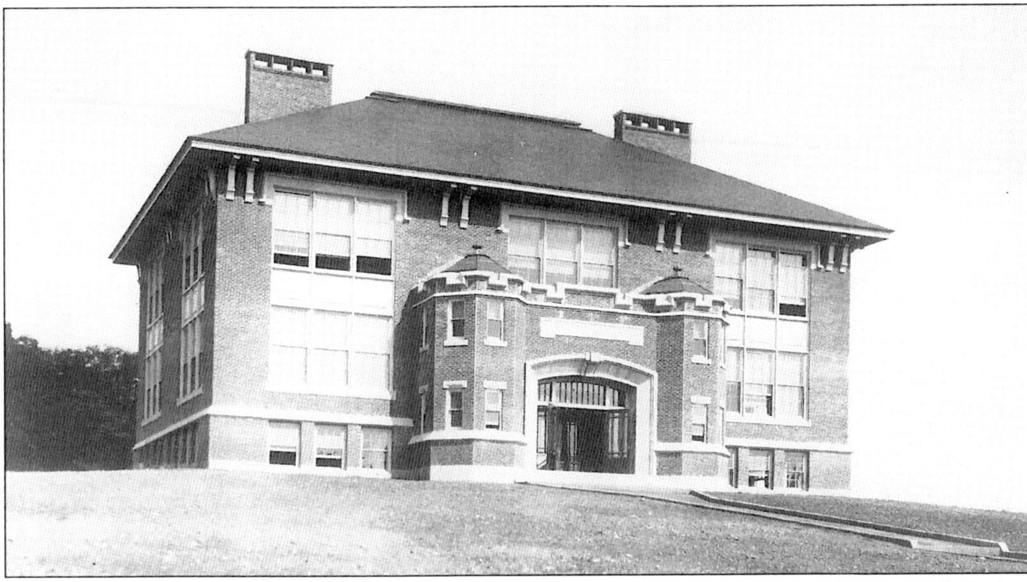

A NEW ELEMENTARY SCHOOL WAS OPENED IN YORK VILLAGE IN 1915. It had eight rooms for eight grades and eight teachers. Grades one through four were on the first floor and grades five through eight were on the second floor. The toilet facilities and the high school industrial arts classroom were in the basement. The upper half of the playground was used by the older students and the lower playground was reserved for the lower grades.

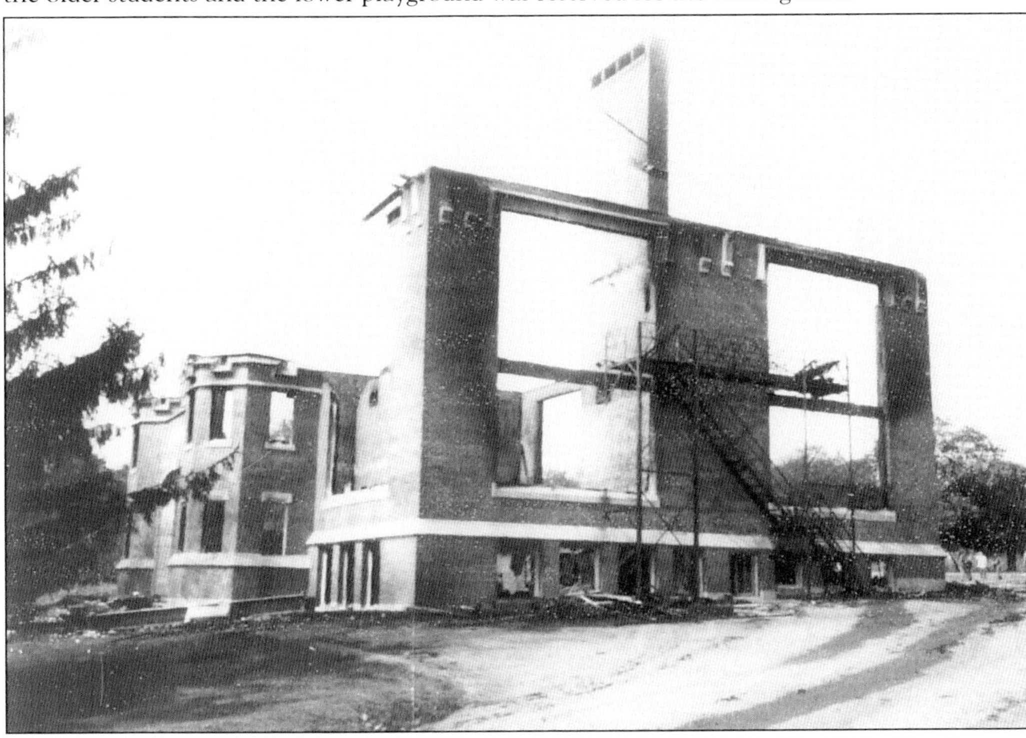

A SPECTACULAR FIRE DESTROYED THE BRICK BUILDING IN 1972. The fire took place at night so there were no students in the building. Additional classrooms being planned for an annex were incorporated into a plan for a completely new school facility.

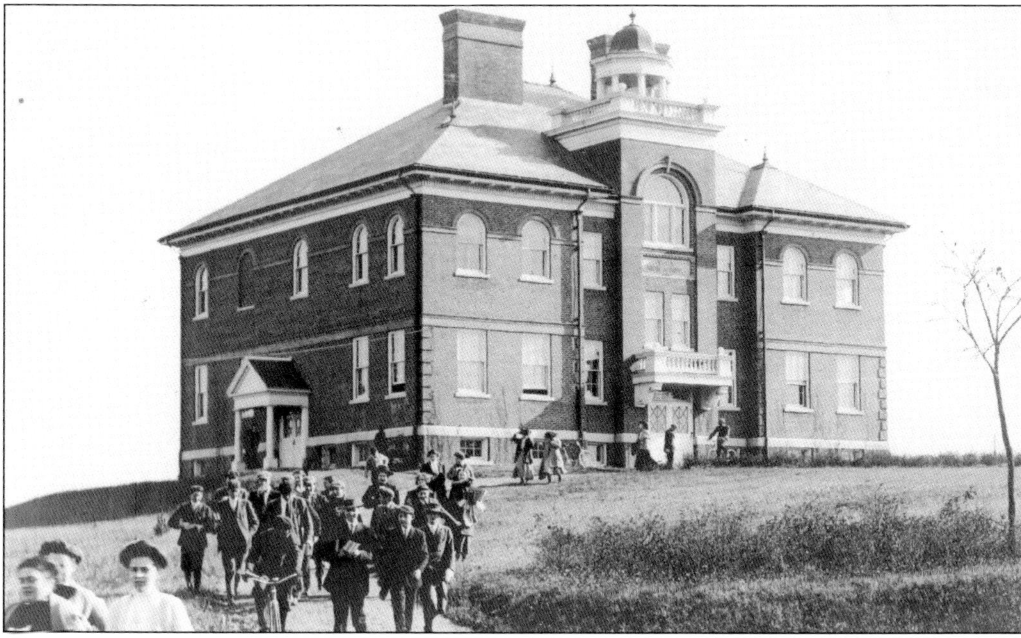

THE VOTERS APPROPRIATED $250 TO PLAN A FREE HIGH SCHOOL AT THE 1893 TOWN MEETING. The planning committee was successful and in 1900 it was decided to raise the sum of $10,000 to build a new school building. A building committee was appointed.

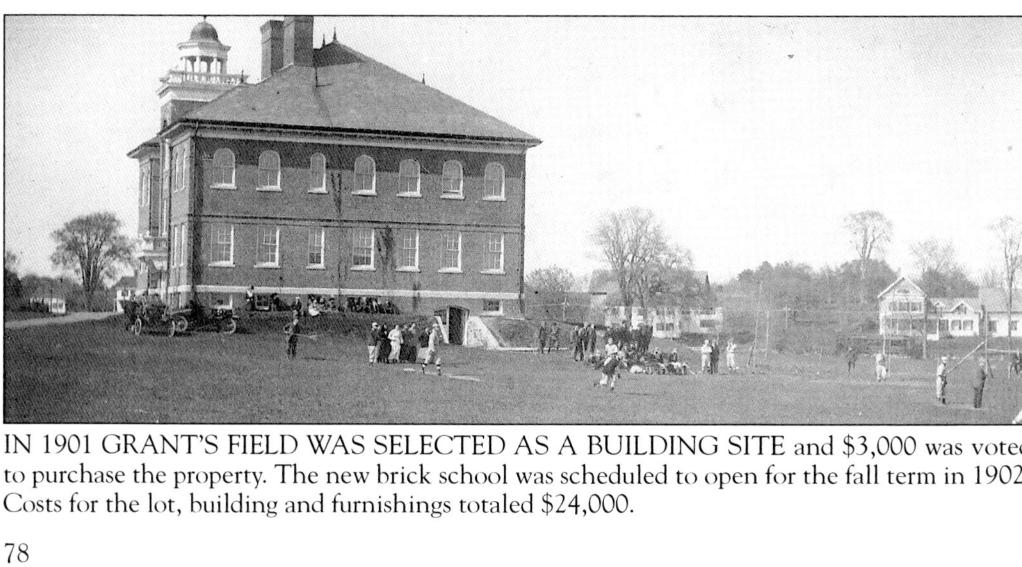

IN 1901 GRANT'S FIELD WAS SELECTED AS A BUILDING SITE and $3,000 was voted to purchase the property. The new brick school was scheduled to open for the fall term in 1902. Costs for the lot, building and furnishings totaled $24,000.

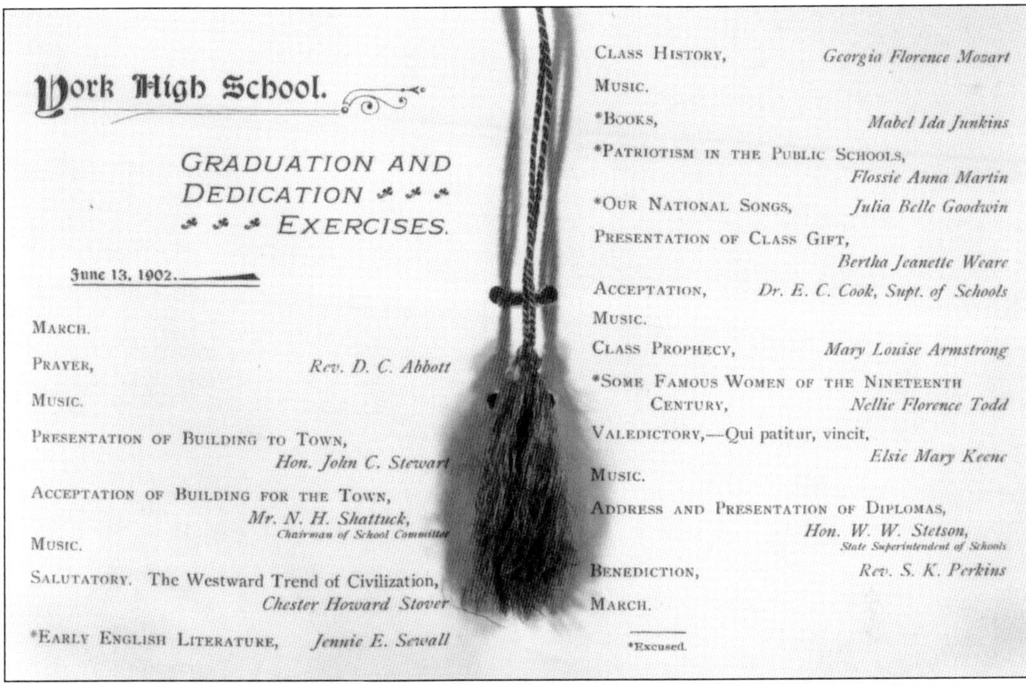

York High School.

GRADUATION AND DEDICATION EXERCISES.

June 13, 1902.

MARCH.

PRAYER, *Rev. D. C. Abbott*

MUSIC.

PRESENTATION OF BUILDING TO TOWN, *Hon. John C. Stewart*

ACCEPTATION OF BUILDING FOR THE TOWN, *Mr. N. H. Shattuck, Chairman of School Committee*

MUSIC.

SALUTATORY. The Westward Trend of Civilization, *Chester Howard Stover*

*EARLY ENGLISH LITERATURE, *Jennie E. Sewall*

CLASS HISTORY, *Georgia Florence Mozart*

MUSIC.

*BOOKS, *Mabel Ida Junkins*

*PATRIOTISM IN THE PUBLIC SCHOOLS, *Flossie Anna Martin*

*OUR NATIONAL SONGS, *Julia Belle Goodwin*

PRESENTATION OF CLASS GIFT, *Bertha Jeanette Weare*

ACCEPTATION, *Dr. E. C. Cook, Supt. of Schools*

MUSIC.

CLASS PROPHECY, *Mary Louise Armstrong*

*SOME FAMOUS WOMEN OF THE NINETEENTH CENTURY, *Nellie Florence Todd*

VALEDICTORY,—Qui patitur, vincit, *Elsie Mary Keene*

MUSIC.

ADDRESS AND PRESENTATION OF DIPLOMAS, *Hon. W. W. Stetson, State Superintendent of Schools*

BENEDICTION, *Rev. S. K. Perkins*

MARCH.

*Excused.

THE GRADUATING CLASS OF 1902 combined graduation exercises with dedication exercises. They were the first class to graduate from the new building.

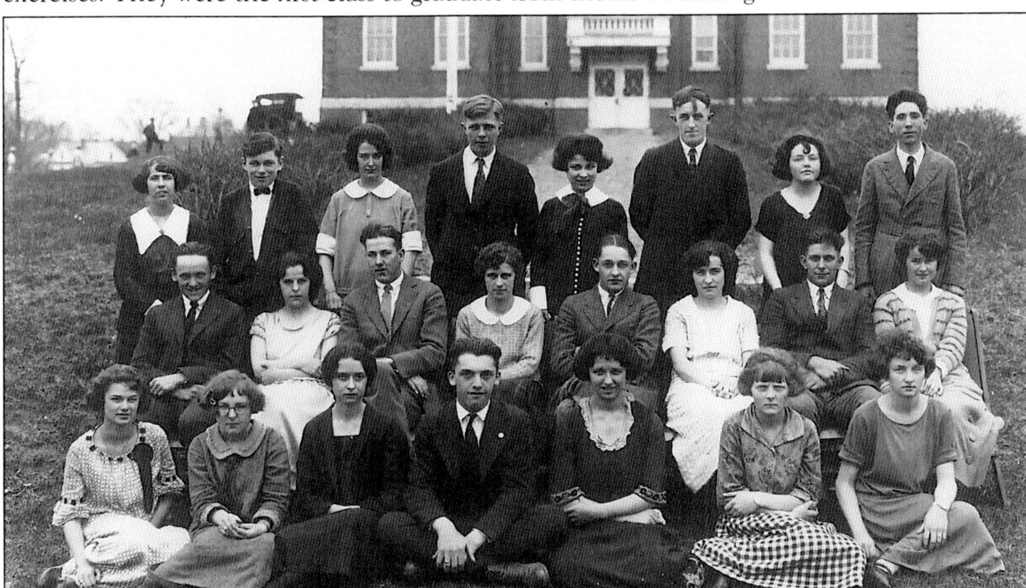

THE CLASS OF 1924. Front, left to right: Elaine Adjutant, Frances Woodward, Pearl Gilchrist, Theodore Blaisdell, Martha Blaisdell, Ellen Woodward and Doris Talpy. Middle row: Charles Donnell, Rita Plaisted, Harry Hutchins, Class Advisor Marion Berry, Charles Young, Genevive Banks, Albert Grover and Susan Lucas. Rear: Ruth Morse, Amenias Hotchiss Bowden, Marian Vinal, Carol Hawkes, Constance Marshall, Jerome Goodwin, Christina Ramsdell and Center Ferrin.

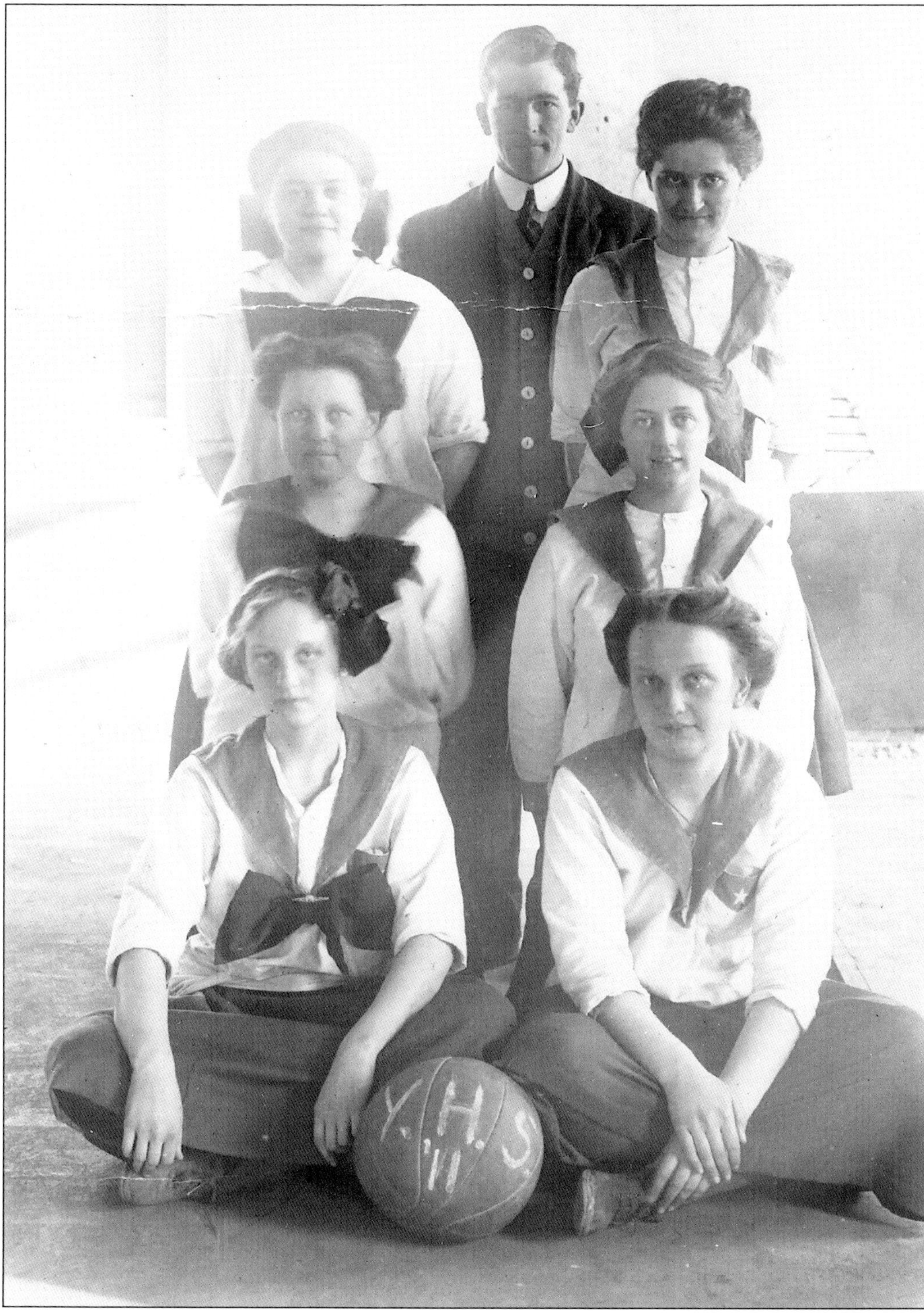

THE GIRLS BASKETBALL TEAM REPRESENTING YORK HIGH SCHOOL IN 1911. Front, left to right: Lutie Plaisted and Helen Plaisted. Second row: Jennie Bunker and Edna Bragdon. Third row: Marion Banks and Coach Melissa Brown. Anson Handy was the principal.

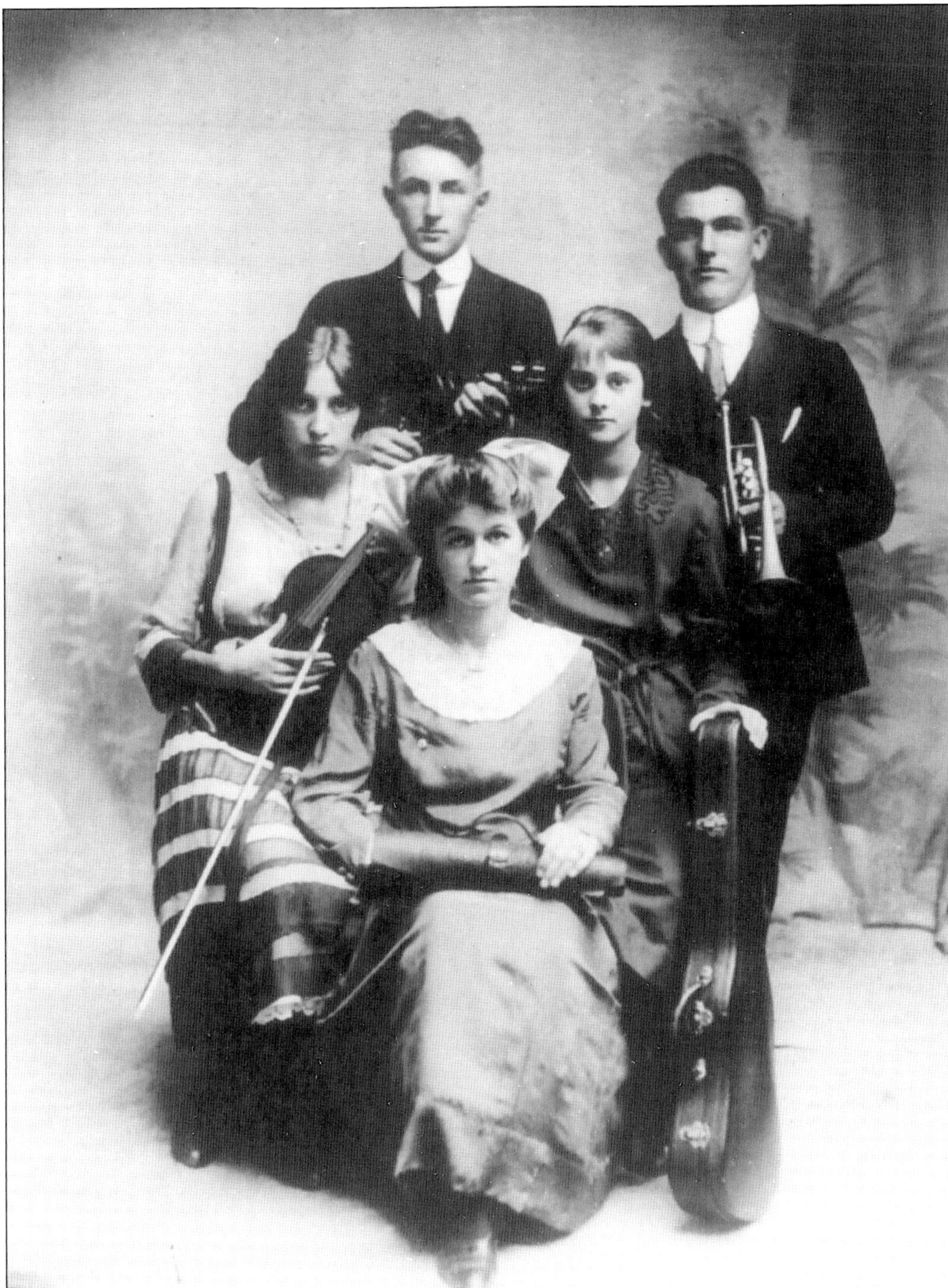

THE YORK HIGH SCHOOL SENIOR ORCHESTRA IN 1922. Front: Marguerite Walker. Second row, left to right: Doris Goodwin and Esther Straub. Back row: Howard Goodwin and Wesley Austin.

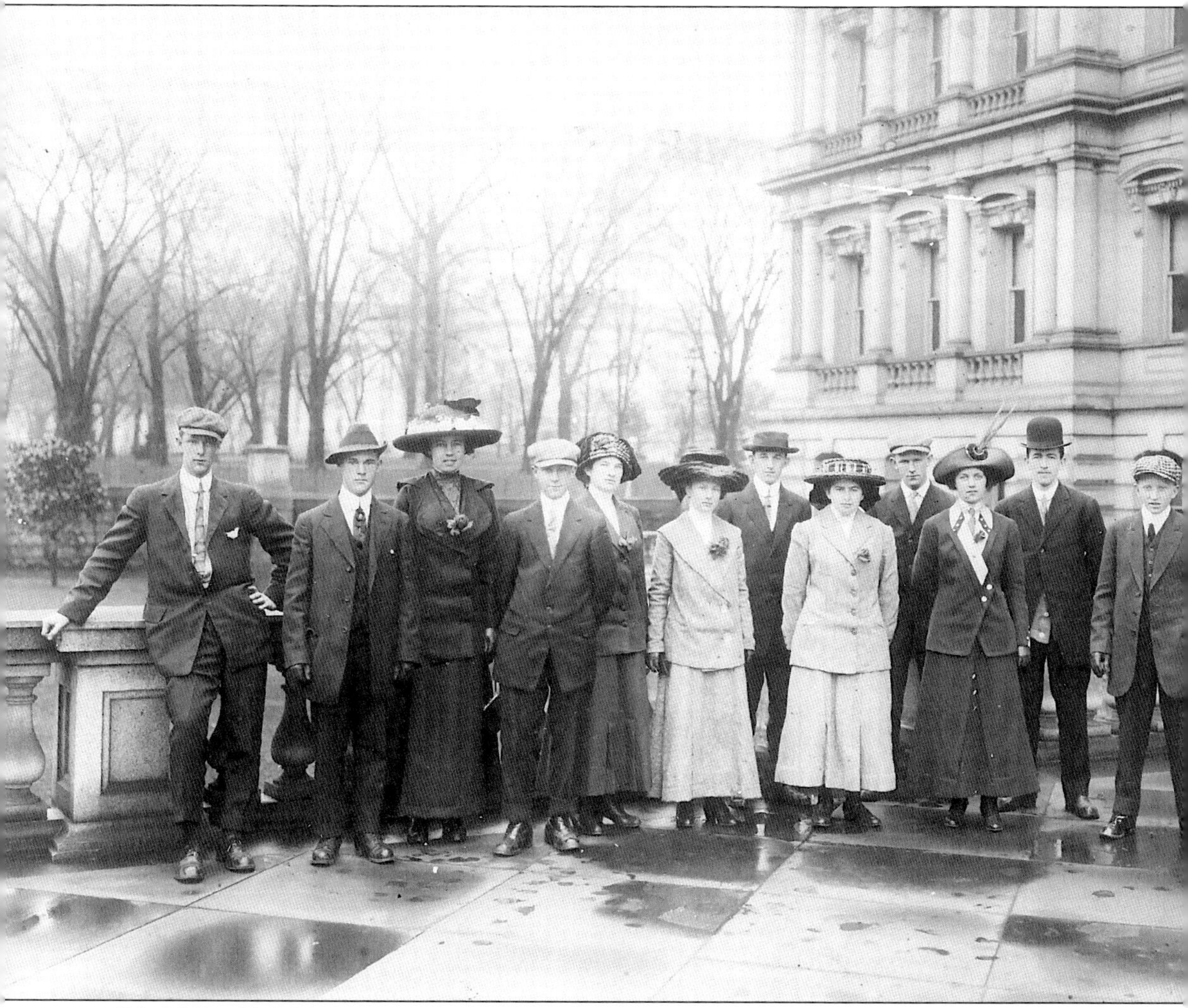

SENIOR CLASS TRIPS WERE A YORK HIGH SCHOOL TRADITION. This group was photographed by the State War and Navy Building in Washington D.C. on March 26, 1912. Left to right: Russell Weare, Mark Caswell, Jennie Hutchins, Clifford Young, Emilie Payne, Georgia Eaton, Harley Freeman, Mattie Langell, Herman Johnson, Edna Bragdon, Principal Anson Handy and Freeman Putnam.

OPPOSITE: THIS ENTERTAINMENT PROGRAM describes the Second Annual Fair, Supper and Entertainment Evening held by the students of York High School in 1928. Music, movies, a dramatic performance and dancing were enjoyed by those who attended.

YHS

Second Annual Fair, Supper and Entertainment, November 23, 1928

ENTERTAINMENT PROGRAM

Music .... High School Orchestra

One-Act Play .... "The Unseen"

CAST

Jeffry Baldwin .... Paul Dozois, '29
Lois, his wife .... Sara Donnell, '30
Hulda, a Swedish servant .... Margaret Cote, 30

Note: Curtain will be lowered one-minute during play to denote the lapse of one week.

Saxaphone Solo .... "Mighty Like a Rose"
Richard Weaver, '31

Violin Solo .... Selected
Paul Dozois, '29

Instrumental Trio .... Selection
F. Hawkes, '30 P. Dozois, '29
D. Earle, '28

Movie .... Two-Reel Comedy

Dancing .... Music by "Harmony Four"

We, the members of Y. H. S., wish to thank most heartedly all citizens and friends who have contributed so generously in making our Fair a success.

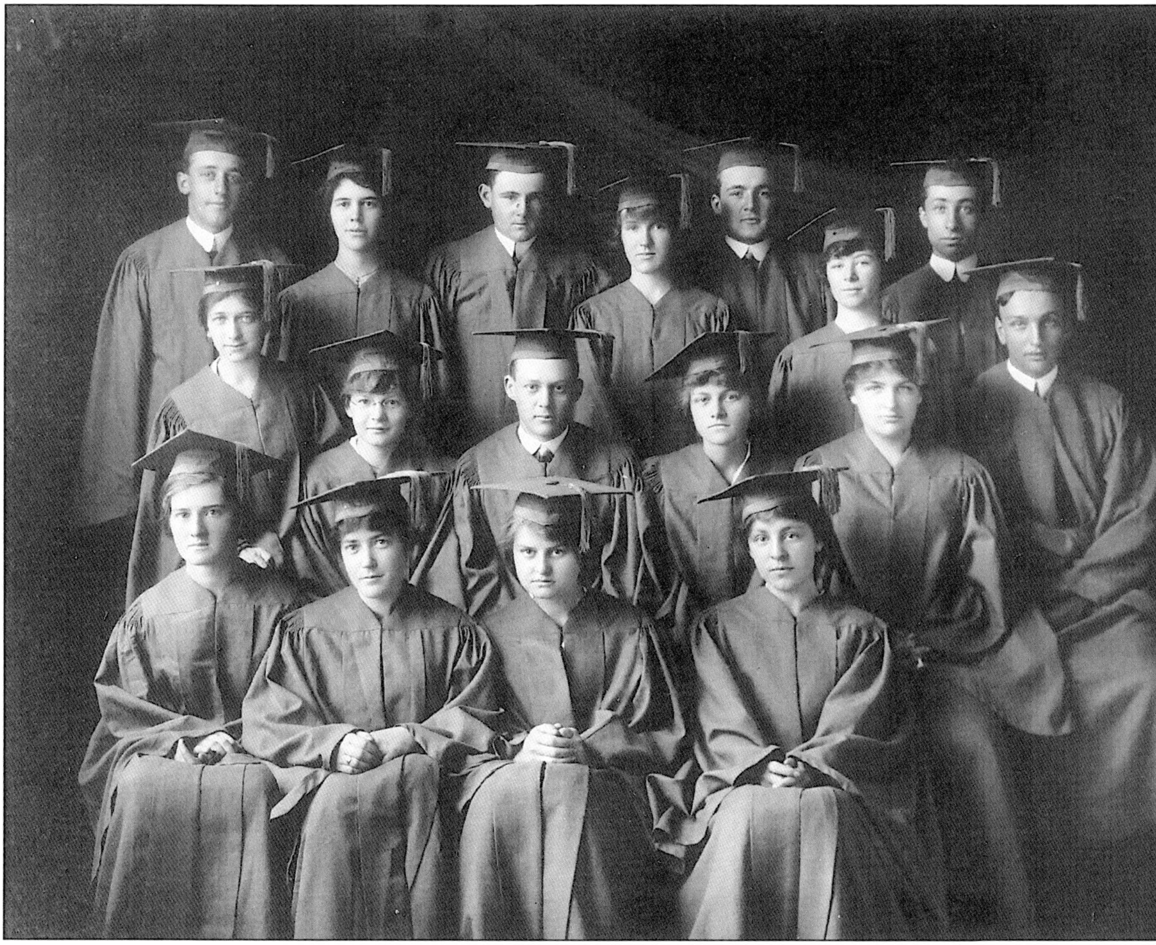

THE CLASS OF 1916 INTRODUCED THE WEARING OF CAPS AND GOWNS AT GRADUATION. Front, left to right: Aubrey Plaisted, Miranda Brooks, Valedictorian Mildred Moulton and Adena Austin. Second row: Rae Littlefield, Grace Philbrick, Class President Peter Weare, Priscilla Bracy, Doris Moore and Ernest Plaisted. Third row: Colburn Blaisdell, Marion Talpy, Arthur Chase, Hazel Ellis, Randolph Goodwin, Agnes Keene and George Blaisdell.

OPPOSITE: THE D.A.R. SPONSORED THE EIGHTH GRADE PRIZE SPEAKING CONTEST IN 1929. The featured speakers included Jennie Donnell, Elizabeth Moulton, Pauline McKowen, Mary McIntire, Anna Littlefield, Edna Kanada, Gordon Freeman, Alice LaBonte, Edna Perkins, Annie Starkey, Edwin Goudy, Charlotte Hooper and Elizabeth MacDonald.

THIRD ANNUAL

D. A. R. EIGHTH GRADE PRIZE SPEAKING CONTEST

Friday Evening, March 15th, 1929

CONGREGATIONAL CHURCH
YORK VILLAGE

Music .... "By the Shores of the Gitche Gumee"
Upper Grades, York Village School

Prayer

Music

"The Soldier's Reprieve" .... Lippard
JENNIE DONNELL

"The Whistling Regiment" .... Anon.
ELIZABETH MOULTON

"Gettysburg Address" .... Lincoln
PAULINE McKOWEN

"The Man Who Hung the Lantern" .... Minot
MARY McINTIRE

Music—"Minnewawa, Said the Pine Trees"

"The Minuteman" .... Hunter
ANNA LITTLEFIELD

"The Banner Betsy Made" .... Anon.
EDNA KANADA

"Valley Forge" .... Gillen
GORDON FREEMAN

"Lexington" .... Holmes
ALICE LABONTE

"The Legend of Walbach Tower"
EDNA PERKINS

Music

"E Pluribus Unum" .... Cutter
ANNIE STARKEY

"The Rider of The Black Horse" .... Lippard
EDWIN GOUDY

"The Angels of Buena Vista" .... Whittier
CHARLOTTE HOOPER

"John Burns at Gettysburg" .... Harte
ELIZABETH MacDONALD

Music—The Rainbow

Decision of Judges

Music taken from cantata, "Childhood of Hiawatha," by Wilson.

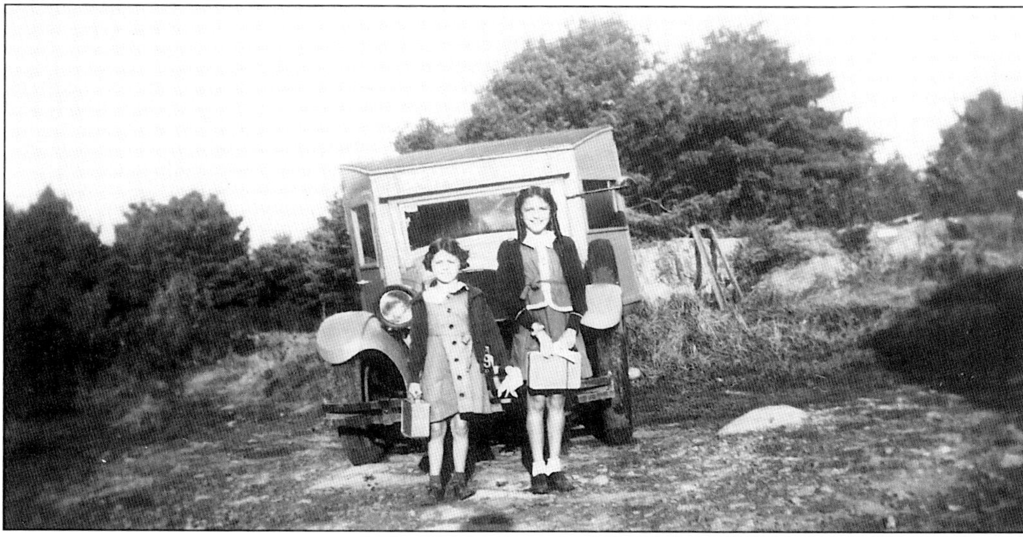

IN THE 1930s, SUPERINTENDENT ELMER SMALL AGREED TO PAY WILLIAM GIFFORD TO TRANSPORT HIS TWO DAUGHTERS TO SCHOOL. A neighbor asked Gifford to take his daughter and he built a bus to carry the girls. Eventually, the bussing of students became a common practice leading to the large fleet of buses that are now employed to transport students. Virginia and Anna Gifford are shown in front of the old blue bus that their father built to carry them to school.

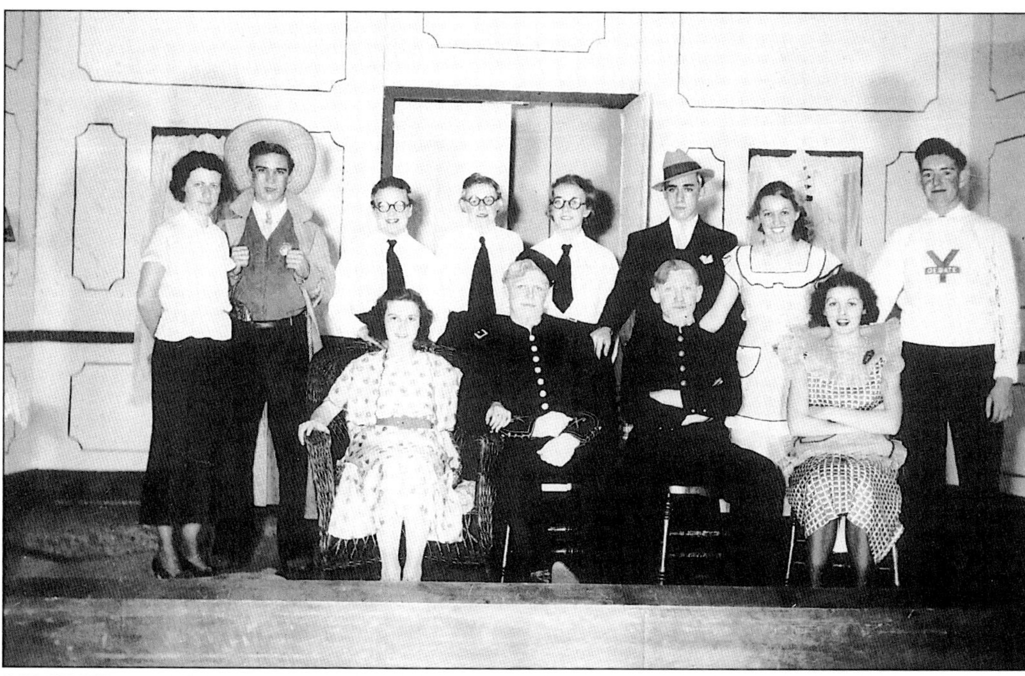

"CLOVER TIME" WAS THE TITLE OF THE PLAY PRESENTED BY THE JUNIOR CLASS IN 1936. Front, left to right: Dorothy Connors, Vernon Mackie, Robert Ronayne and Georgia Scarborough. Second row: Coach Marion Berry, Herbert Craig, Pauline Hall, Helen Sullivan, Edith Perkins, Russell Woodward, Rosie Tonnetti and Daniel Donnell.

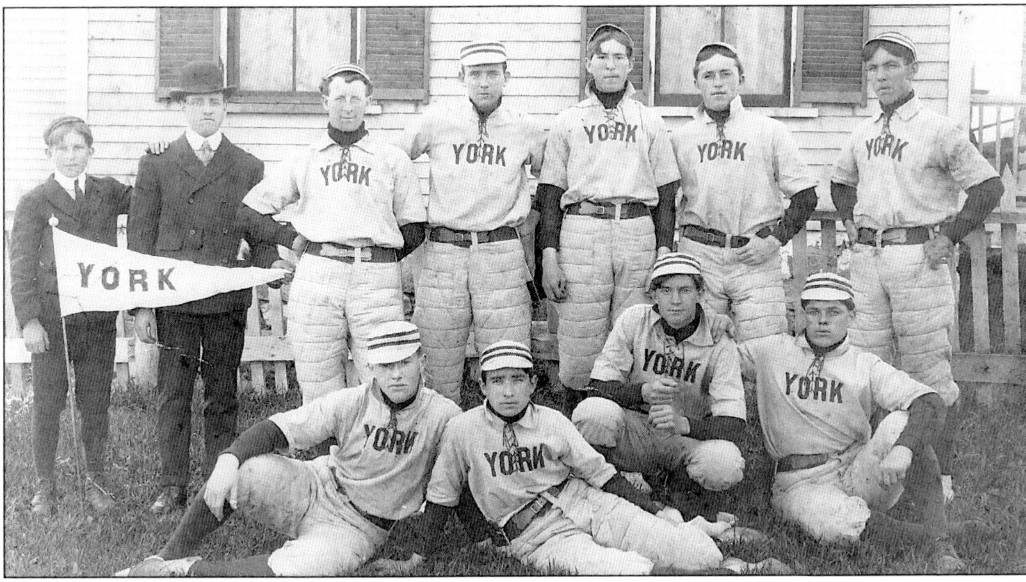

THE 1910 YORK HIGH SCHOOL BASEBALL TEAM even included their banner in the team picture. Seated, left to right: Ed Hawkes, Don Wakefield, Fred Martin and Bill Littlefield. Standing: Marshall Putnam, Harry Thompson, Sam Moulton, Art Baker, John Ladd, Leslie Bragdon and John Stover.

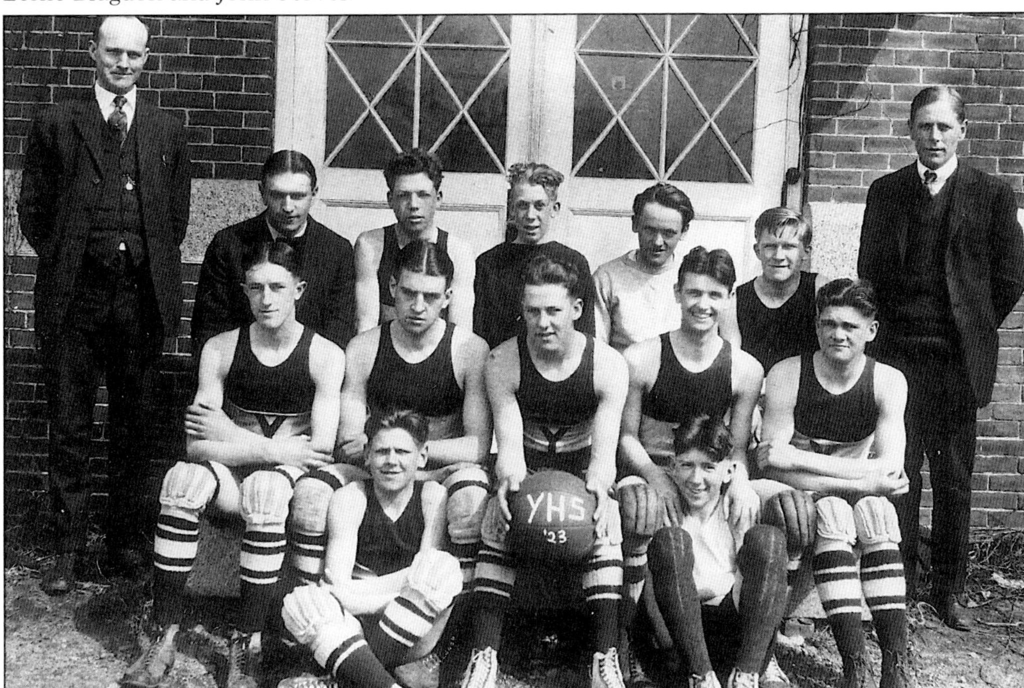

THE 1923 YORK HIGH SCHOOL BASKETBALL TEAM on the steps outside the gym. Front, left to right: Fred Ellis and Antonio LaPlante. Second row: Jerome Goodwin, John Banks, Harry Hutchins, Ned Lucas and Gerald Goudy. Third row: Principal Merle F. Hunt, Manager William Parsons, Ted Cook, Wilmont Dyar, Charles Donnell, Lloyd Moulton and Coach Myron Cox.

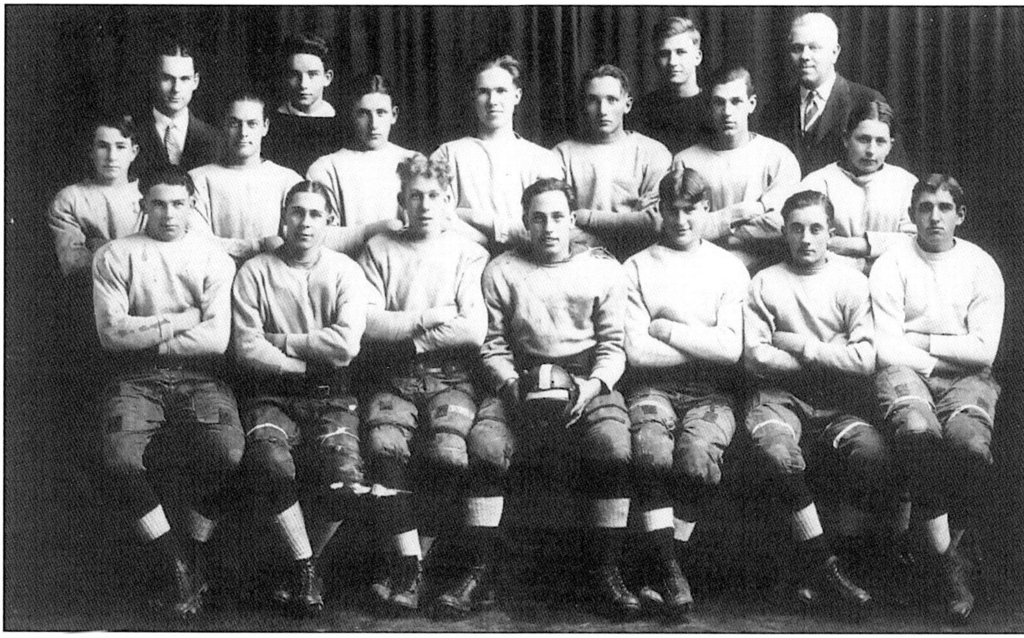

THE 1925 YORK HIGH SCHOOL FOOTBALL TEAM. Front, left to right: Philip Nason, Ivan Churchill, Wilmont Dyer, Howard Vickery, Willis Bardwell, Eugene Banks and William Adams. Second row: Chester Tobey, Lester Roberts, Thomas Bridges, Maurice Weare, Joseph Donnell, John Hutchins and Charles Weaver. Third row: Coach Chauncey Fish, Michael McKenna, Alonzo Skillings and an unidentified coach.

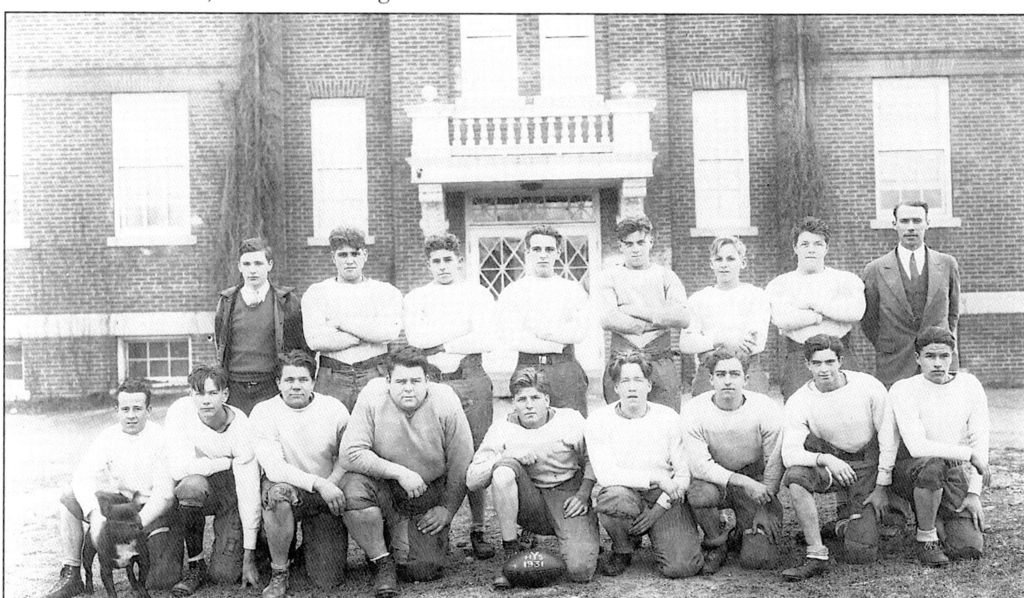

THE 1931 FOOTBALL TEAM WAS ONE OF THE BIGGEST TEAMS IN THE LEAGUE. Front, left to right: Tinker Moulton, Robert Lucas, Earl Ladd, "Soup" Moulton, D. Bracy, Martin Chase, Russell Marston, Ed Starkey and Art Davis. Standing: Hank Goudy, George Philbrick, Kip Smith, Richard Littlefield, Unknown, Unknown, Arnold Mitchell and Coach John Schroeder.

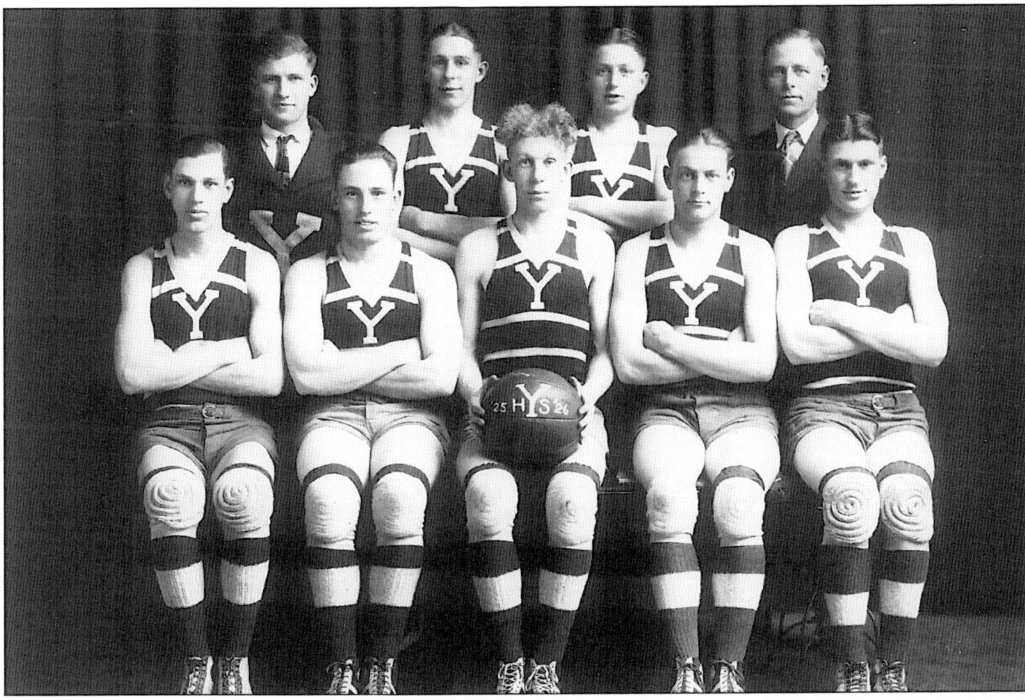

THE 1925 BASKETBALL TEAM CLOSED THE MOST SUCCESSFUL SEASON IN THE SCHOOL'S HISTORY WITH TWELVE WINS AND TWO LOSSES. A story about the team was published in the Boston Globe. Seated, left to right: John Hutchins (RG), Howard Vickery (C), Captain Wilmont Dyar (LF), Lester Roberts (RF) and Willis Bardwell (LG). Standing: Manager E.L. Horr, Ivan Churchill, Charles Weaver and Coach Myron Cox.

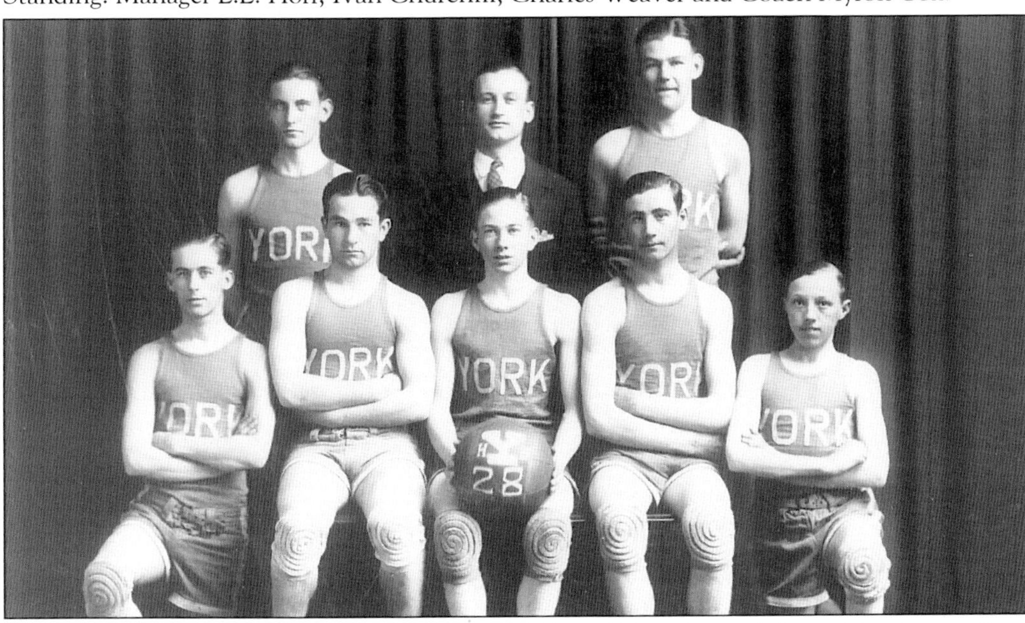

THE 1928 YORK HIGH SCHOOL BASKETBALL TEAM. Front, left to right: Robert Prest, Chester Tobey, Eddie Cooper, Charles Bridges and Cecil Perkins. Standing: Kenwood Thumith, Coach Chauncey Fish and James Cote.

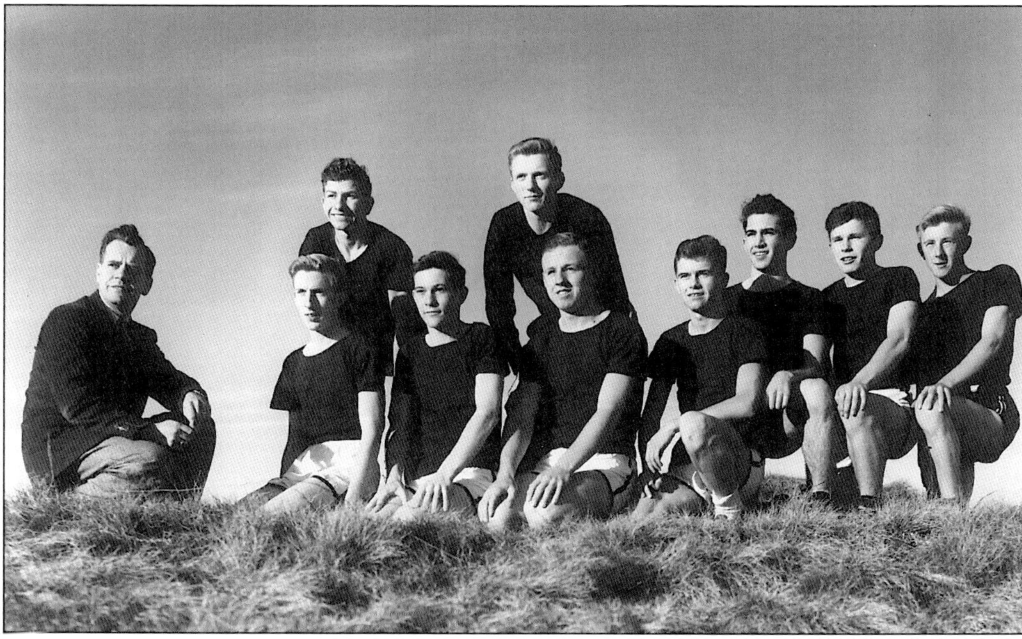

THE 1948 CROSS COUNTRY TEAM WON THE STATE CHAMPIONSHIP. Kneeling, left to right: Coach William Fisher, Alex Turner, David Bardwell, Charles Ballentine, Conrad Freeman, George Cooper, William Sawyer and Alan Roberts. Standing: Charles Childs and Linwood Carville.

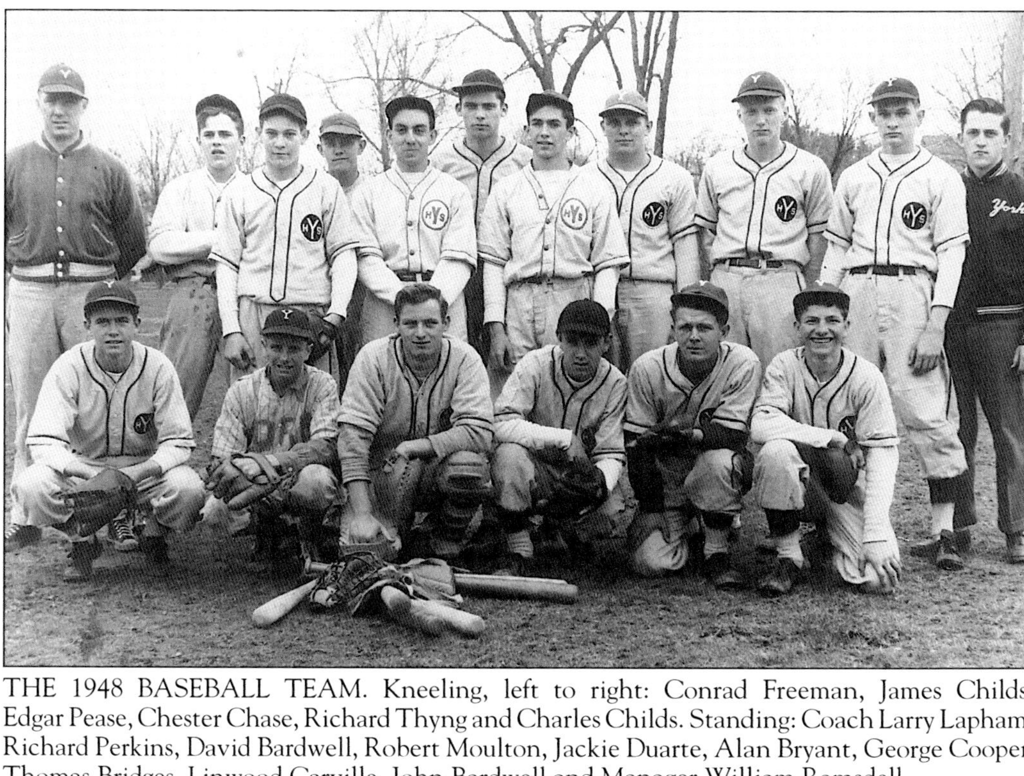

THE 1948 BASEBALL TEAM. Kneeling, left to right: Conrad Freeman, James Childs, Edgar Pease, Chester Chase, Richard Thyng and Charles Childs. Standing: Coach Larry Lapham, Richard Perkins, David Bardwell, Robert Moulton, Jackie Duarte, Alan Bryant, George Cooper, Thomas Bridges, Linwood Carville, John Bardwell and Manager William Ramsdell.

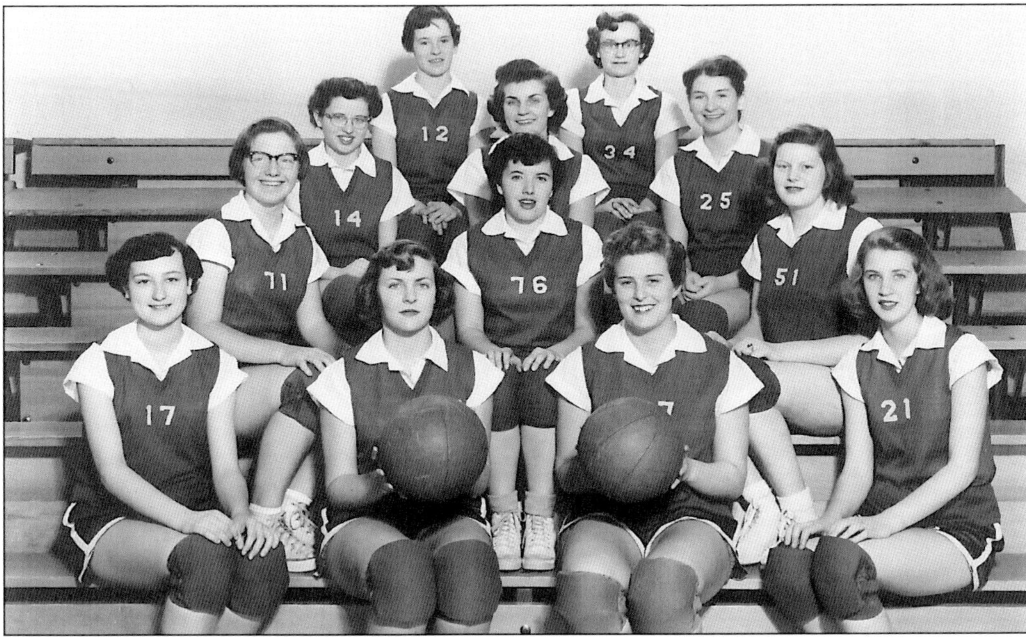

THE YORK HIGH SCHOOL GIRLS BASKETBALL TEAMS COACHED BY LARRY LAPHAM WERE RARELY BEATEN. In an eight year span his teams collected 125 wins against four losses and one tie. Elizabeth Sawyer was one of the first York athletes to score over one thousand points in a season. Front, left to right: Janice Sylvester, Jane Gates, Elizabeth Sawyer and Sylvia Day. Second row: Mary Olive Spiller, Fran Cooper and Sally Pease. Third row: Ann Briley, Margaret Hackett and Faith Hutchins. Fourth row: Loretta Warner and Lois Suitor.

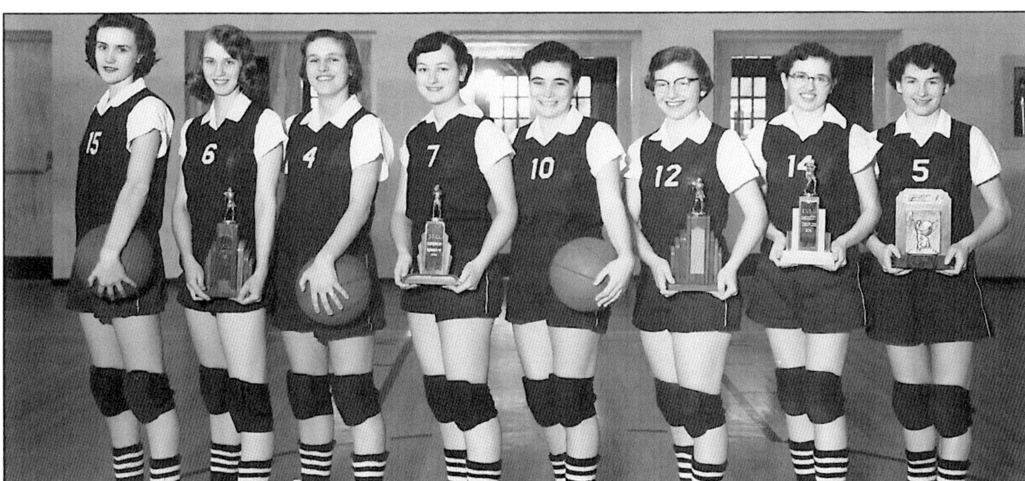

THE YORK HIGH GIRLS WON FIFTY-TWO VICTORIES OVER A THREE YEAR SPAN. The 1954-45 team won the Southern York County League Championship and collected a display case full of trophies over an eight year period in which they outscored their opponents 7,817 points to 4,295. They also produced three state foul shooting champions during the first seven years of the tournament. They included Jean Donnell (1950), Faith Hutchins (1955) and Sis Fontaine (1956). Left to right: Jane Suitor, Sylvia Day, Sis Fontaine, Janice Sylvester, Ann McManus, Mary Olive Spiller, Ann Briley and Faith Hutchins.

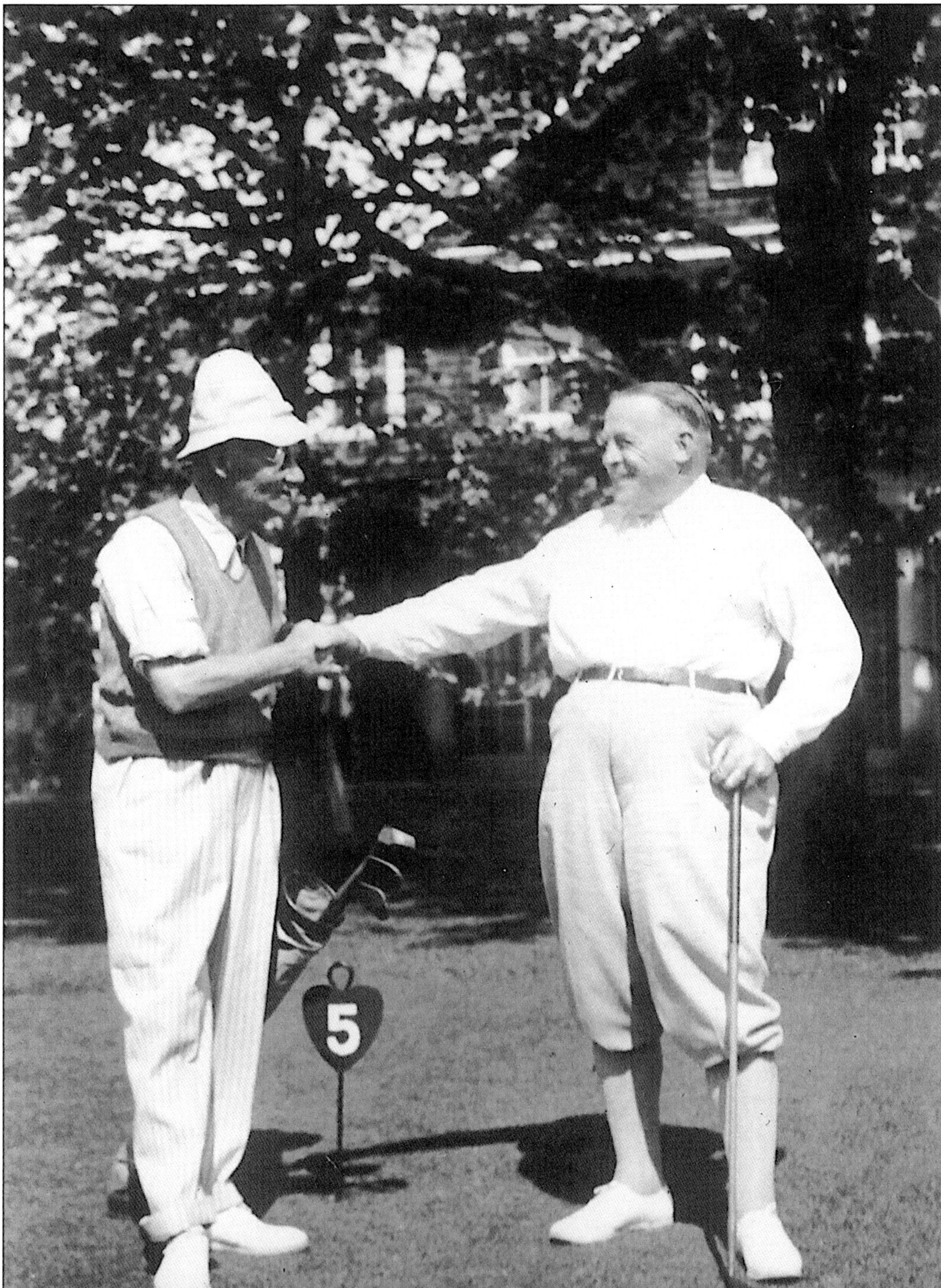

ALEX B. LAGARE AND JOHN G. BATES EXCHANGE GREETINGS ON THE FIFTH TEE. Golf was very popular in York but the course was primarily used by members of the summer colony.

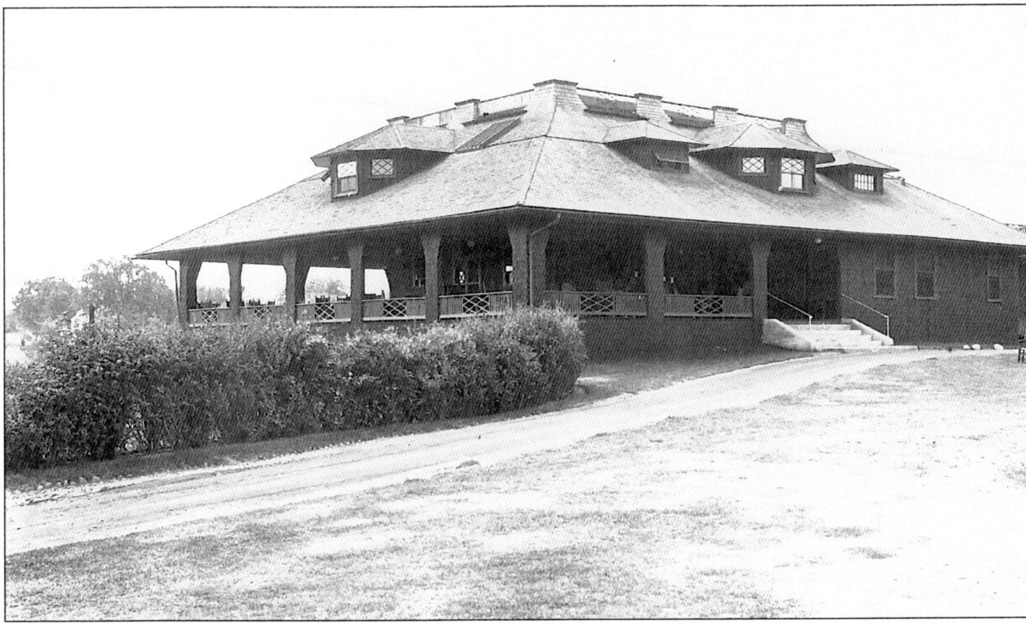

THE CLUB HOUSE AT THE COUNTRY CLUB WAS BUILT IN 1900-01. The brown-shingled building was designed and built by E.B. Blaisdell. High on a bluff overlooking the York River, patrons could watch the flow of traffic across Sewall's Bridge, including the electric trolley cars that were patronized by golfers and tennis players.

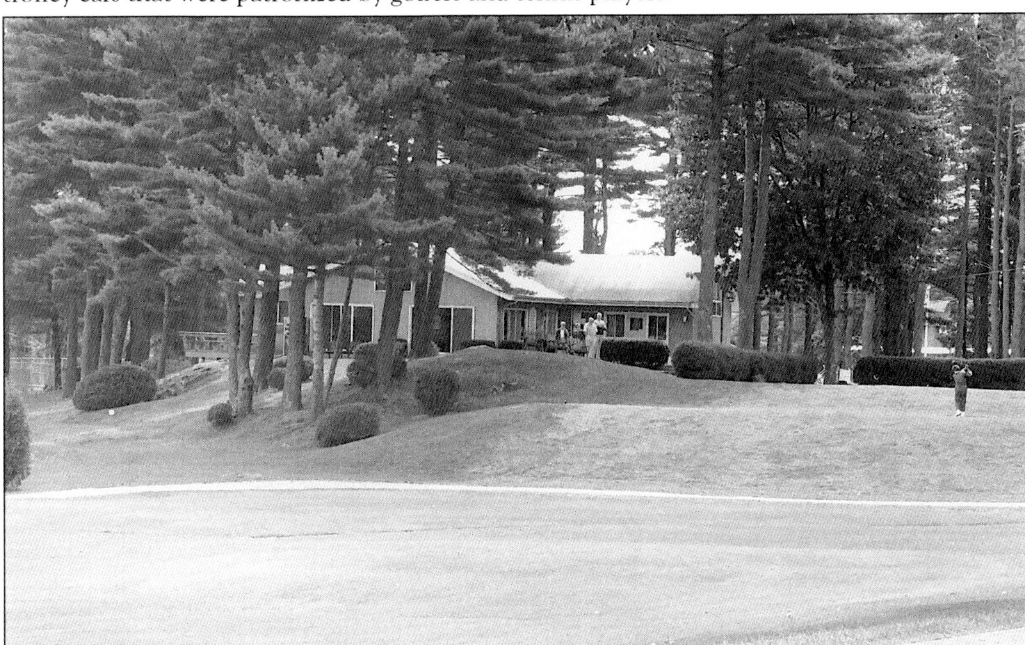

YORK COUNTRY CLUB WAS LEASED TO THE PINEHURST-MARSHALL HOUSE CORPORATION IN 1957. Under the direction of Richard Tufts, the golf clubhouse was relocated near the first tee. The first phase, which included a pro shop and locker rooms, was completed in 1963. An addition provided space for a snack bar and housing for the increasing number of electric golf carts.

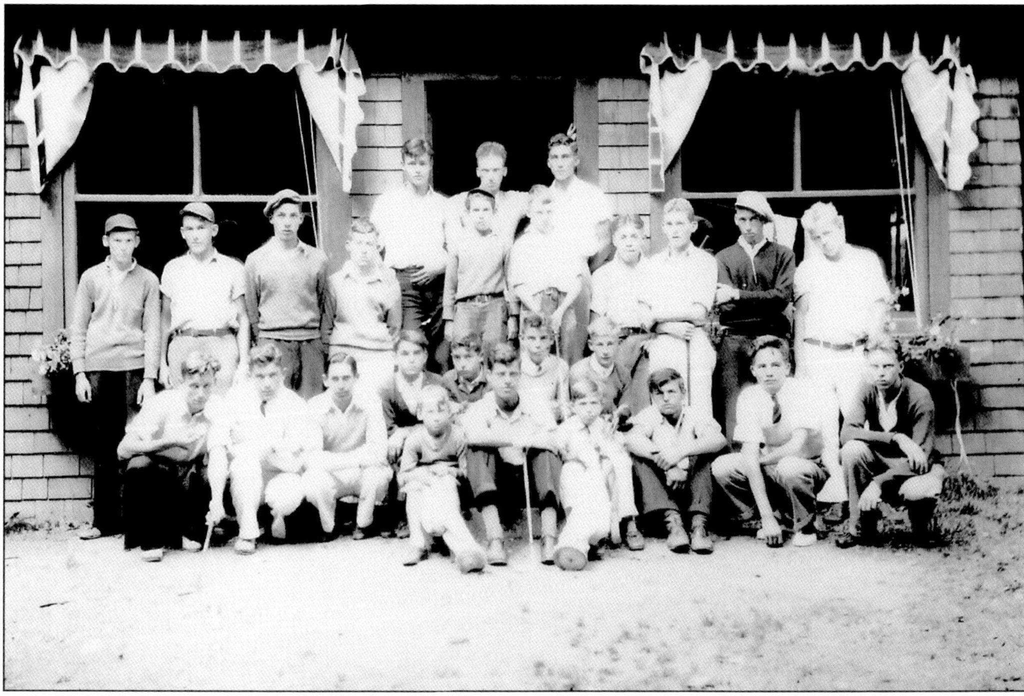

CADDIES CAME FROM KITTERY AND YORK ON THE TROLLEY CARS. Some came from the brickyard boarding house. This group, gathered in front of the golf pro shop, is in one of the few group photographs taken of caddies. Caddymaster Herb Bracy is standing in the doorway.

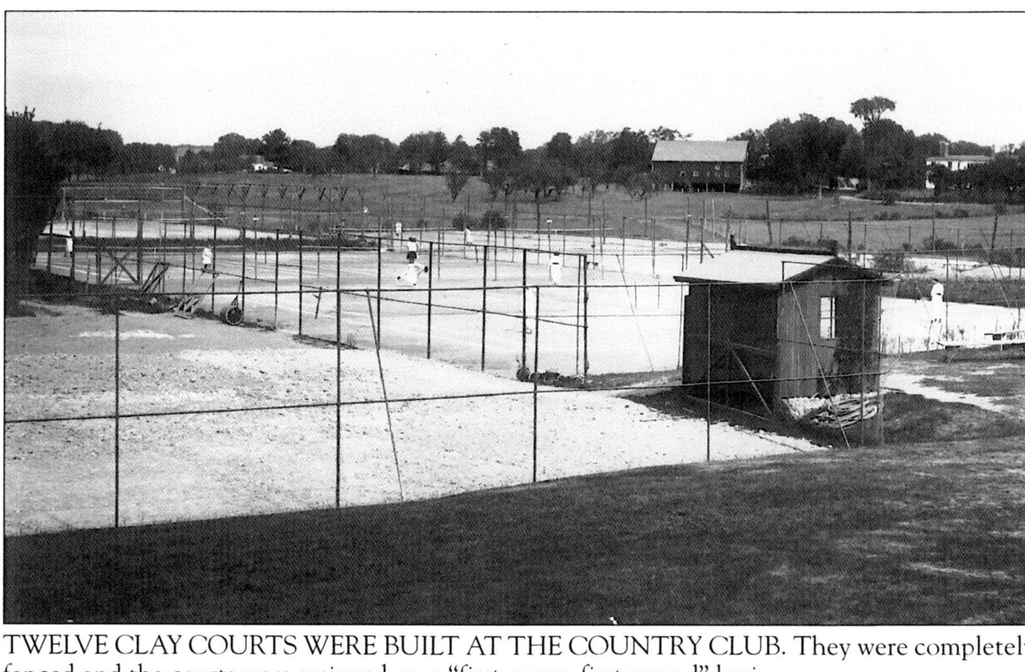

TWELVE CLAY COURTS WERE BUILT AT THE COUNTRY CLUB. They were completely fenced and the courts were assigned on a "first come, first served" basis.

Four

The Back Country

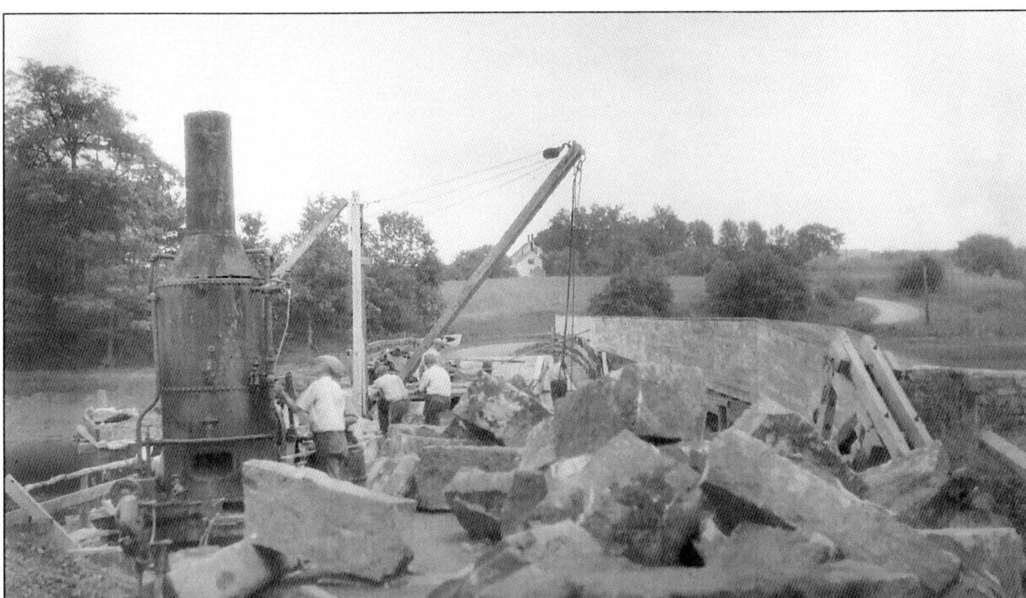

SCOTLAND BRIDGE WAS THE SECOND BRIDGE CONSTRUCTED ACROSS THE YORK RIVER. The original bridge was replaced after being carried away in a freshet in 1811. This bridge was being constructed in 1930 under the supervision of Angevine Gowen.

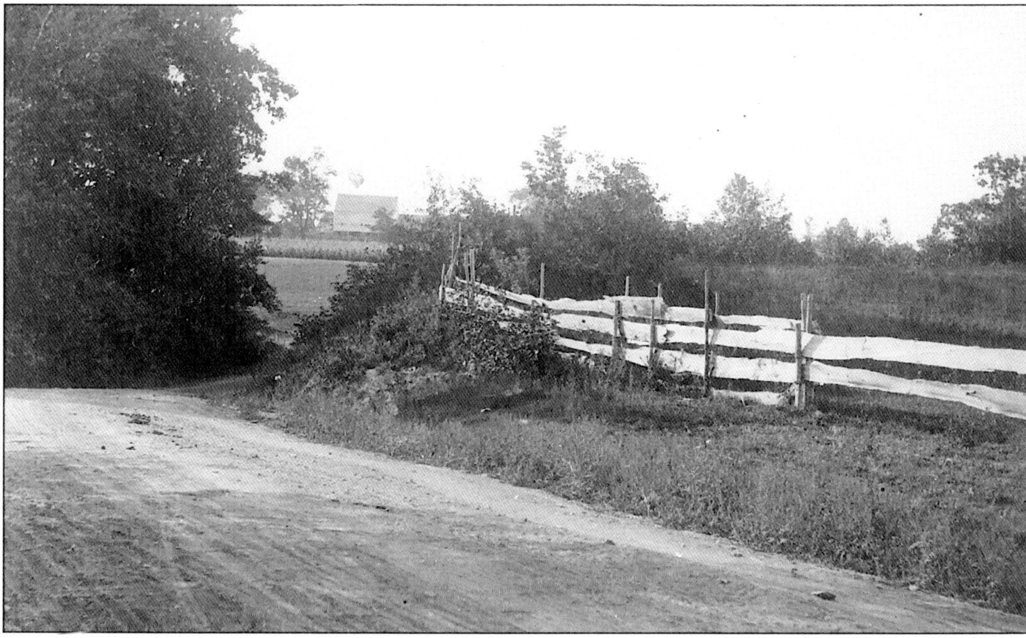

THIS RURAL SCENE ON ROUTE 91 may be looking toward the Junkins Farm on Scotland Bridge Road. In 1900, the farm was a popular stop for summer boarders. It is now a "Bed and Breakfast."

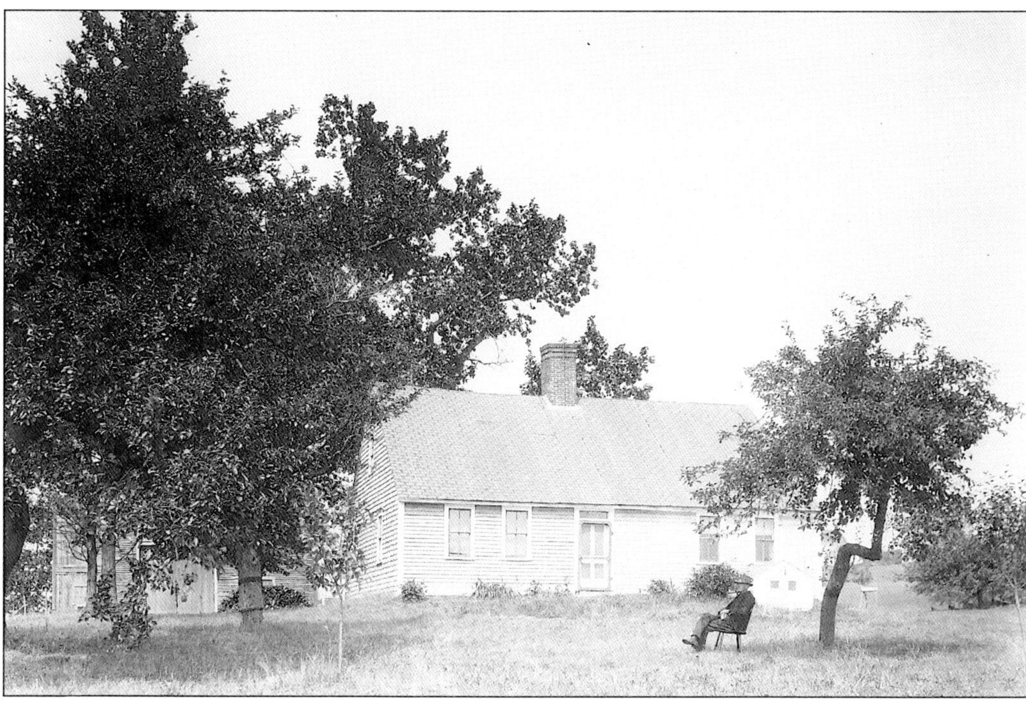

THE JOSEPH MOULTON FARM IS AT THE END OF GOWEN LANE off Cider Hill Road. It was built in 1714 by Joseph Moulton, son of the first Jeremiah Moulton, who once owned all of the meadow between this lane and the York River. It was also known as the Gowen Farm because it was the home of Angevine Gowen for many years.

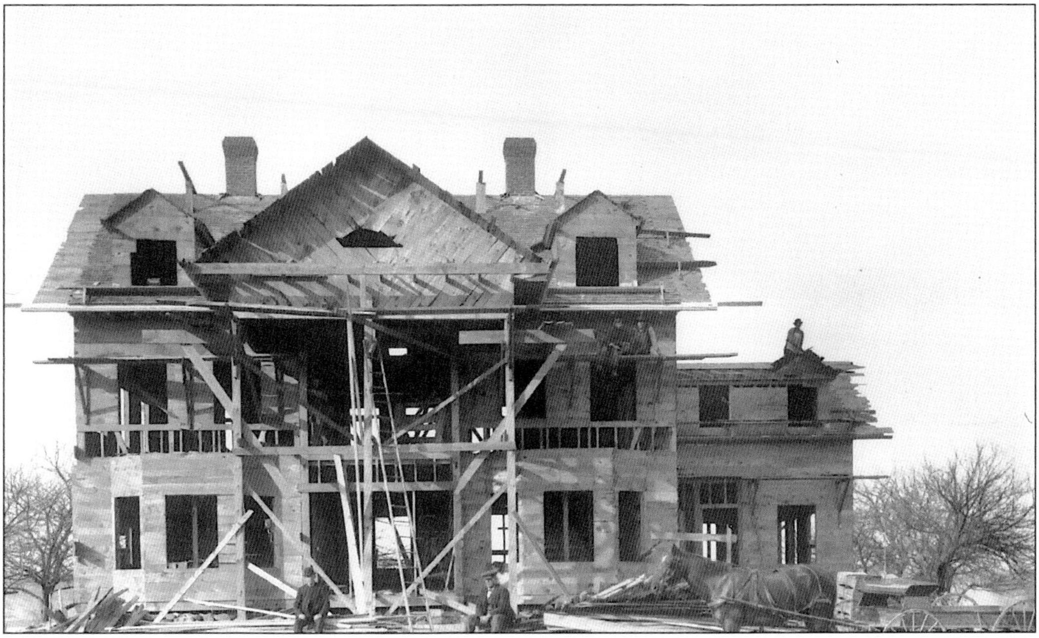

YOUNGHOLME, A LARGE WHITE HOUSE ON THE CREST OF THE HILL near the intersection of Route 91 and Pudding Lane, has been a Cider Hill landmark for many years. Charles H. Young built the large home to house his growing family. Angevine Gowen lived nearby and he took pictures at several phases of the construction.

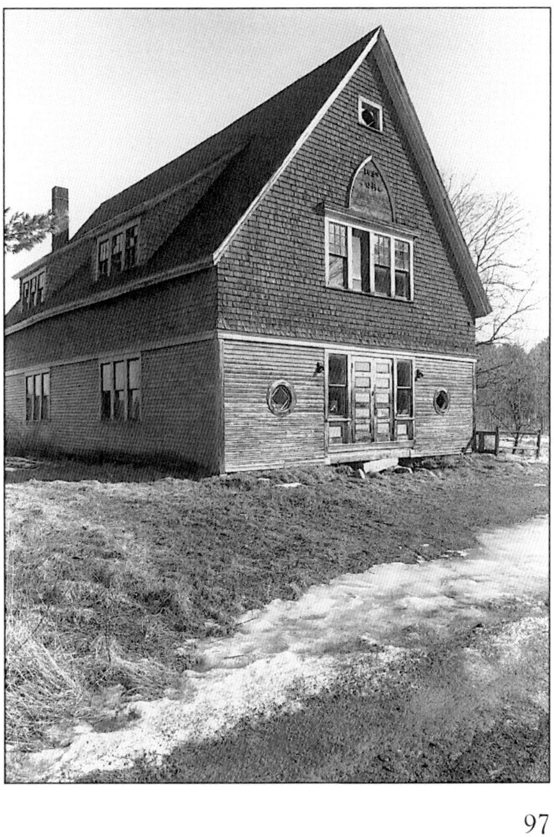

THE BRIXHAM GRANGE HALL was constructed at a cost of about $2,000. It was dedicated by State Master Obadiah Gardner on October 19,1899.

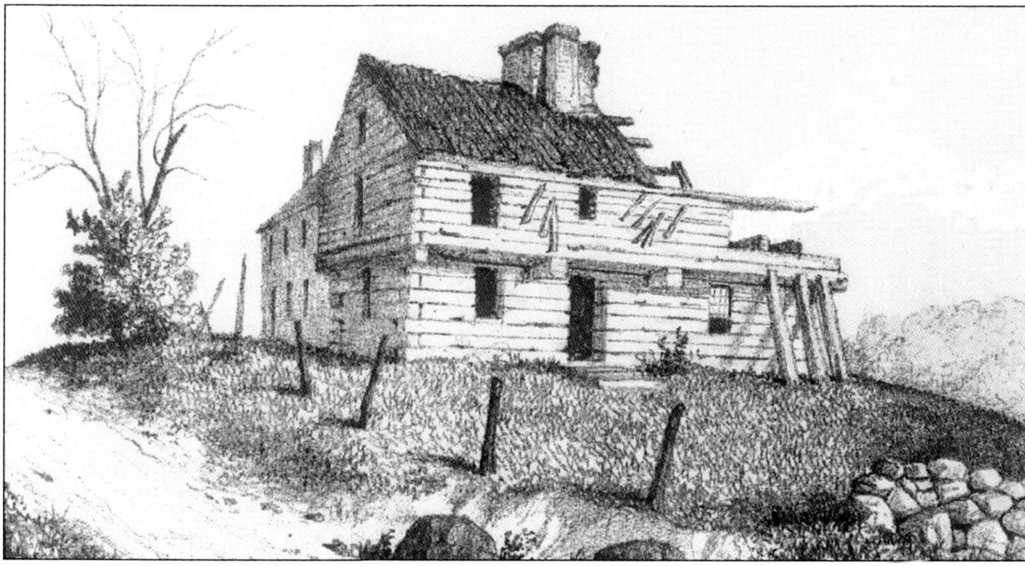

THE JUNKINS GARRISON HOUSE. A garrison house was not a specific style of architecture, but a place of refuge or a place to base militia. Located in York's Scotland district, this garrison was probably built later than most: it was not listed in 1711 as one of the defensive refuges in the town.

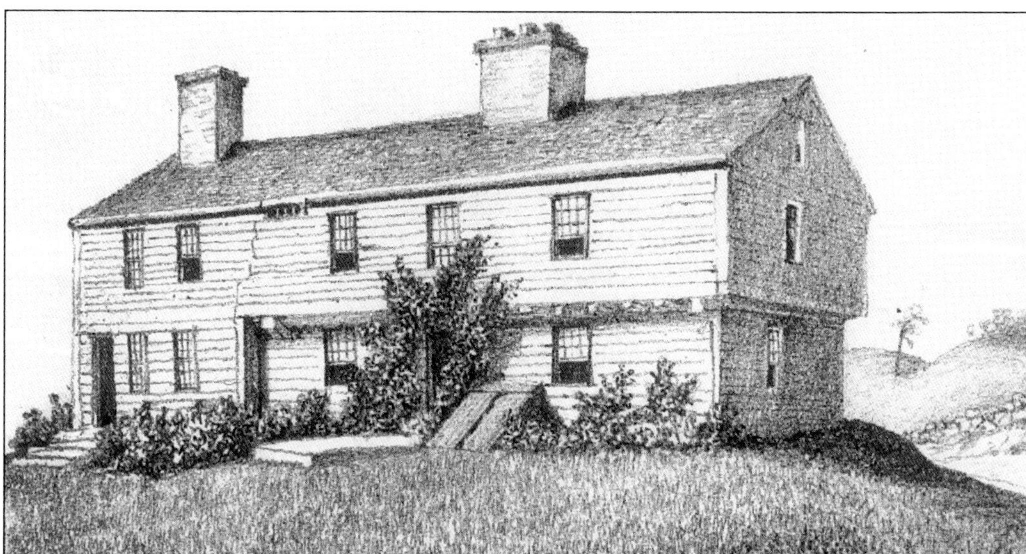

THE MCINTIRE GARRISON. The McIntire Garrison and the Junkins Garrison were both built with a conspicuous overhang of the second story. This structural detail developed in medieval Europe to compensate for crowded, narrow streets.

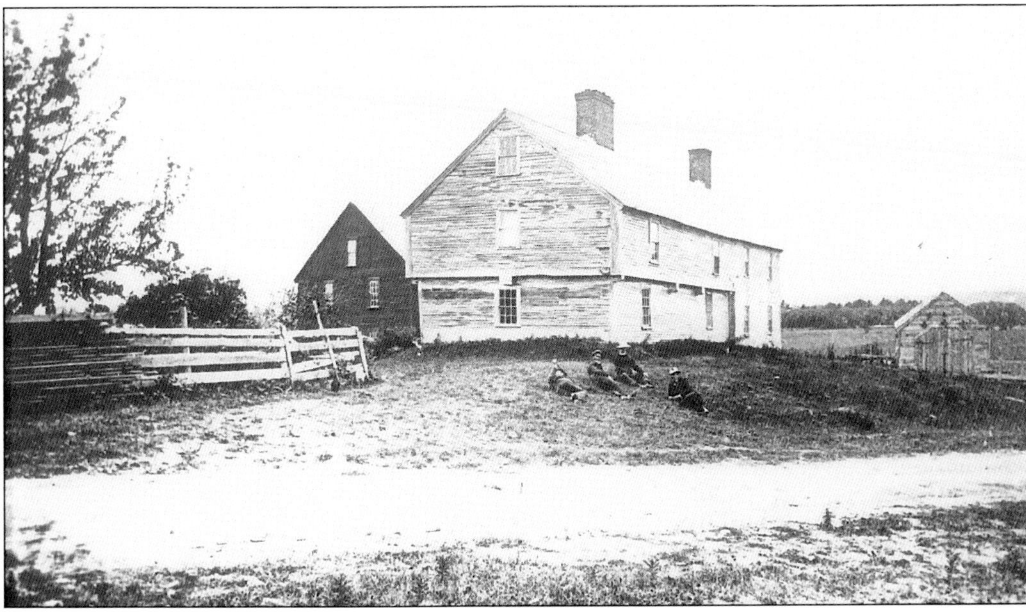

GARRISON HOUSES WERE USUALLY BUILT IN LOCATIONS WHERE GUARDS COULD SEE IN EVERY DIRECTION. Soldiers were quartered in them in times of danger. The McIntire Garrison was thought to have dated from 1645 but recent research has placed the date at sometime after 1707. However, it is still considered a remarkable survival.

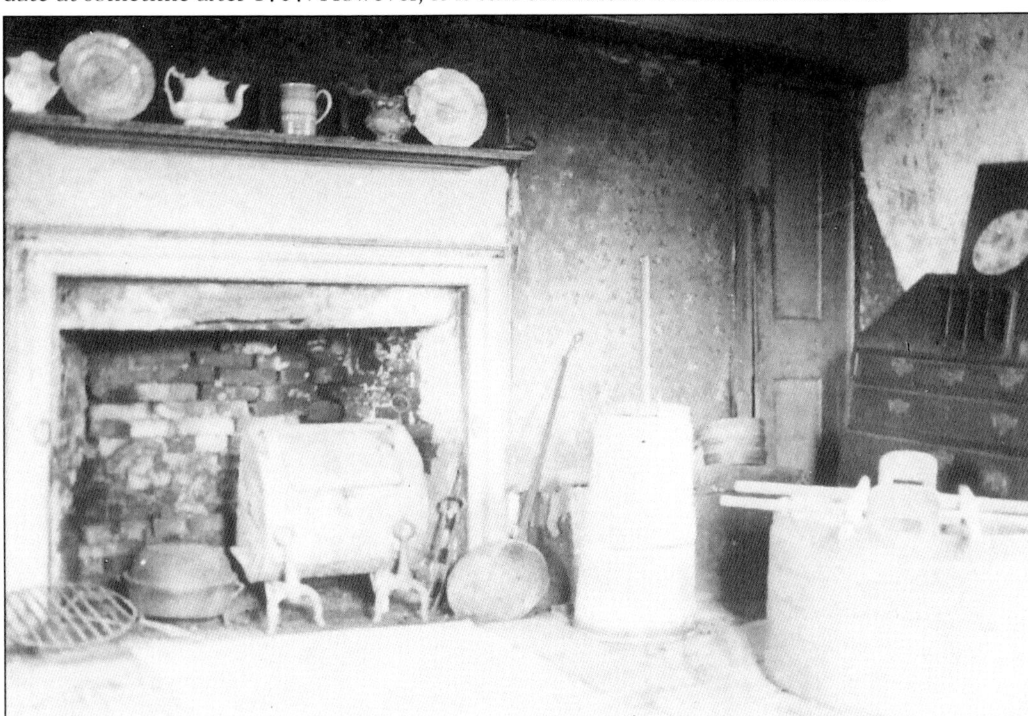

KEEPING ROOM OF THE McINTIRE GARRISON HOUSE. Families were instructed to go to a particular garrison house at the first sign of trouble. Supplies were stored there to feed these people while they were in protective custody.

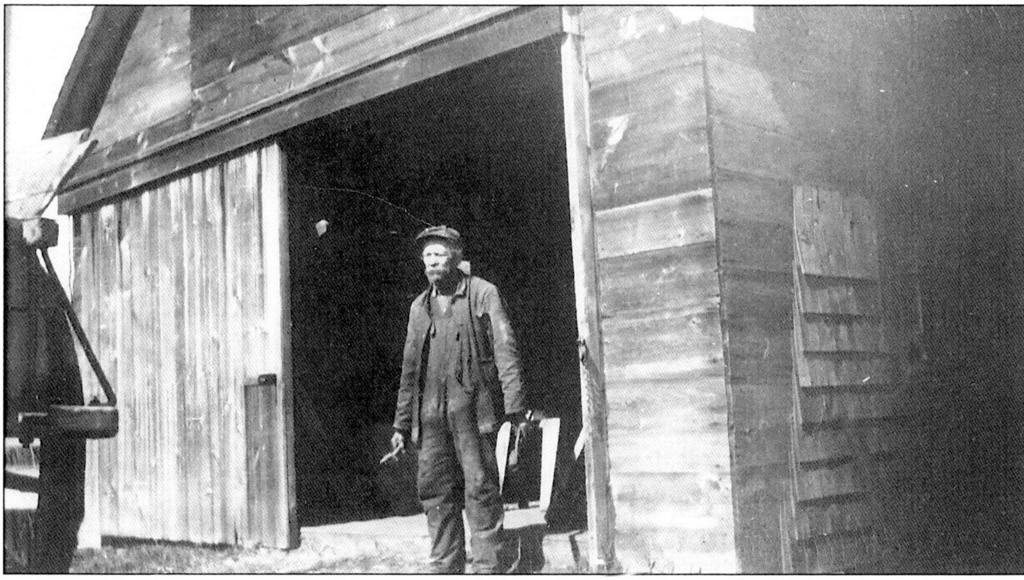

ALBERT SIMPSON (1847–1925) STANDING IN THE DOORWAY OF HIS BLACKSMITH SHOP at the intersection of Route 91 and Brixham Road. Simpson was also a skilled woodworker who was employed by many area residents to work on the interiors of their homes.

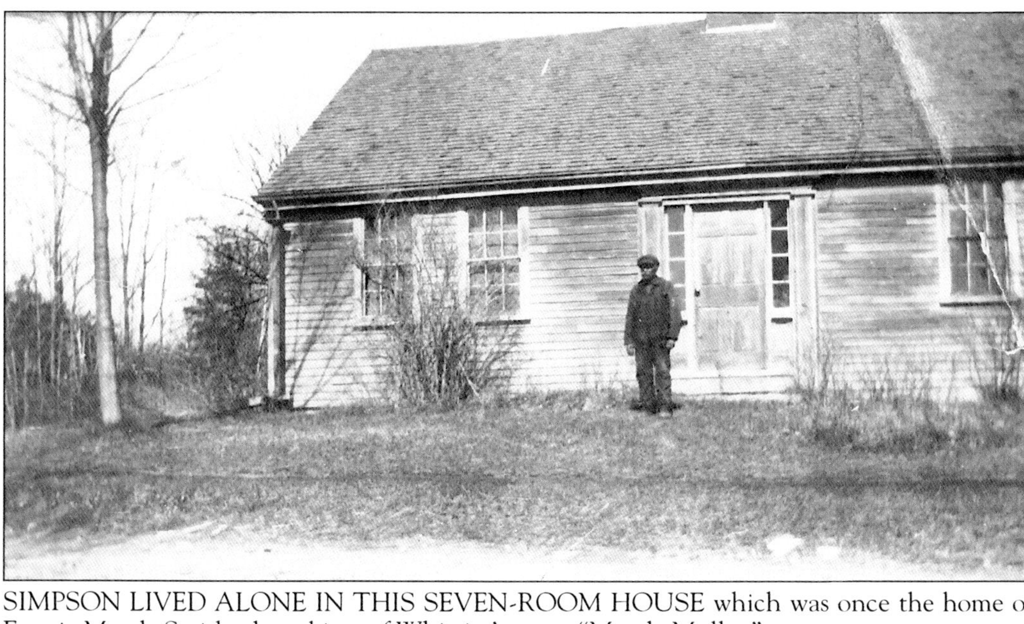

SIMPSON LIVED ALONE IN THIS SEVEN-ROOM HOUSE which was once the home of Fannie Maude Smith, the subject of Whittier's poem "Maude Muller."

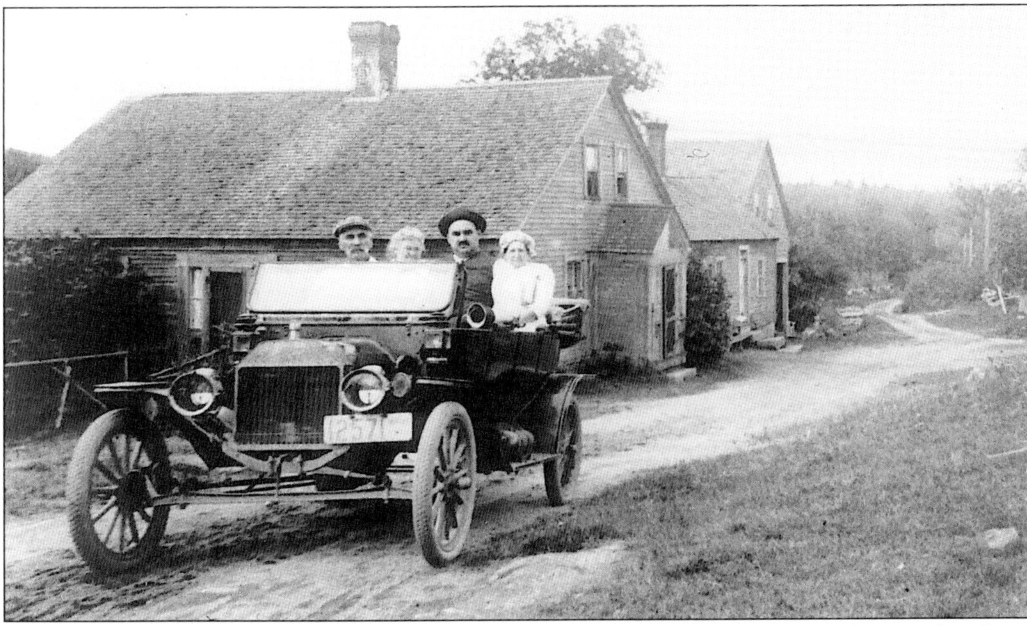

THE JOSIAH NORTON PLACE. In the background is the farm that was known locally as the "sire Norton Place." Josiah Norton is being chauffered by his son Chester. The ladies in the back seat are Josiah's daughter Alice Caswell on the left and Chester's wife Helen on the right.

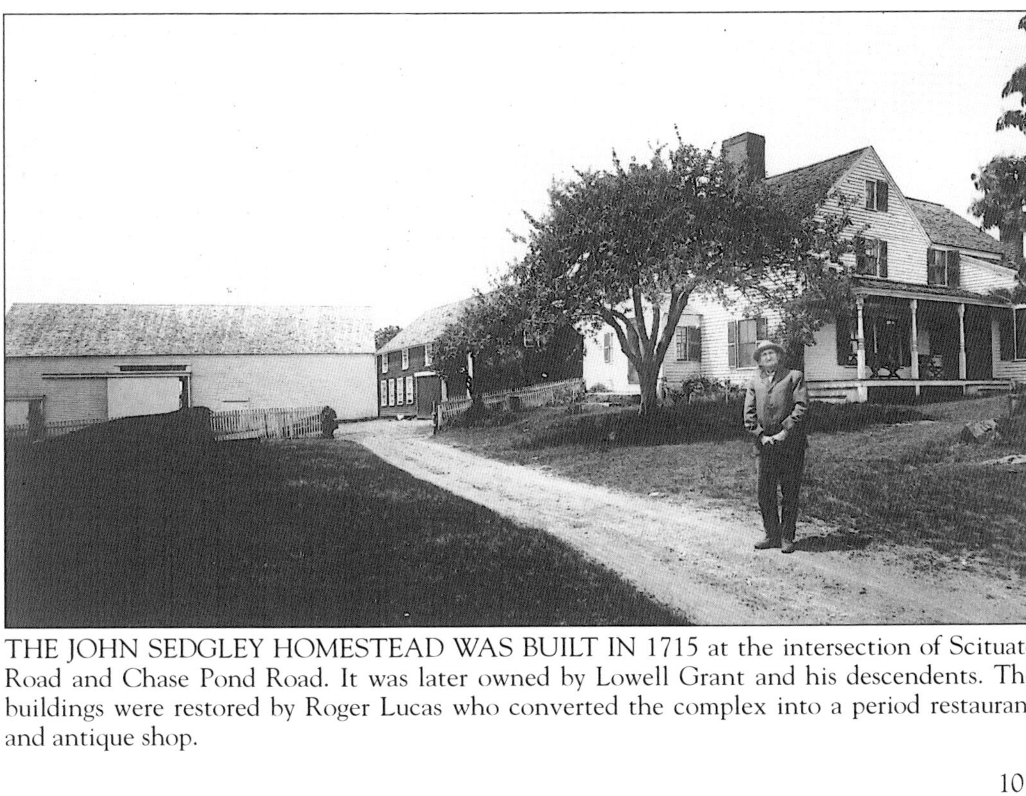

THE JOHN SEDGLEY HOMESTEAD WAS BUILT IN 1715 at the intersection of Scituate Road and Chase Pond Road. It was later owned by Lowell Grant and his descendents. The buildings were restored by Roger Lucas who converted the complex into a period restaurant and antique shop.

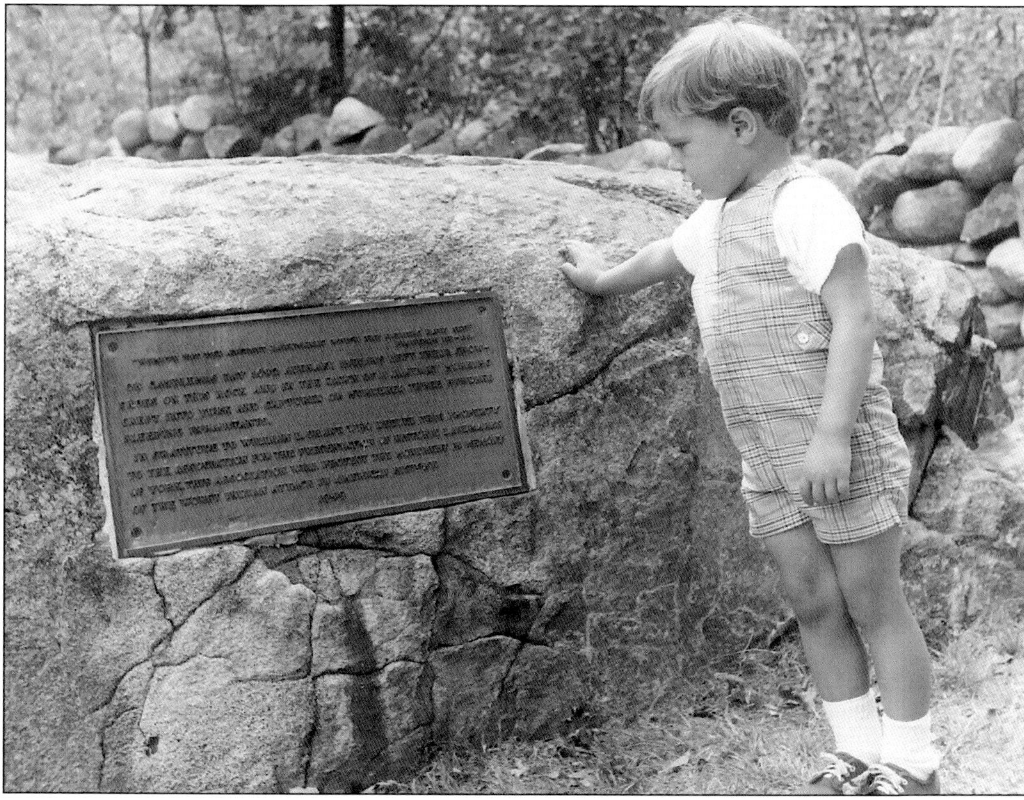

THIS MARKER IS ON "SNOWSHOE ROCK" near the site where the Indians stacked their snowshoes before the Candlemas Day attack on York in 1692.

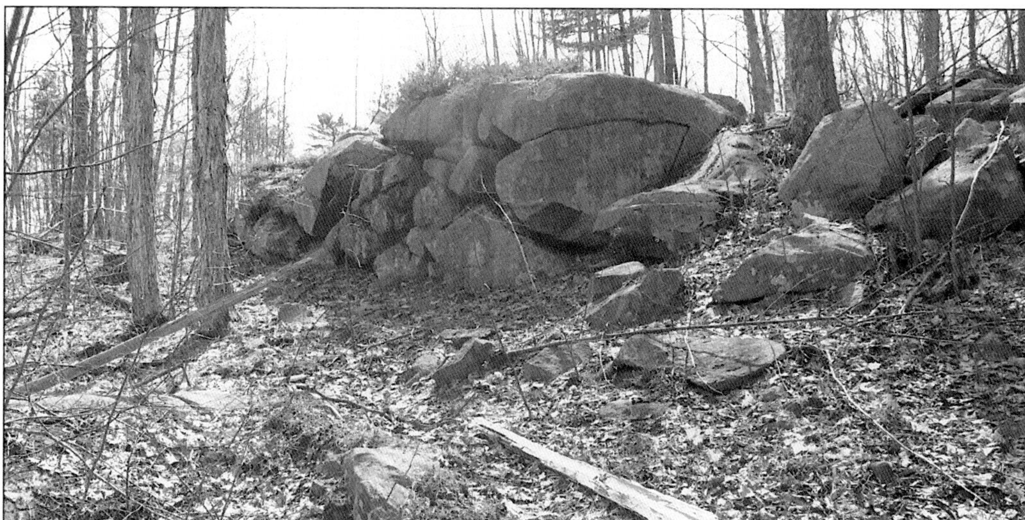

ABOUT ONE HUNDRED AND FIFTY ABENAKI INDIANS CAMPED FOR THE NIGHT AT THE FOOT OF MOUNT AGAMENTICUS. This high rock ledge probably provided shelter for the attackers and was an appropriate place for them to stack their snowshoes. It is estimated that there were about three hundred people in York and about forty houses. The weather was bad and the snow was deep so the Indians decided to attack immediately.

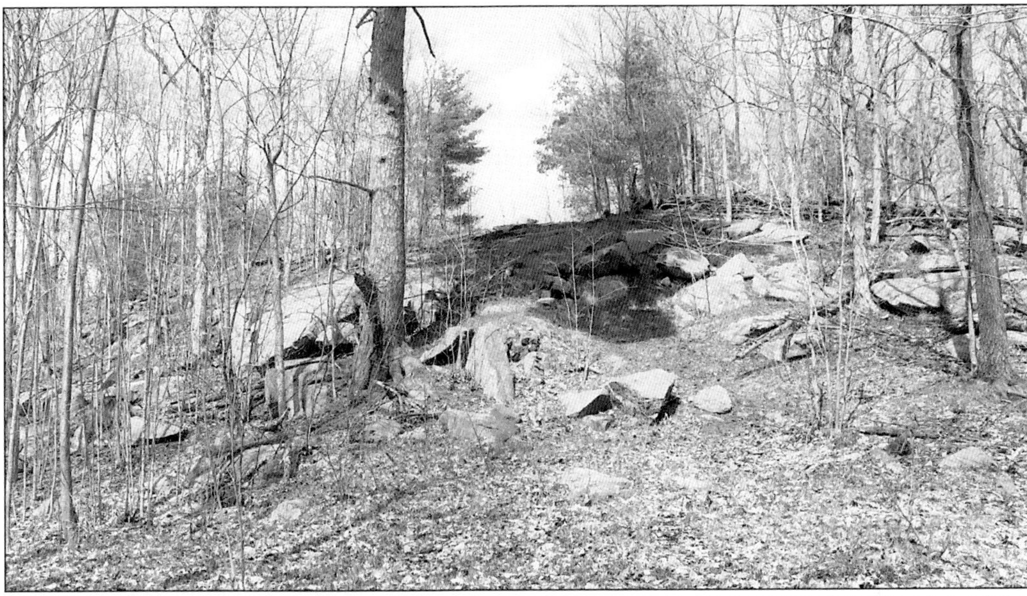

NEAR SNOWSHOE ROCK IS HIGH GROUND FROM WHICH THE INDIANS COULD LOCATE THE HOUSES BY THE SMOKE FROM THEIR CHIMNEYS. They proceeded to attack each house in groups of two or three. In less than three hours they burned most of the dwellings, killed nearly one hundred residents, took eighty captives, and killed large numbers of domestic animals.

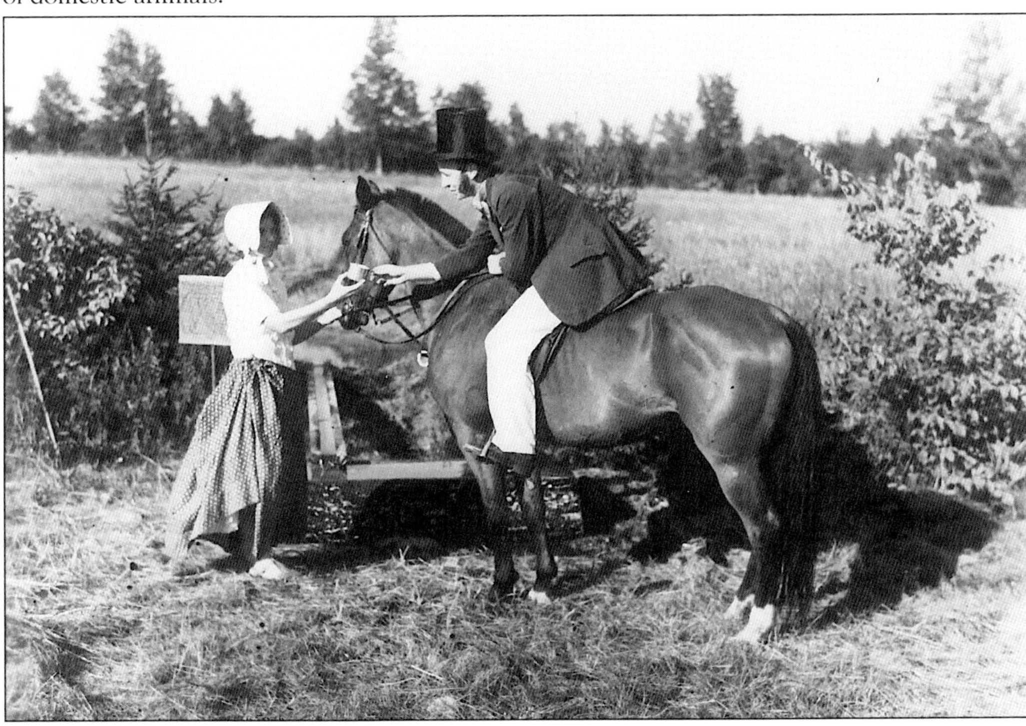

THE DEDICATION OF MAUDE MULLER SPRING IN 1942. As Whittier's poem was read, a young girl in costume raked the newly mown hay and the judge rode up the hill on horseback and stopped to quench his thirst.

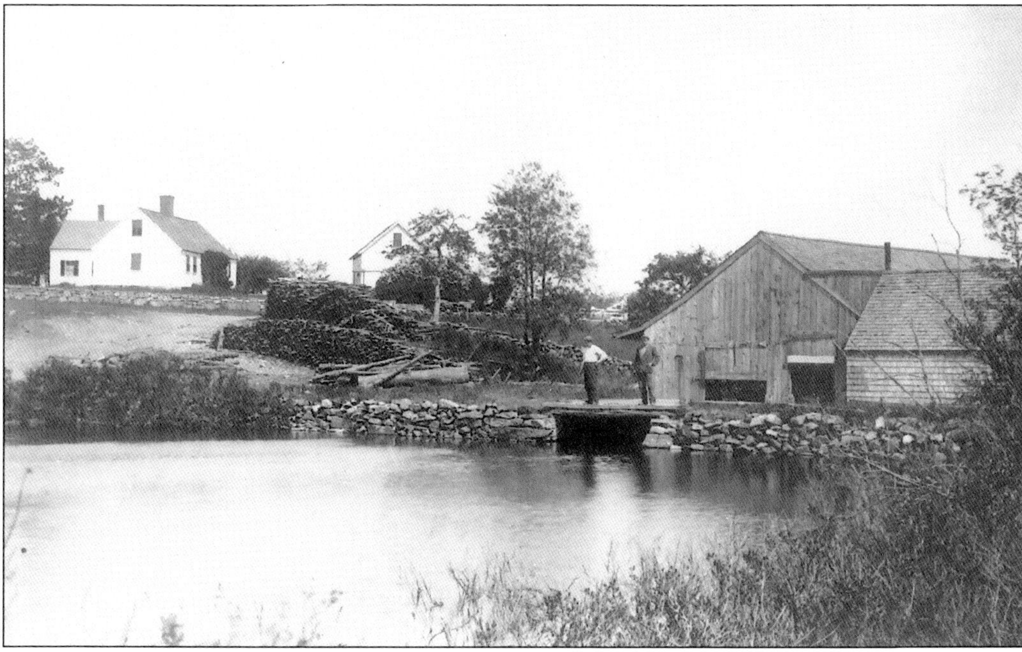

HENRY WOODWARD'S SAWMILL AT SCITUATE POND. Sawmills were common in this community and they provided a source of employment for many local men. Early mills were located near a source of water power and logs were floated to the mill.

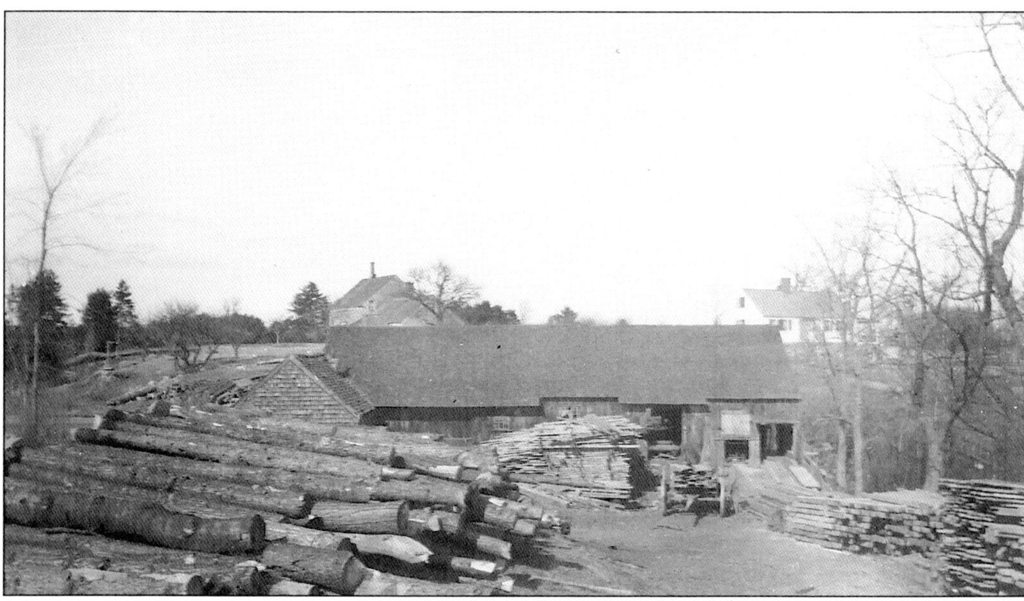

LATER MILLS WERE STEAM-POWERED and they could be located close to the wood lot that was being cut at the time. The only requirement was a small bog or pond that could provide water for the boiler.

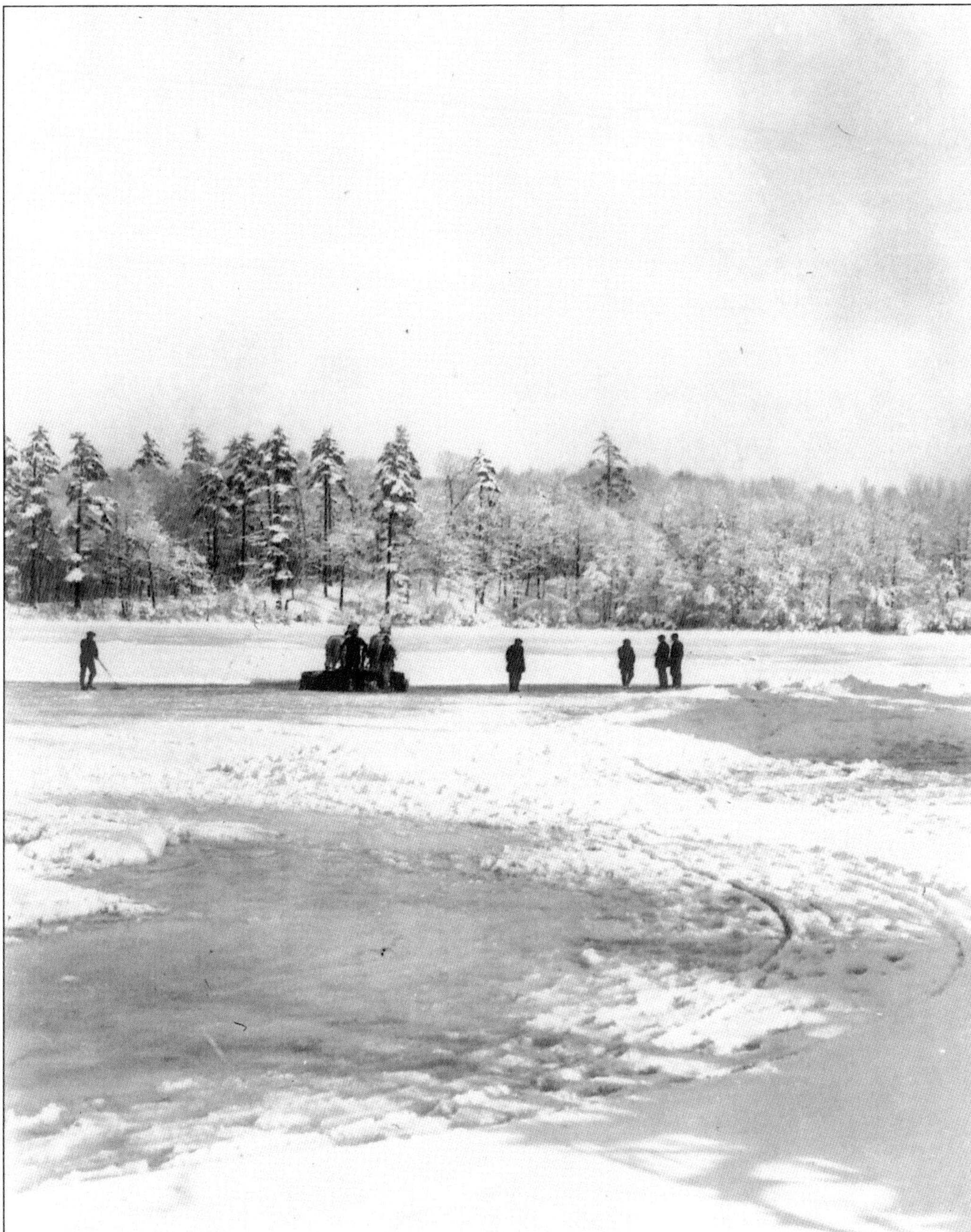

ICE CUTTING ON SCITUATE POND IN 1940.

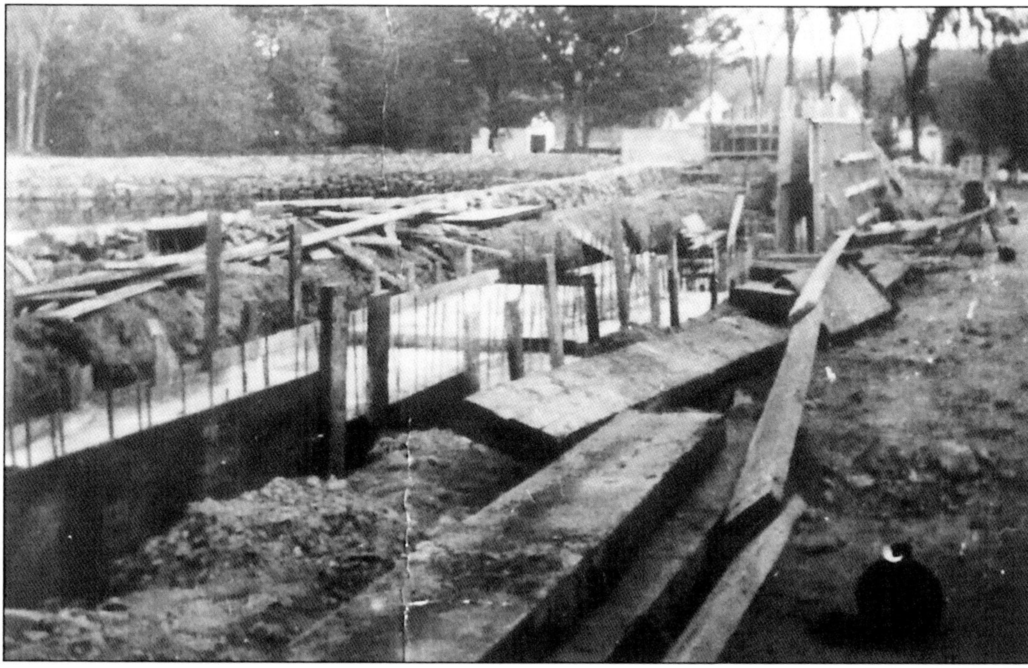

DAM CONSTRUCTION AT CHASE'S POND. The higher dam caused the pond to rise and increase the amount of water in the reservoir.

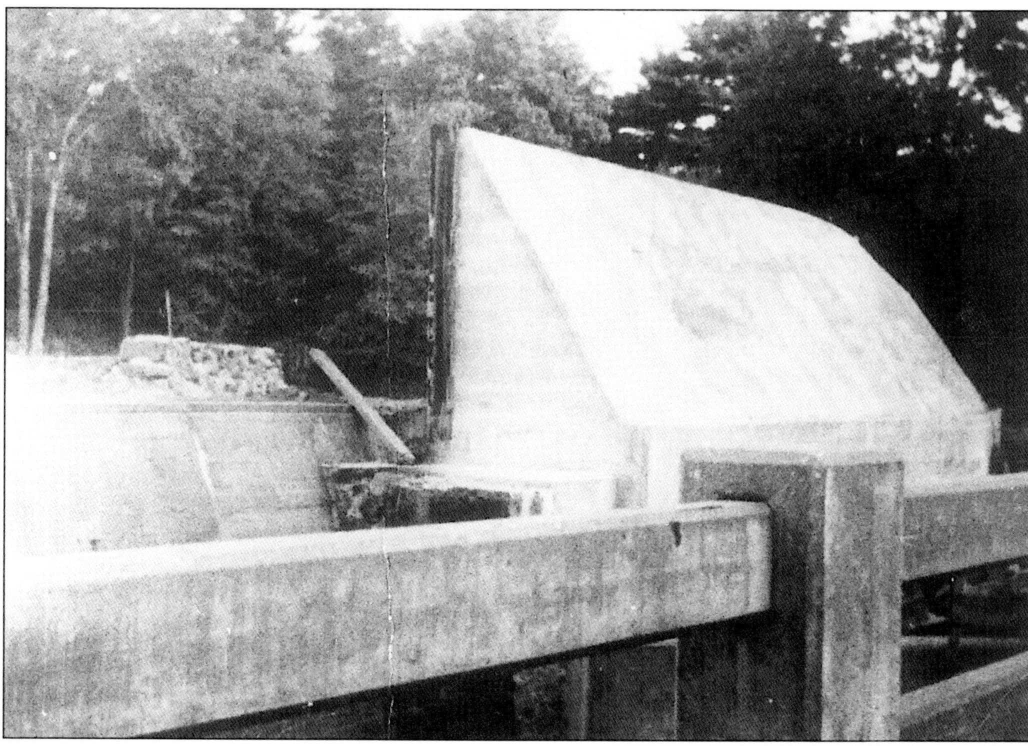

A SECTION OF THE NEW SPILLWAY AT THE CHASE'S POND DAM. This reservoir contains the water supply for the town of York.

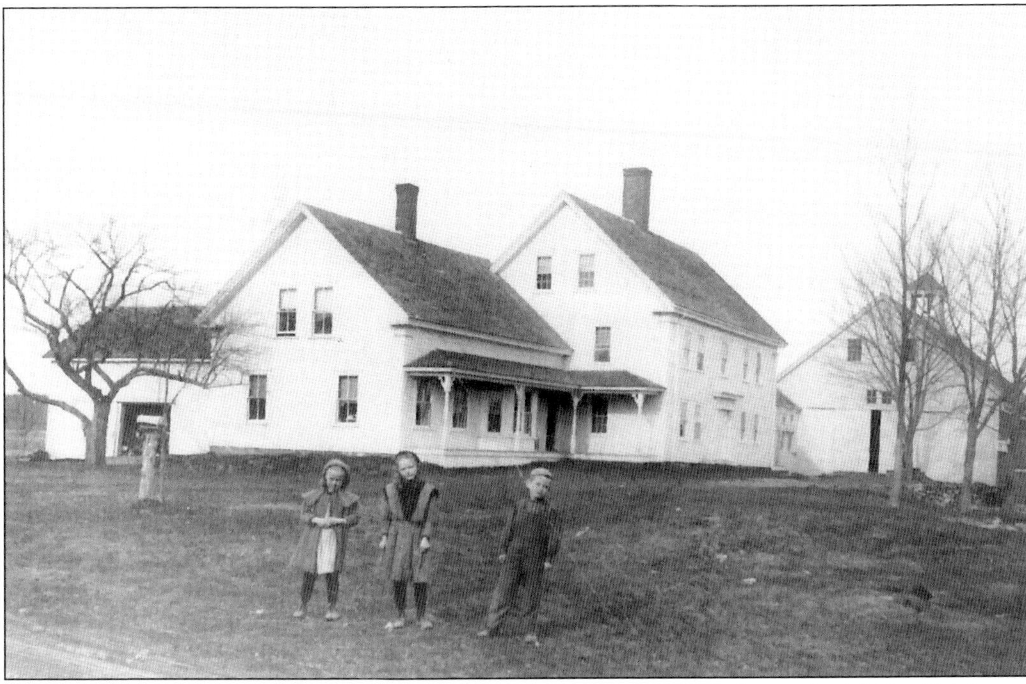

GUY H. McINTIRE'S FARM ON BIRCH HILL ROAD IN 1910. Left to right: Mildred McIntire, Dorothy McIntire and Donald McIntire.

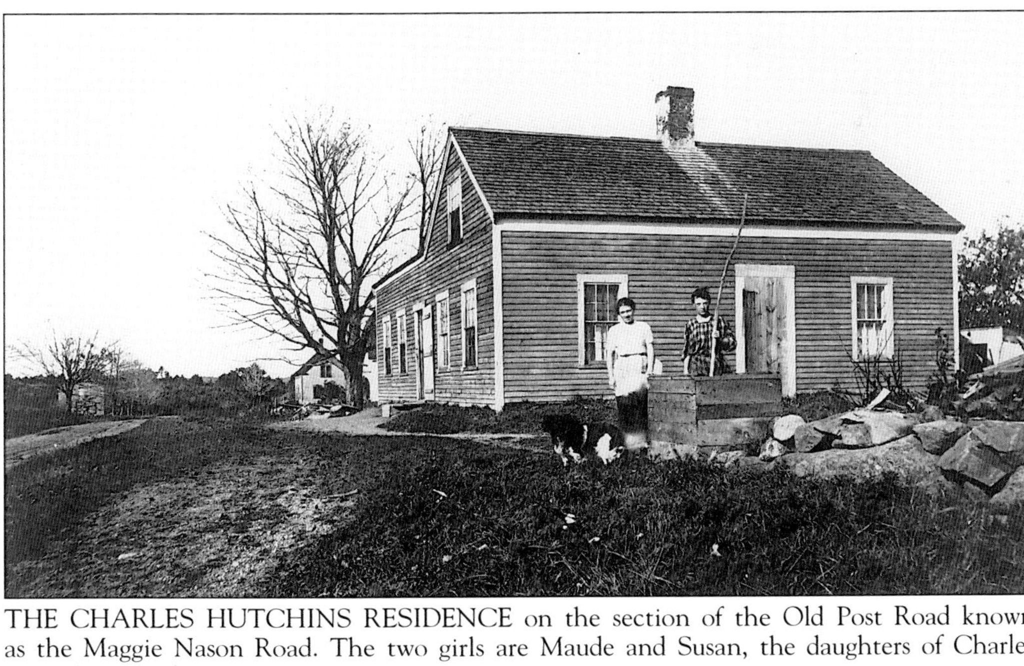

THE CHARLES HUTCHINS RESIDENCE on the section of the Old Post Road known as the Maggie Nason Road. The two girls are Maude and Susan, the daughters of Charles and Juliet Hutchins.

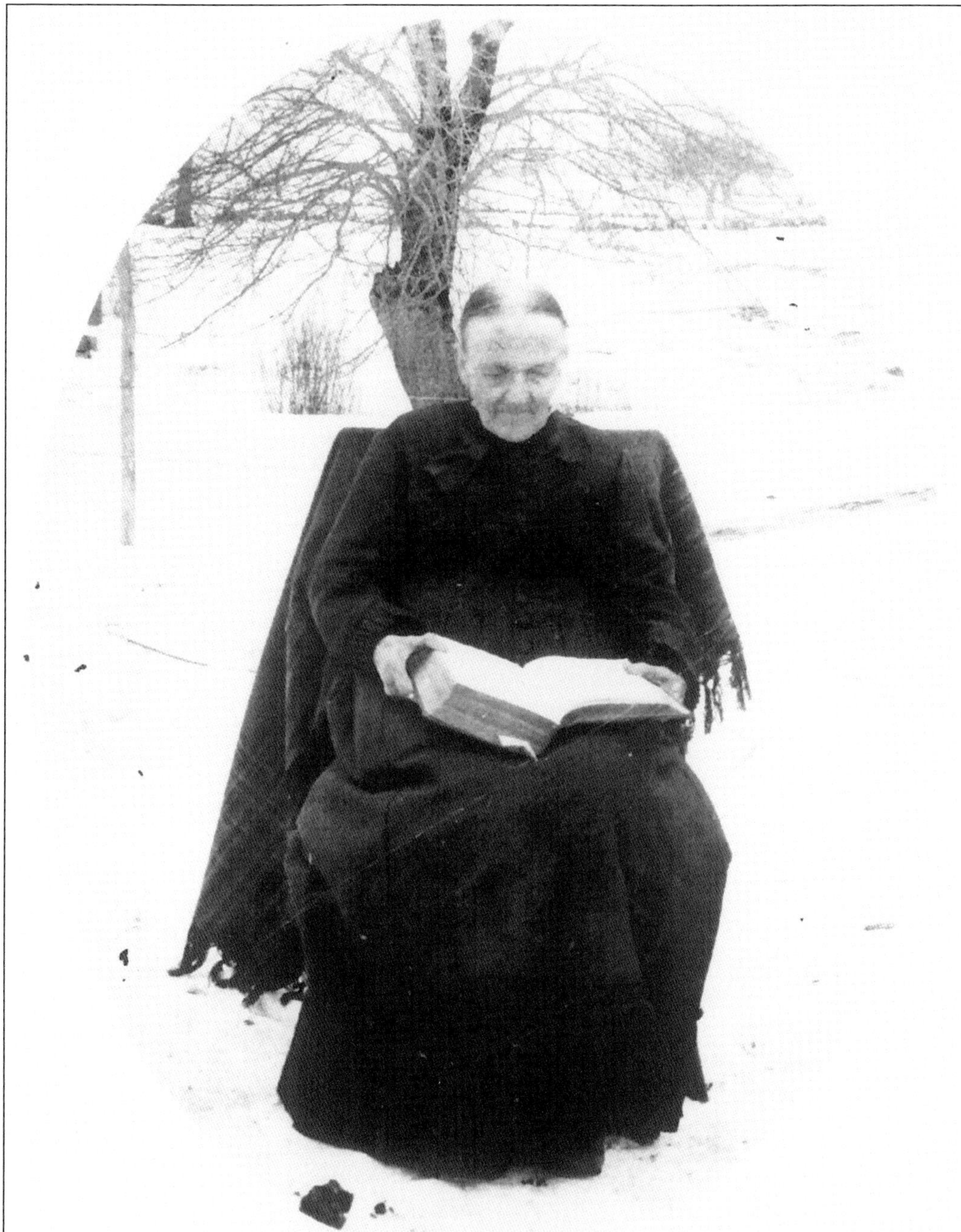

TEZIAH EMERY FIRST CAME TO PUNKINTOWN WHEN IT WAS KNOWN AS "PLANTATION OF THE PISCATAQUA." One of ten children, Teziah was born in the garrison house belonging to her grandfather, Stephen Emery. She was 101 years of age when this picture was taken. Her hearing was unimpaired and she was able to read ordinary print without the aid of glasses. She died in 1898 at the age of 103.

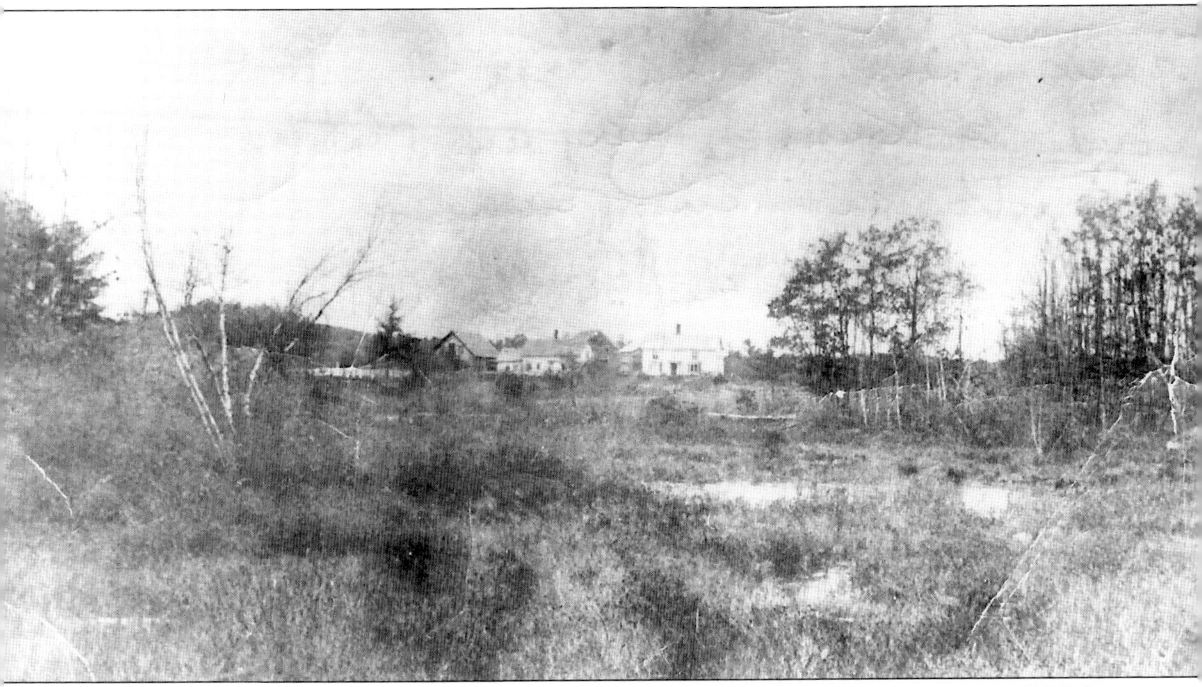

PUNKINTOWN IS ON THE ROAD BETWEEN BRIXHAM AND DOVER THAT LEADS TO YORK POND. It was here that Major Charles Frost or his son built a dam to harness the water power from York Pond. They operated a sawmill and a gristmill. Other mills were built nearby and people moved there to find jobs. The Emerys, the Plaisteds and the Paynes were among the families that lived there.

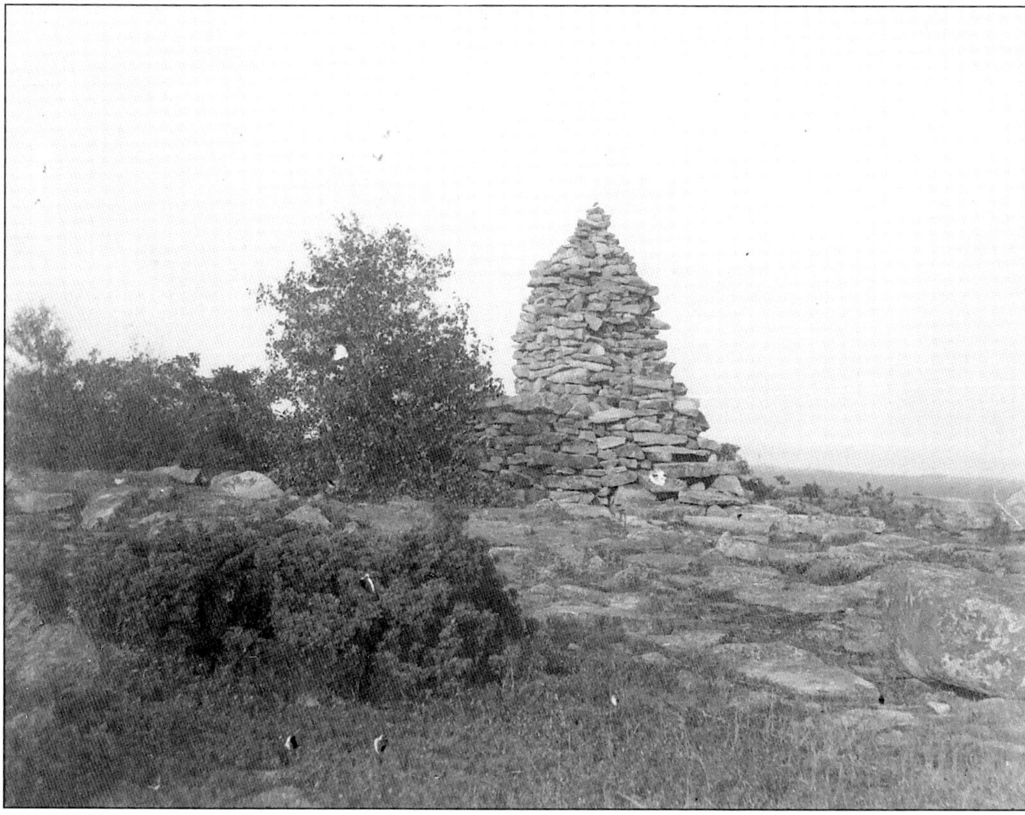

THE SUMMIT OF MOUNT AGAMENTICUS IN 1900. Somewhere on the mountain top is the burial site of St.Aspinquid, a great Indian sachem. John Eliot converted him to the Christian faith and he spent the rest of his long life spreading the word of God among the Indians. A large cairn on the summit marked the approximate location of his grave site for many years.

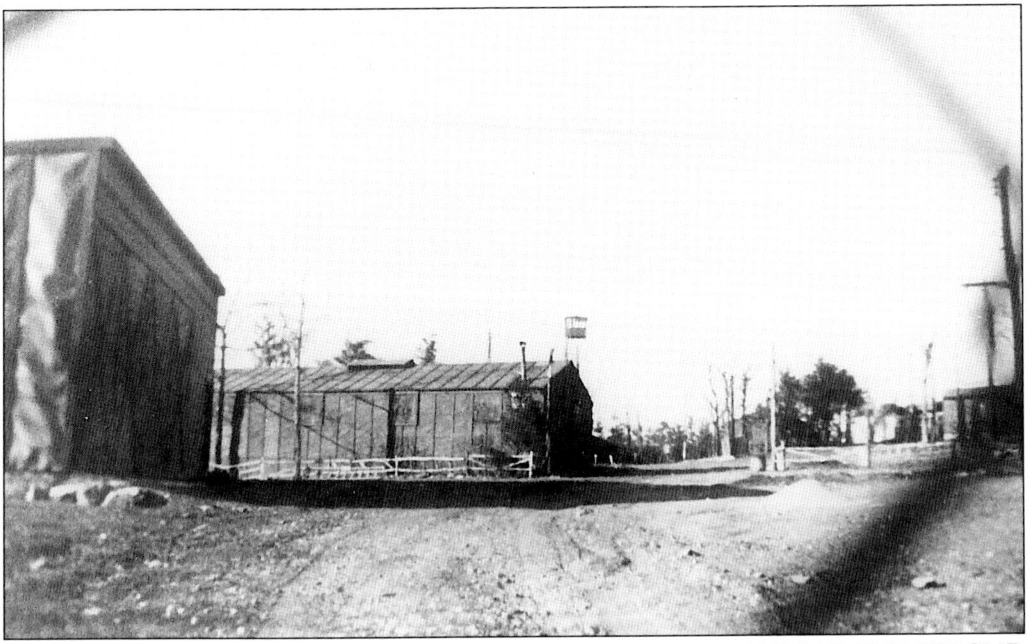

BUILDINGS CONSTRUCTED ON MOUNT AGAMENTICUS DURING THE SECOND WORLD WAR to house the 551st Signal Battalion of the United States Army.

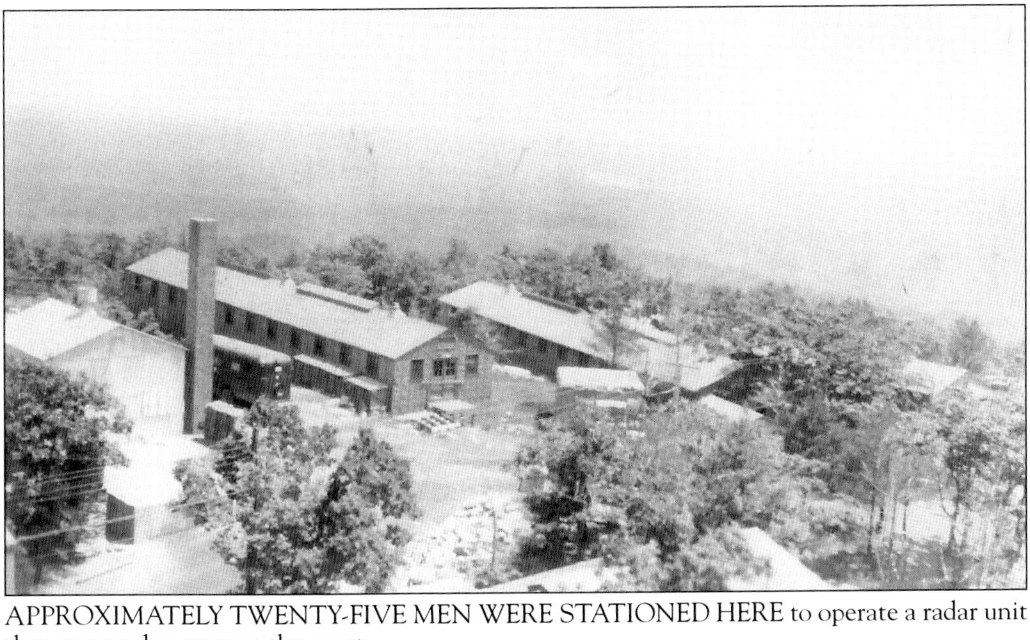

APPROXIMATELY TWENTY-FIVE MEN WERE STATIONED HERE to operate a radar unit that was used to protect the coast.

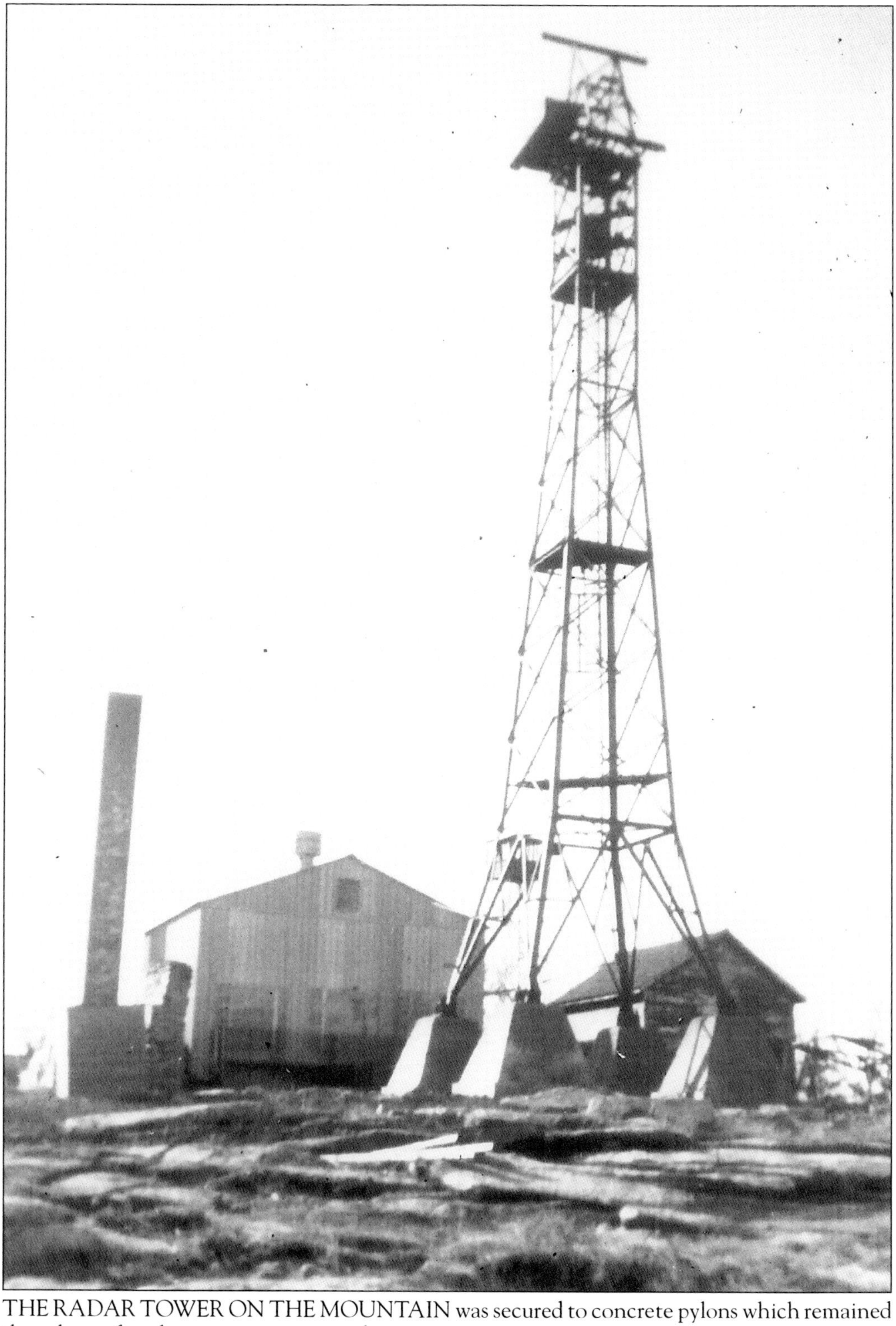

THE RADAR TOWER ON THE MOUNTAIN was secured to concrete pylons which remained there long after the tower was removed.

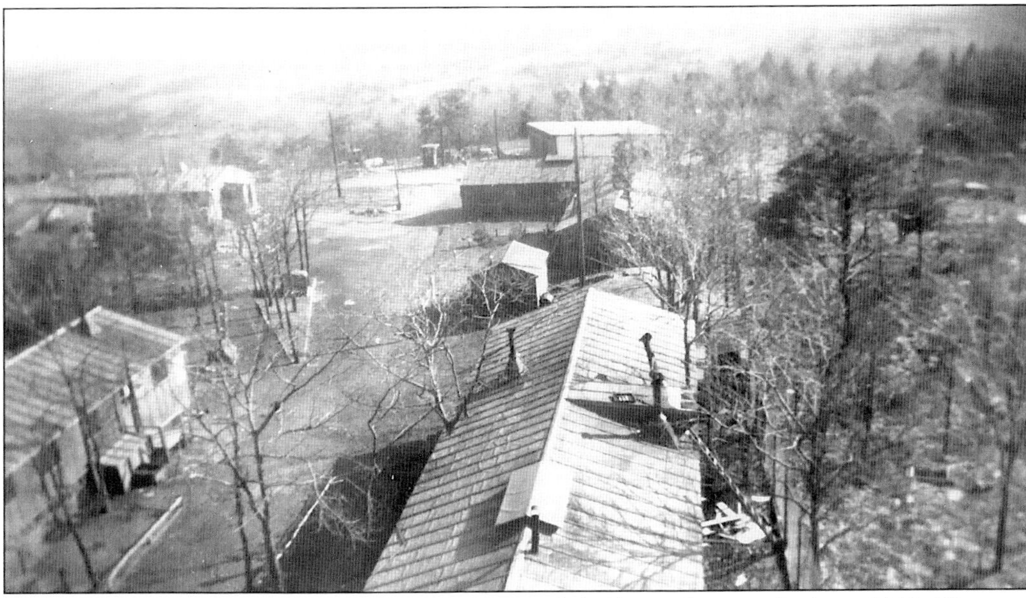

THE FIRST ARRIVALS LIVED IN TENTS until the barracks were built in 1942. The road up the mountain was in poor condition and had to be rebuilt so that they would have regular access to the mountain top.

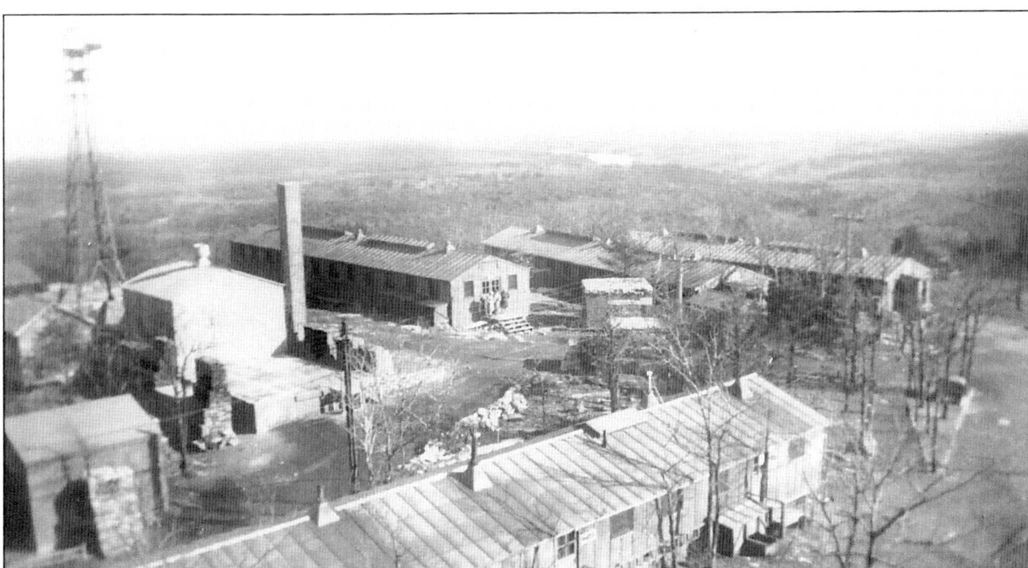

THE UNIT INCLUDED COOKS, CARPENTERS AND RADAR OPERATORS. There was one civilian on site who worked in the lookout tower.

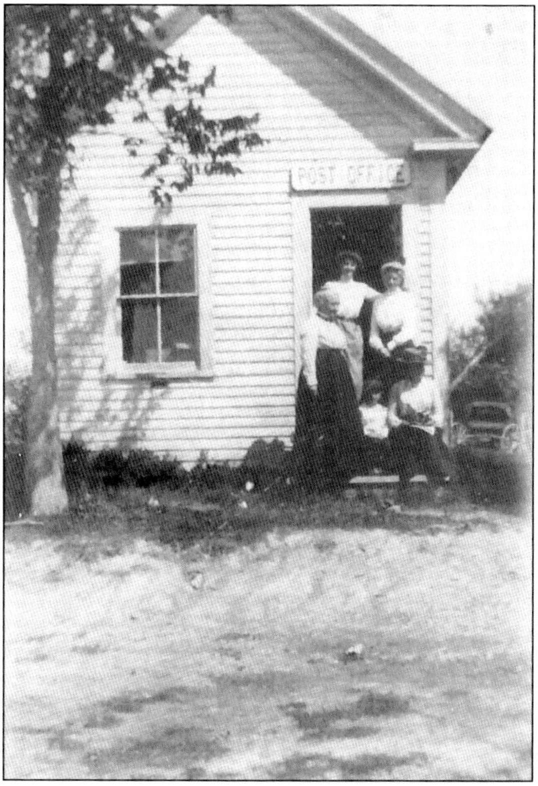

BRIXHAM HAD ITS OWN POST OFFICE for a five year period from February 24, 1898 to April 16, 1903. The small white building was located between Mill Lane Road and the Brixham Grange Hall at Brixham Four Corners.

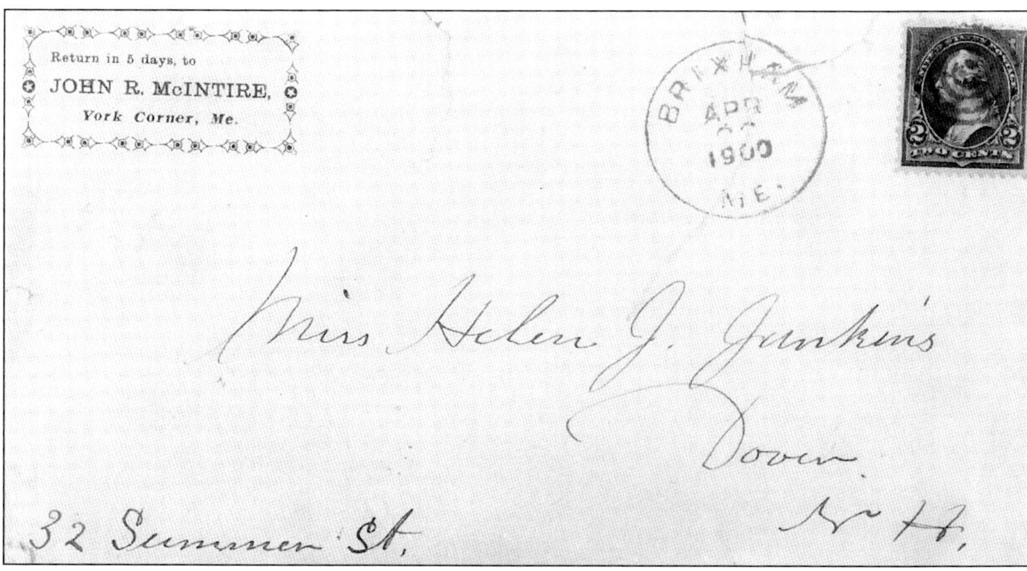

THIS LETTER WAS POSTMARKED AT THE BRIXHAM POST OFFICE. John R. McIntire wrote Helen J. Junkins to inform her of an offer of $2,500 for the purchase of Highland Farm. McIntire was selling the property for her.

Five

Special People and Special Events

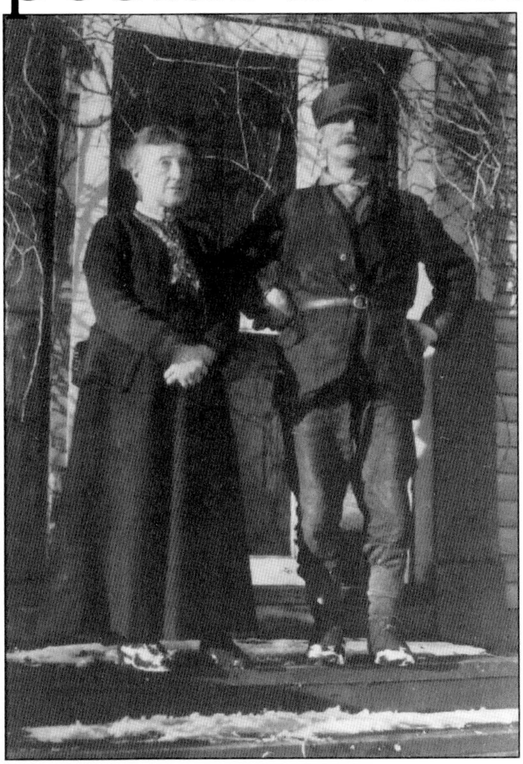

MALCOM PAYNE SPENT HIS LIFE AT THE HOMEPLACE ON SEABURY ROAD. Industry, frugality, hospitality and rugged individualism made up a large part of his character. The hospitality of his home, where he lived with his sister Elena Payne Riley, was proverbial. No one left their homestead unfed.

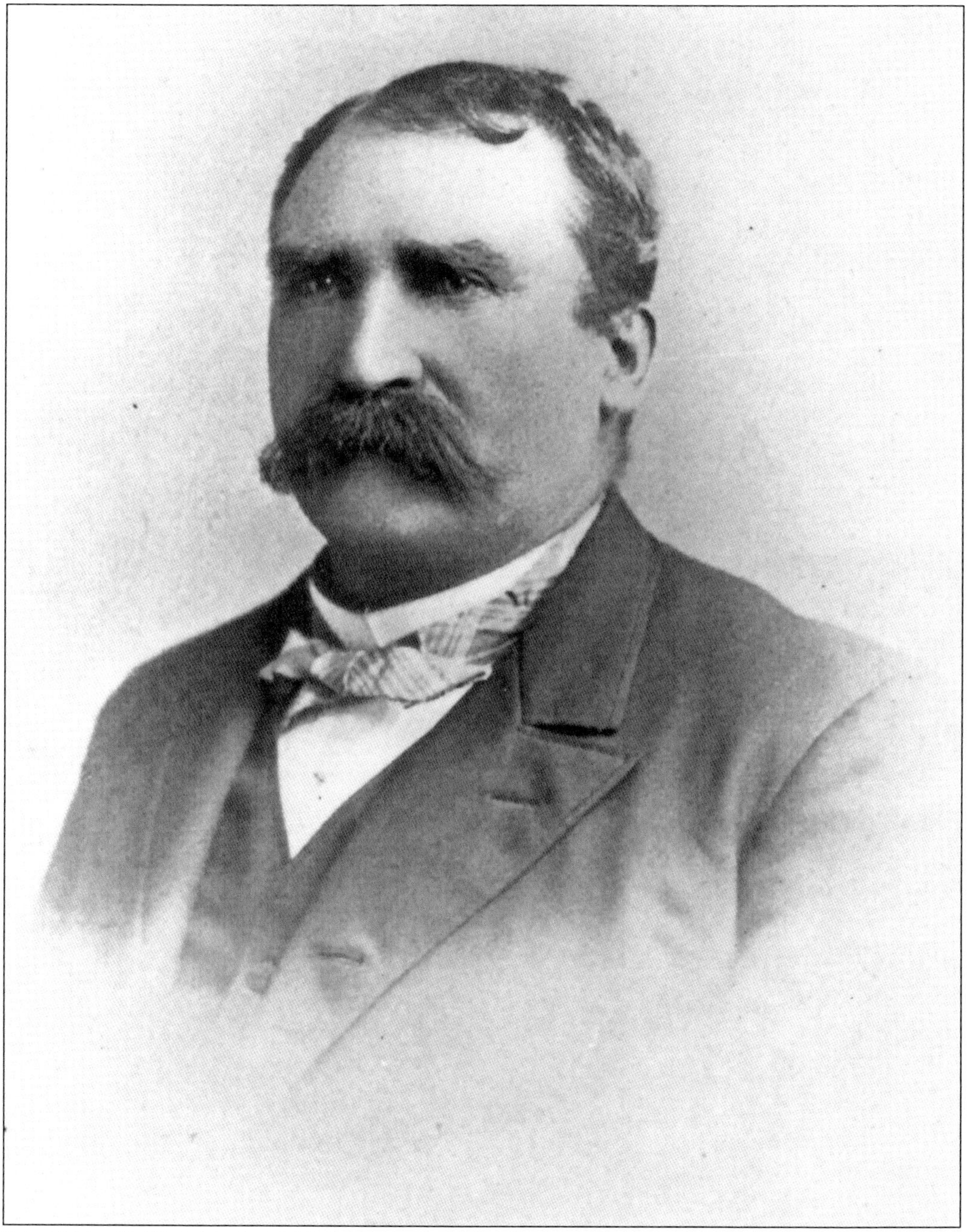

IN 1884, JOTHAM P. NORTON BOUGHT THE GEORGE GOODWIN FARM on the banks of the York River. With the purchase, he acquired 50 acres of good clay. Norton established a brickyard to make bricks for the Boston market and employed between fifty and one hundred men.

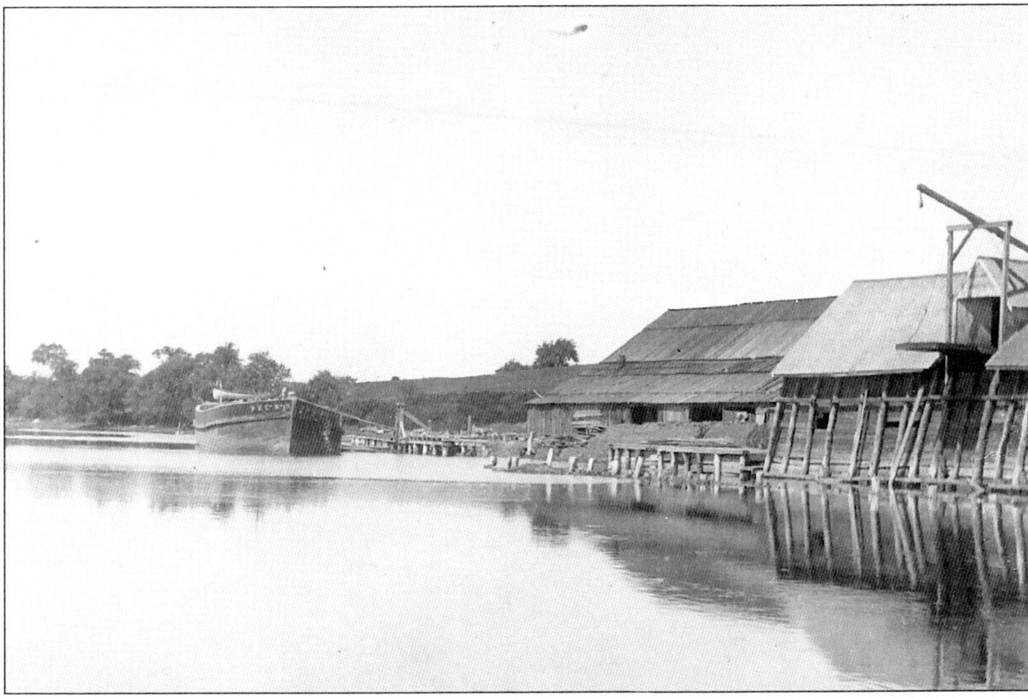

THE NORTON BRICKYARD AND THE YORK HARBOR BRICKYARD WERE BOTH LOCATED ON THE YORK RIVER. Norton bought additional land, built docks, bought a schooner and set up a sawmill. The production capacity of his yard increased to 80,000 bricks per day.

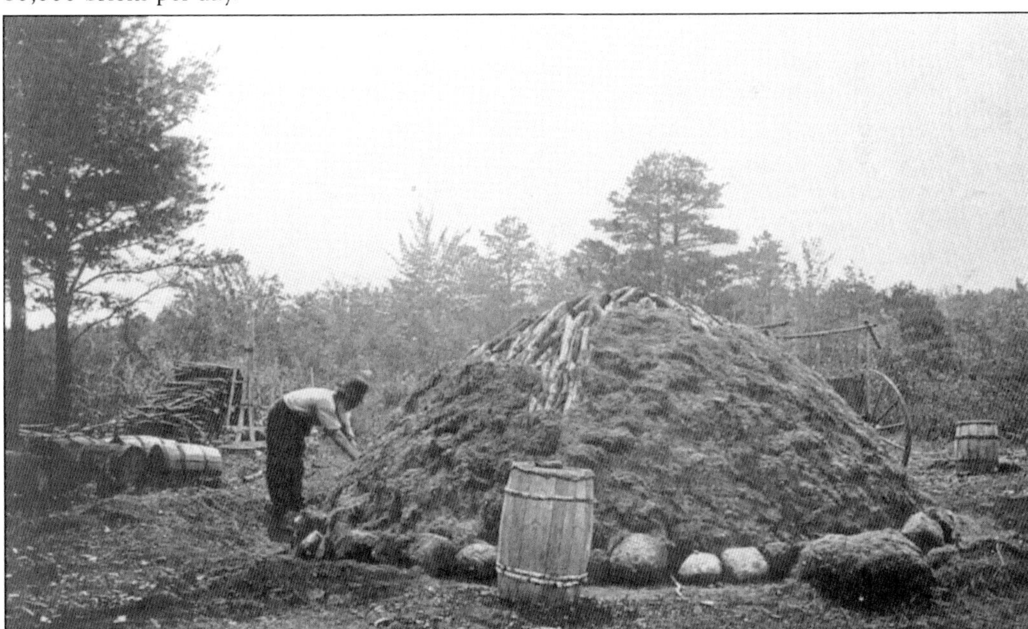

NORTON EMPLOYED MEN TO CHOP CORDWOOD FOR THE KILNS. It was converted to charcoal for use in the brickyard. Company officials also purchased wood from local residents. The going rate was $1.00 per cord for firewood and $1.25 per cord for 5-foot lengths.

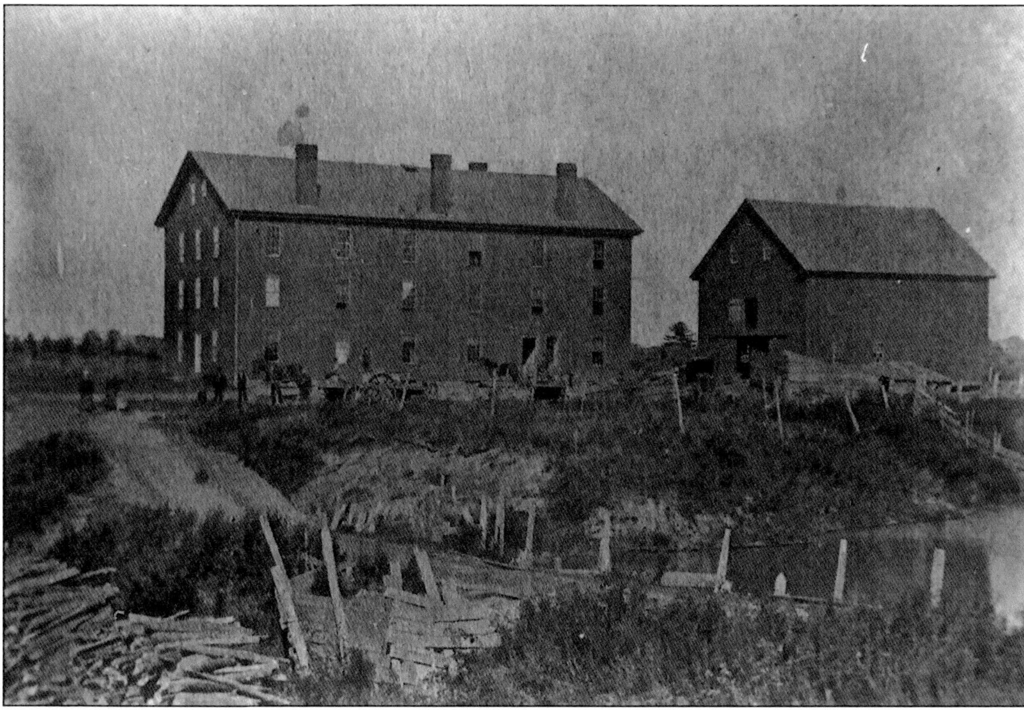

A BOARDING HOUSE PROVIDED FOOD AND SHELTER FOR THOSE WHO NEEDED IT. Mrs. Philip Cushing ran the boarding house for the Norton company. In 1903, the board fees ranged from 39 cents to 89 cents per day.

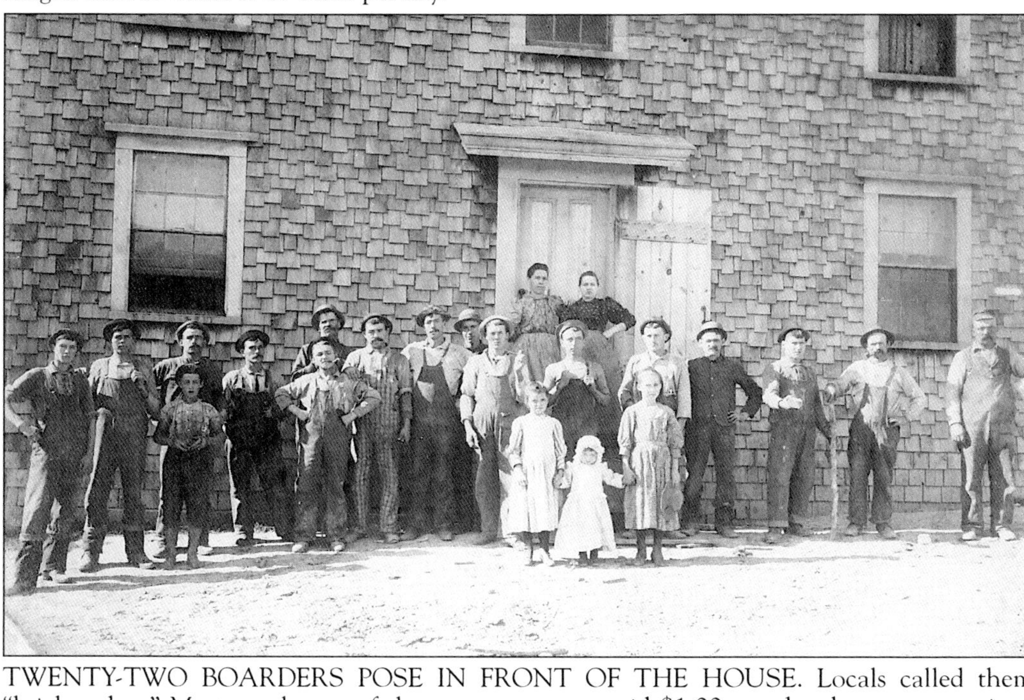

TWENTY-TWO BOARDERS POSE IN FRONT OF THE HOUSE. Locals called them "brickyarders." Most employees of the company were paid $1.00 per day, but some received $2.00. Their charges at Plaisted's store were deducted from their monthly pay envelopes.

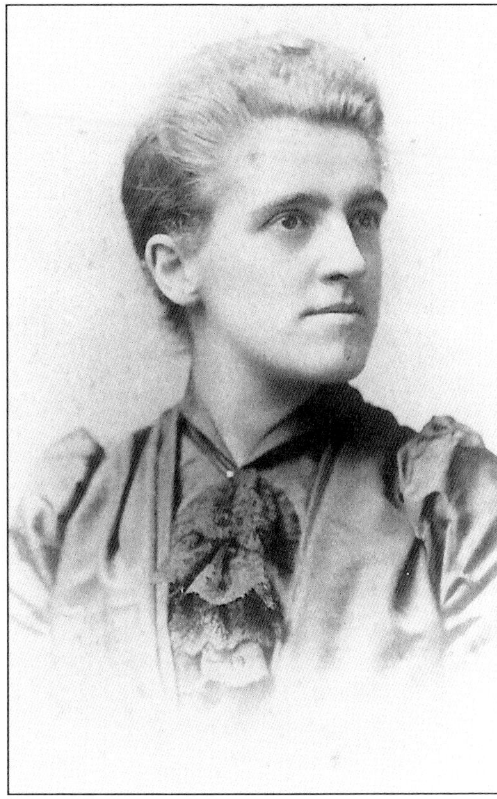

DR. MARY E. BARRELL was probably the first woman from York to become a medical doctor. She was born in York on December 15, 1862 and died in York Hospital on March 13, 1935. She is buried in Beech Ridge Cemetery with her brothers Charles and George who were also doctors.

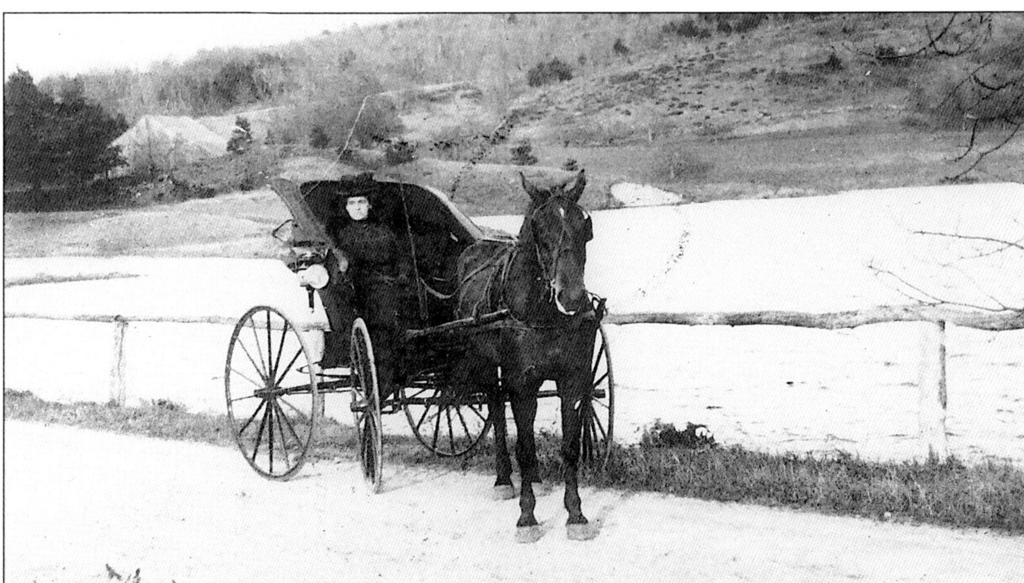

DR. BARRELL VISITING PATIENTS with her horse and buggy.

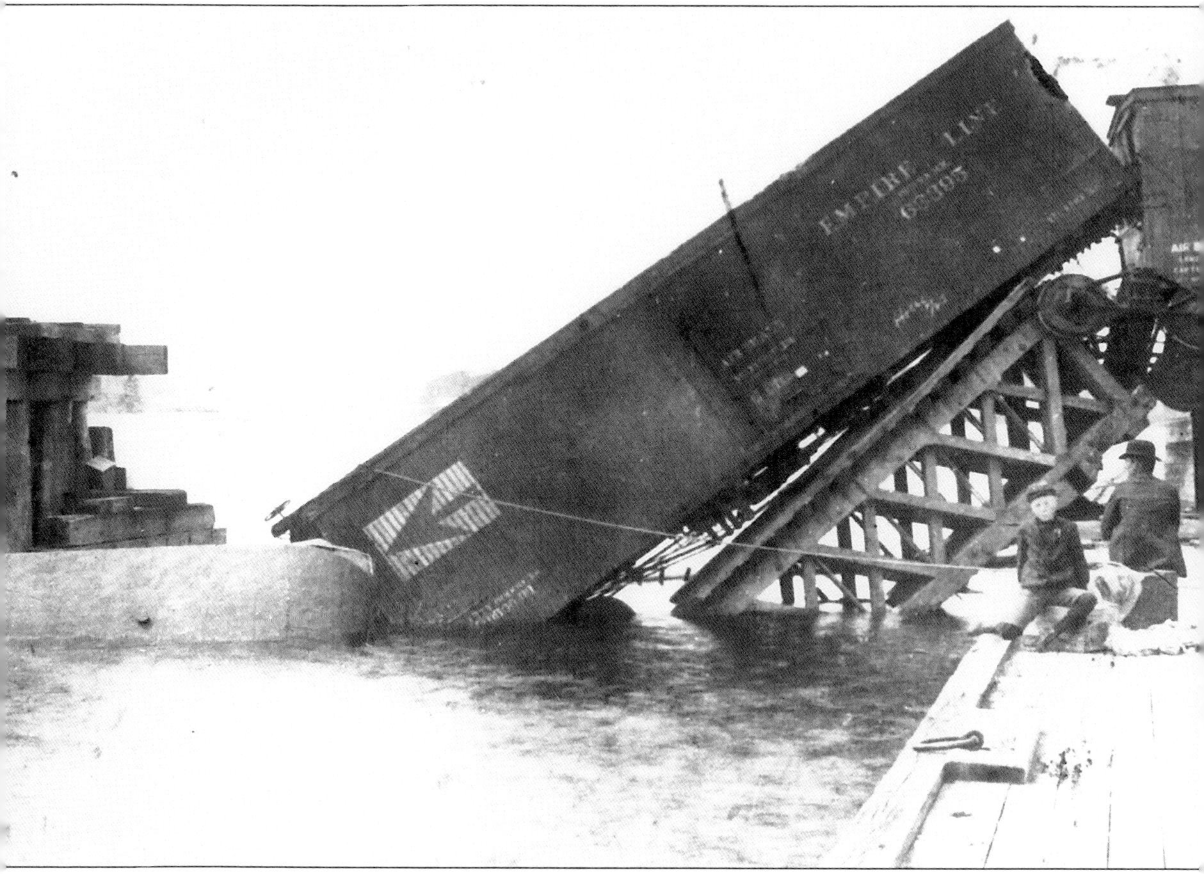

THE ONLY MAJOR WRECK ON THE YORK HARBOR AND BEACH RAILROAD occurred on April 30, 1900 with four crewmen and nine passengers on the train. Five cars broke loose at the top of a grade after the train had crossed the York River. All nine passengers managed to jump before the cars reached the bridge, which was being opened for a tugboat towing a barge. Fred Emery had his legs crushed so badly that one had to be amputated. Cyrus Smith broke his wrist but the others escaped without injury.

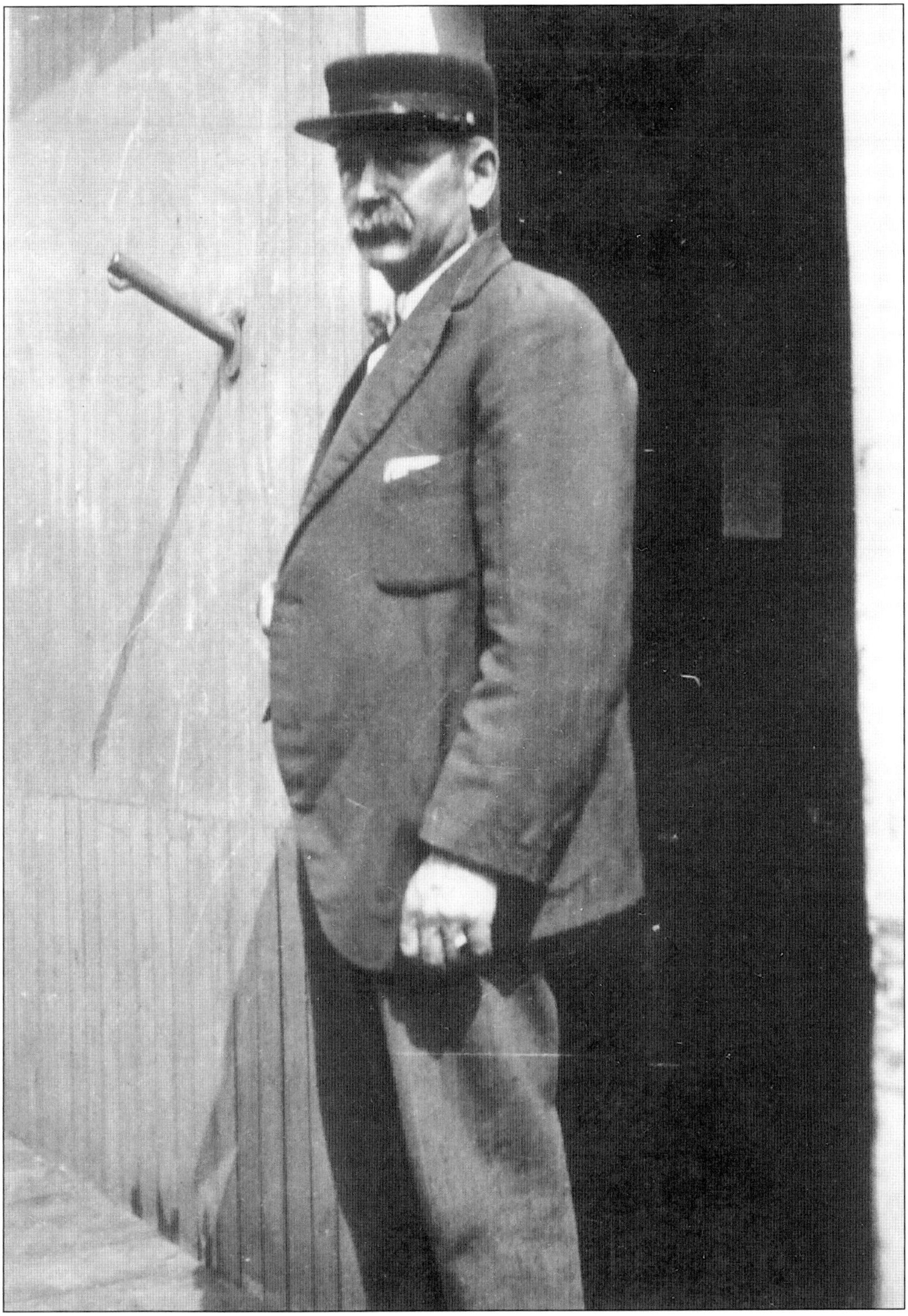

FRED MOORE WAS THE TRAIN AGENT AT THE SEABURY STATION FOR MANY YEARS.

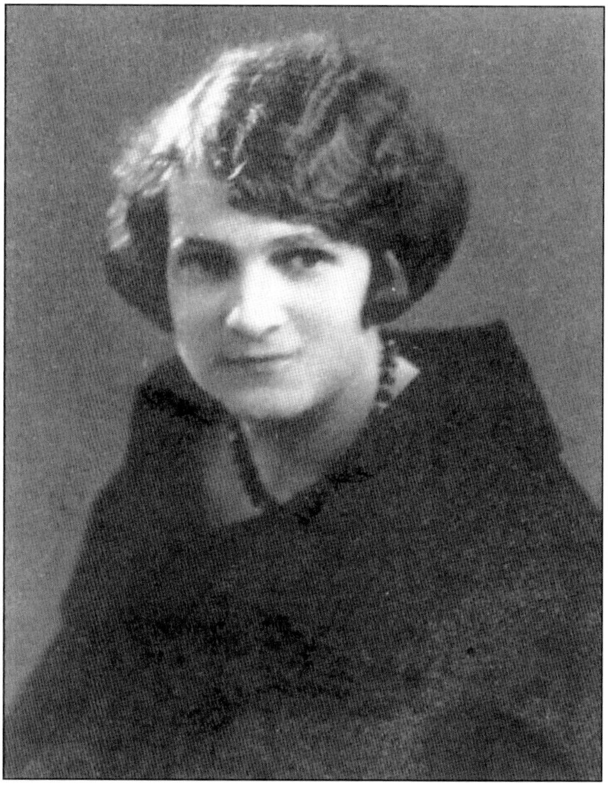

ELSIE BARDWELL, SCHOOL TEACHER AND LONG-TIME LIBRARIAN. Elsie succeeded Myrtie Banks as librarian at the York Public Library. She introduced modern cataloging and classification systems.

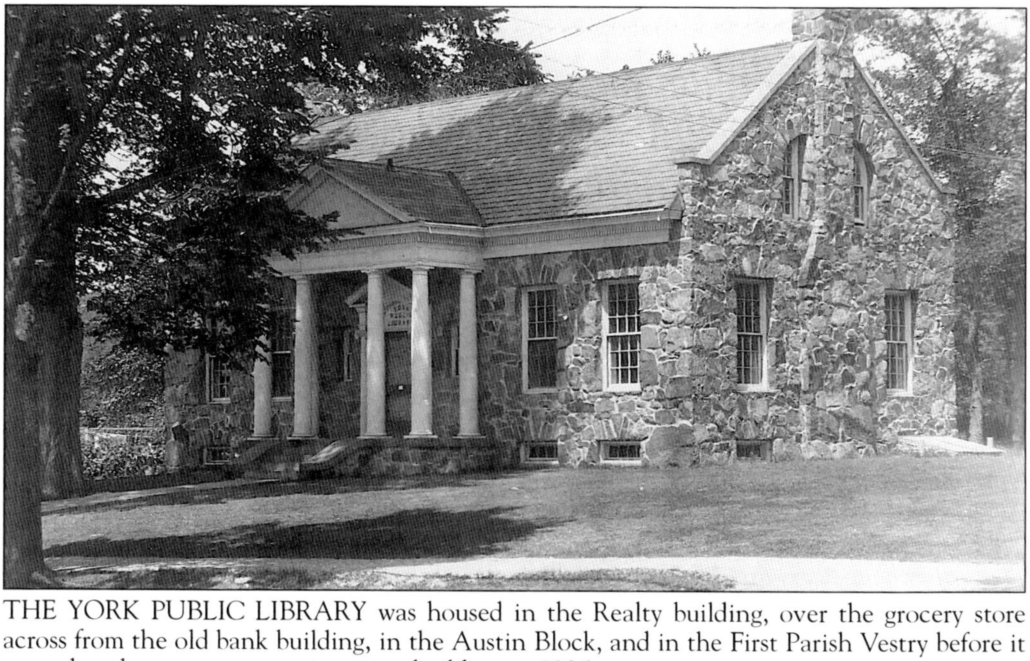

THE YORK PUBLIC LIBRARY was housed in the Realty building, over the grocery store across from the old bank building, in the Austin Block, and in the First Parish Vestry before it moved to the present attractive stone building in 1926.

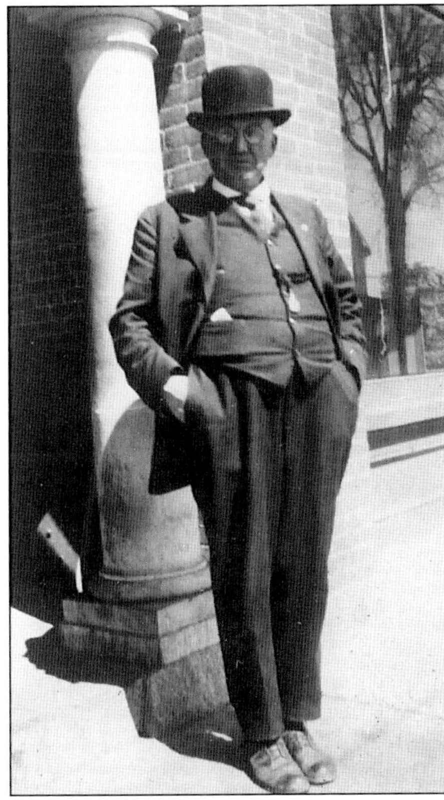

ERNEST F. HOBSON IN FRONT OF THE REALTY BUILDING. Hobson came from Buxton to work for Putnam's Express. He opened one meat market in the old Central Maine Power Company block and another in Wells. Hobson was a sharp businessman who became a dealer in antiques and used furniture. He accumulated land by lending money to people in financial difficulty and accepting wood lots as a form of repayment.

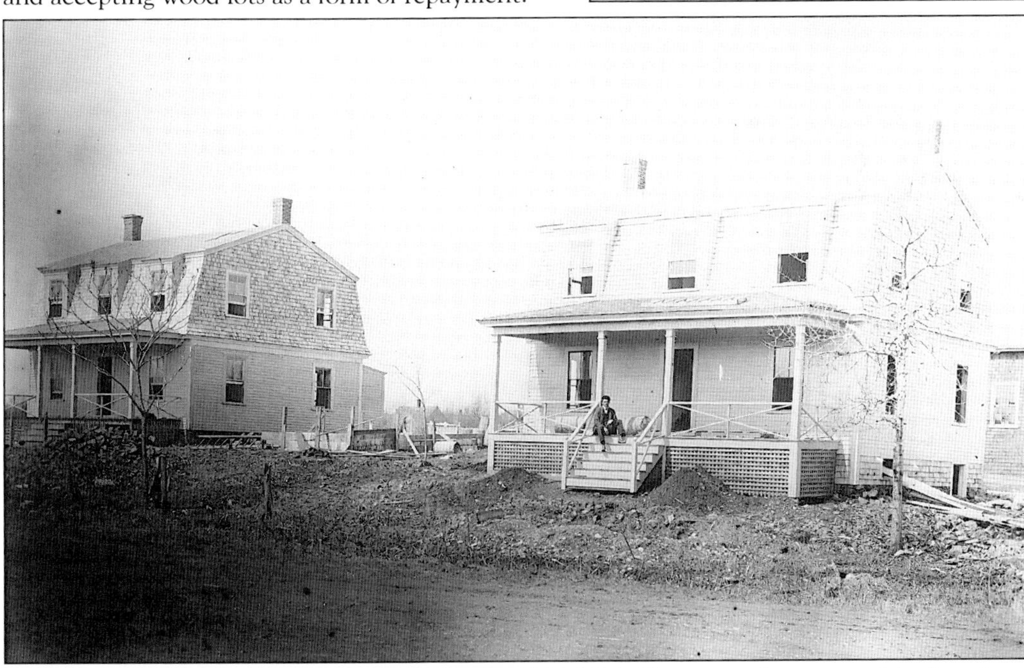

HOBSON ALSO SOLD AND RENTED COTTAGES. These two houses on Moulton Lane were built near the old Putnam Express Office, which flourished as long as the trains came to York Harbor station.

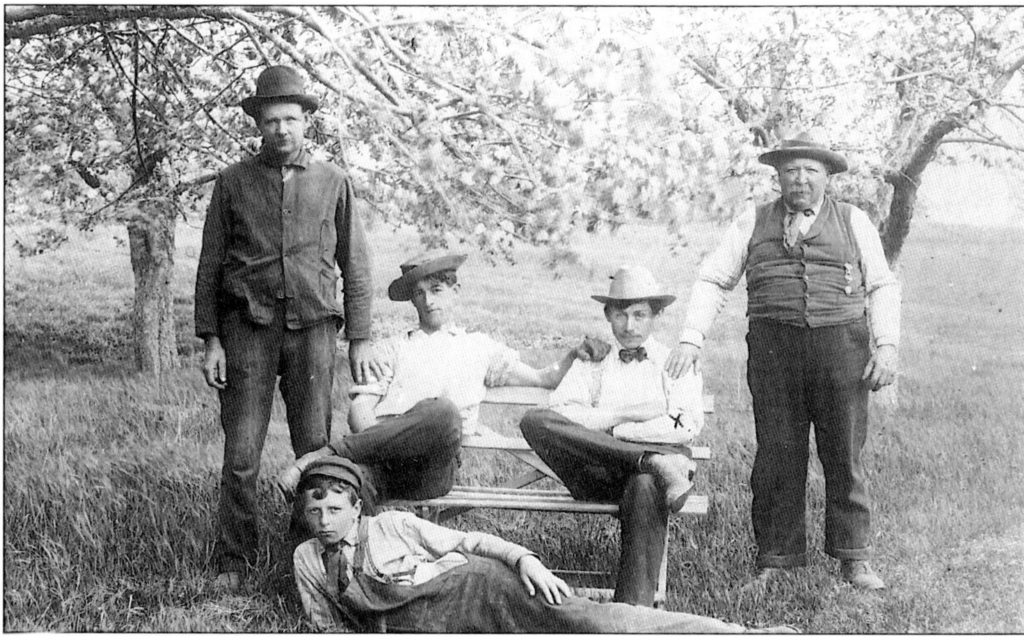

MEMBERS OF THE GYPSY MOTH CREW that moved about the countryside destroying gypsy moth eggs. They wrapped tree trunks with burlap that had been soaked in creosote and removed rocks from stone walls in search of egg masses. This crew operated during the 1912 to 1920 period. Fred Blaisdell is on the right.

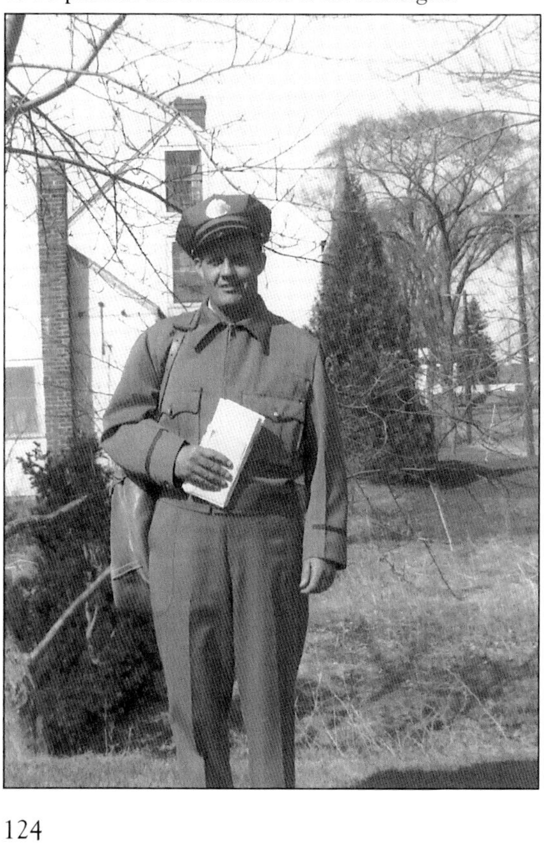

KEN TOWNE DELIVERING MAIL ON ORGANUG ROAD. Ken was one of the first carriers when the York Post Office instituted home delivery in York Village. Service began on a cold morning on March 3, 1962.

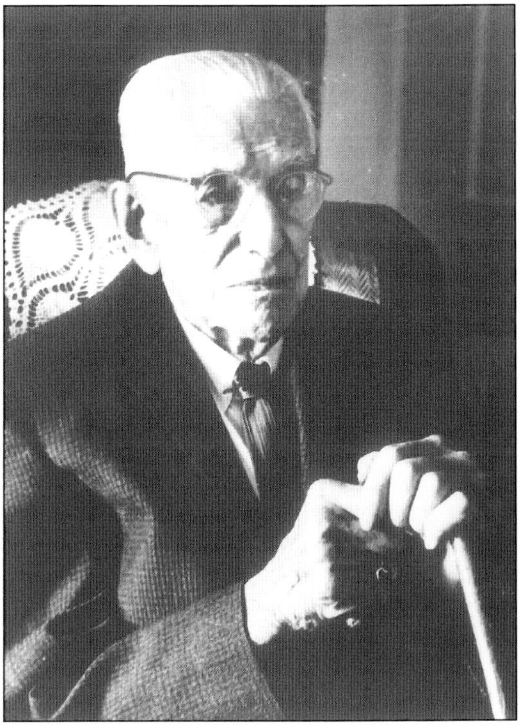

DR. ALBERT E. McCOLLUM WAS BORN IN CHERRYFIELD, MAINE IN 1870, but practiced dentistry in York for many years. He was a long-time trustee of the York Public Library which was across the street from his home and office.

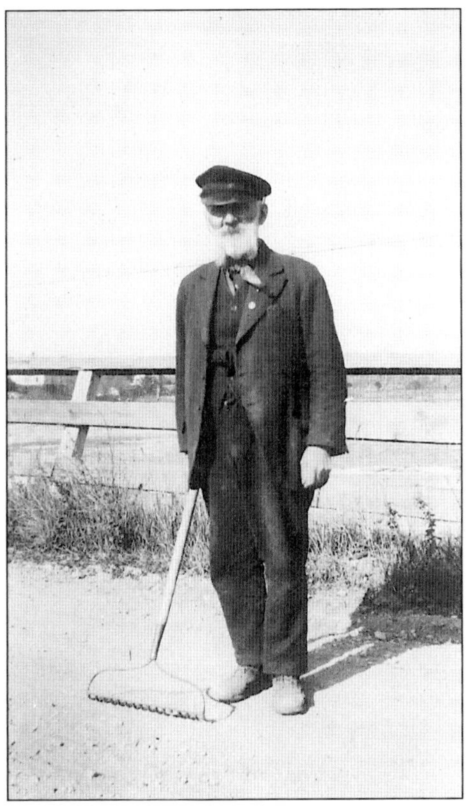

THE HONORABLE EDWARD C. MOODY RAKING ROCKS FROM THE ROAD. He lived at the Moody Farm on Ridge Road. At that time the road was simply a lane leading to the farm. Moody's Handbook History of the Town of York: 1623–1914, was read by many generations of York residents who were interested in the history of the community.

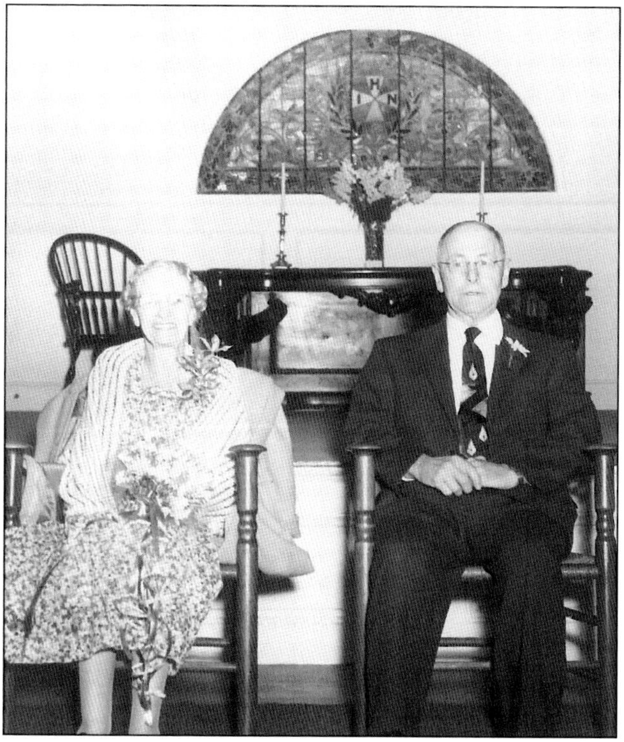

MYRON AND EFFIE COX AT THEIR FIFTIETH ANNIVERSARY PARTY AT THE PARISH HOUSE. Myron Cox edited and printed the weekly newspaper, photographed community events, coached high school sports teams, served as police chief and operated the Cox Store with the support of his wife, who was also active in community affairs. She was a strong supporter of the library and played a major role in its success.

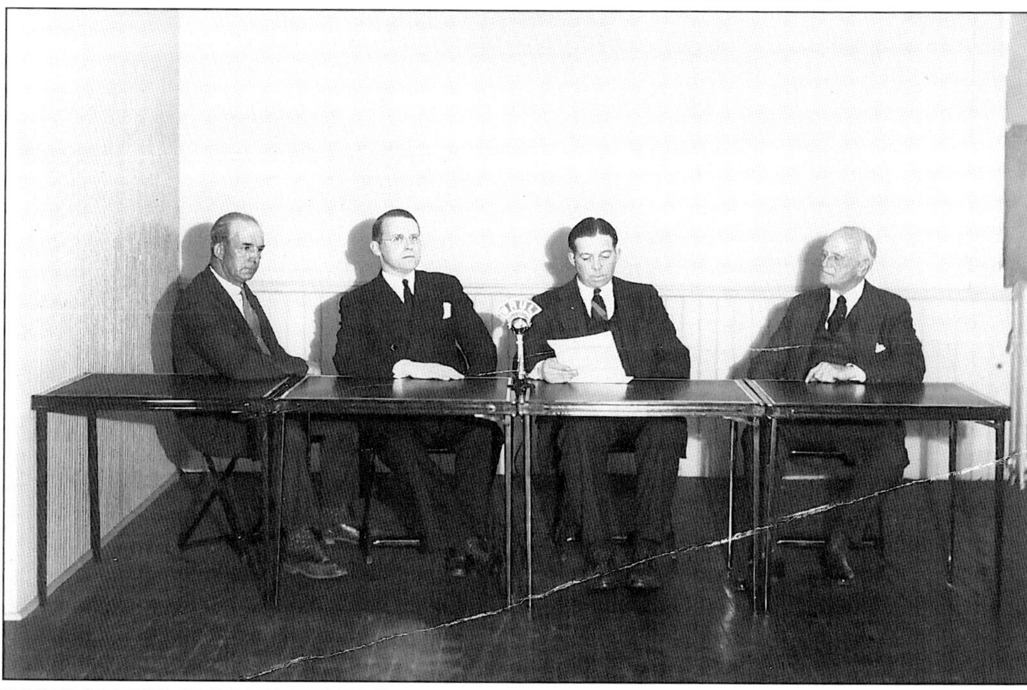

DURING THE SECOND WORLD WAR York maintained a strong bond with its sister city of York, England. Selectman Nathaniel G. Marshall is broadcasting a radio message of hope and encouragement from the town hall to the citizens of York, England. Left to right: William Foster, Rev. Harold Millinger, Nathaniel G. Marshall and an unknown participant.

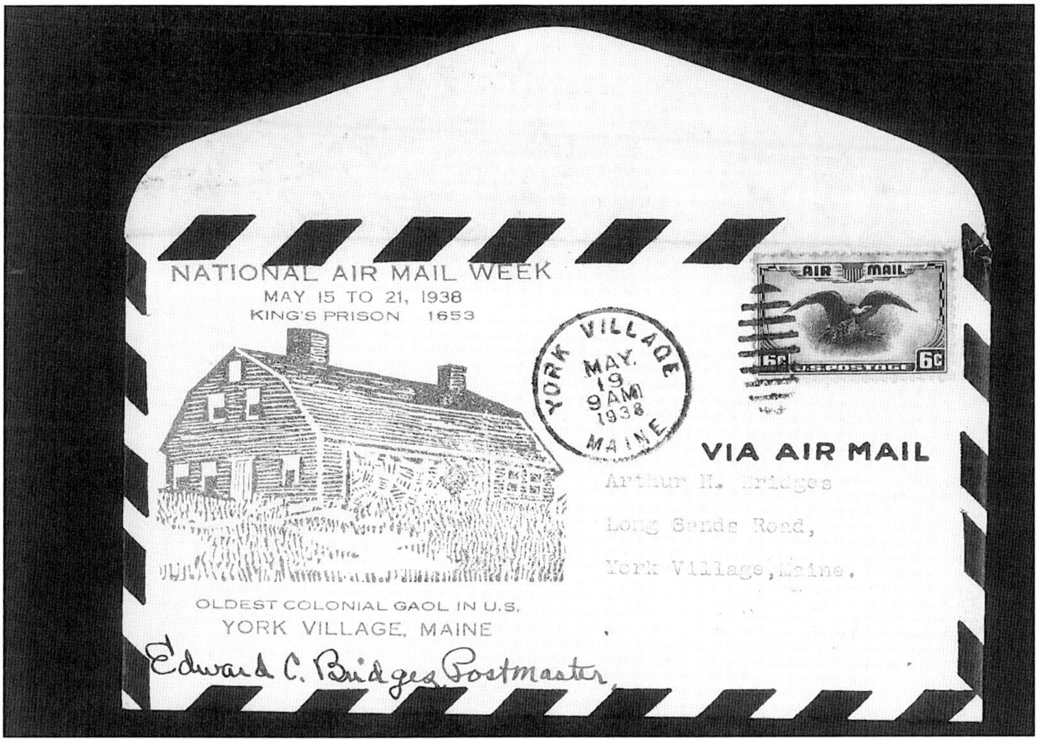

AIRMAIL COMES TO YORK. On the morning of May 19, 1938, a little black biplane landed on Long Sands Beach. Postmasters from Kittery, Eliot and York came to pick up their mail pouches. The pilots had flown from Portland to introduce air mail services to the rural areas of Maine.

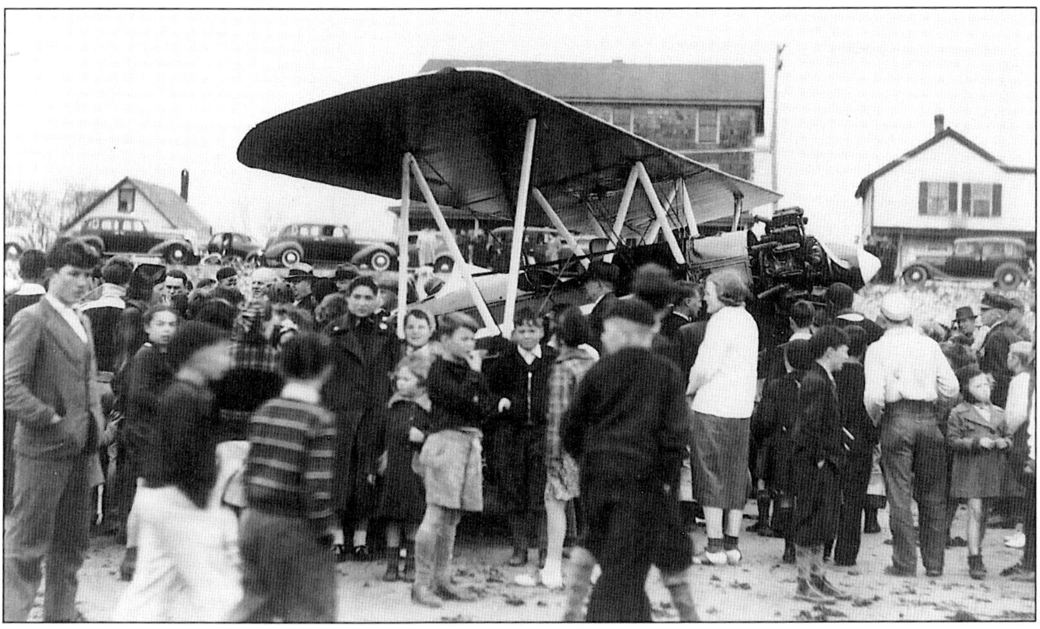

POSTMASTERS AND SPECTATORS GATHERED AT THE BEACH to meet the first airmail delivery.

Acknowledgements

Ted Bragdon, Wesley Austin, Arthur Bridges, Alice Freeman, Frank Parsons, Edward Hipple, Freda Weaver, Philip Gordon, Gertrude Blaisdell, Maurice Payne, Martha O'Neil, Bert Ciampa, David Hilton, Peter Moore, Joseph W.P. Frost, Robert Donnell, William Foster, Stephen Small, O.R. Cummings, Jo Randolph, Everett Norton, Calvert Leemen, Roger Currier, Mary Ellen Wood, Wayne Perkins, Andrew Renney, Ruth Freeman, Susan Christmas, Theodore Blaisdell, Howard Martin, Jim Williams, Perry Turner, Donald Stover, David Lowell, Leon Ramsdell, Eunice Graham, Bainbridge Parsons, Russell Freeman, Elsa Adams, Marion Woodward, Edna Morando, Douglas Starbird, Marguerite McDonough, Virginia Bean, Edith Woodward, Linda Thurston, Buelah McIntire, David Bardwell, Faith Webster, Forbes Wilson and the St. Aspinquid Masonic Lodge.